Typed Feature Structure Grammars

European University Studies
Europäische Hochschulschriften
Publications Universitaires Européennes

Series XXI
Linguistics

Reihe XXI Série XXI
Linguistik
Linguistique

Vol./Bd. 319

PETER LANG
Frankfurt am Main · Berlin · Bern · Bruxelles · New York · Oxford · Wien

Anders Søgaard / Petter Haugereid (eds.)

Typed Feature Structure Grammars

PETER LANG
Internationaler Verlag der Wissenschaften

Bibliographic Information published by the Deutsche Nationalbibliothek
The Deutsche Nationalbibliothek lists this publication in the Deutsche Nationalbibliografie; detailed bibliographic data is available in the internet at <http://www.d-nb.de>.

Printed with financial support of the Faculty of Arts at the Norwegian University of Science and Technology and the Center for Language Technology at the University of Copenhagen.

ISSN 0721-3352
ISBN 978-3-631-57550-5

Internationaler Verlag der Wissenschaften
Frankfurt am Main 2009

www.peterlang.de

To Peter Rossen Skadhauge.

Contents

Introduction

Anders Søgaard*
University of Copenhagen

Petter Haugereid†
Norwegian University of Science and Technology

1 Introduction

Typed feature structures (TFSs) are employed in a variety of linguistic theories. In this volume, four of these theories are represented: Combinatory Categorial Grammar (CCG), Construction Grammar (CG), albeit somewhat indirectly, Head-driven Phrase Structure Grammar (HPSG) and Lexicalized Tree-Adjoining Grammar (LTAG). TFSs have been studied from a mathematical point of view and employed in a wide range of empirical analyses and technological applications. The seven papers in this volume represent this diversity.

Six of the seven papers were presented at the 1st International Workshop on Typed Feature Structure Grammars in Aalborg, Denmark in the summer of 2006. The one-day workshop was a satelite event of the 22nd Scandinavian Conference of Linguistics. Nine papers were presented at the workshop. Two authors did not submit their paper to the post-conference proceedings, whereas the ninth paper remains unpublished for truly tragic reasons. Peter Rossen Skadhauge, a researcher at the Center for Computational Modelling of Language in Copenhagen, died only a few weeks after the workshop. His death is a great loss for computational linguistics, and this volume is dedicated to his memory.

2 Types

Untyped universes, such as naïve set theory, are organized in every day use whether we want it or not. This sometimes leads to slightly embarassing situations when we encounter objects in our universe that violate our informal organization. In naïve set theory, for instance, what is the set union of the function successor and the function predecessor? Similar situations may arise in linguistics, for instance with untyped feature structures. What is, for instance, the status of nonterminals in untyped feature structures?

* University of Copenhagen, Njalsgade 80, DK-2300 Copenhagen S, Denmark. Email: anders@cst.dk
† Norwegian University of Science and Technology, Dragvoll, N-7491 Trondheim, Norway. Email: petterha@hf.ntnu.no.

Some untyped universes, like naïve set theory, were found to be logically inconsistent, and typed versions were proposed to eliminate inconsistencies. Similarly, type signatures have been used to validate linguistic theories and grammars that make use of (typed) feature structures (Wintner and Sarkar, 2002).

In polymorphic typed languages, values and variables may have more than one type. We are only interested in finite universal polymorphism here, i.e. languages where functions work universally on a range of types, and the total set of types is finite. (In programming languages, the number of types is usually infinite. In most linguistic applications, finiteness has been assumed.) Two kinds of polymorphisms are typically employed with TFSs: parameterized and inclusion polymorphism. The paradigmatic programming languages that exemplify these two alternatives, are, respectively, Simula 67 and ML. If the reader has no idea what a parameterized type is, consult Remark 1.

3 Typed feature structures

TFSs are sisters of feature structures, also known as attribute-value structures or, simply, category structures – a data structure widely employed in linguistics. Feature structures were introduced in theoretical and computational linguistics in the seventies, and the theoretical notion was formalized in terms of automata and terms. See (Wedekind, 1997) for a traditional introduction to feature structures. It was later noted that feature structures also correspond closely to Kripke models (Blackburn, 1994). One form of notation employed frequently in this volume is in terms of attribute-value matrices (AVMs):

$$\begin{bmatrix} \text{FEAT}_1 & \begin{bmatrix} \text{FEAT}_2 \ \text{value}_2 \\ \text{FEAT}_3 \ \text{value}_3 \end{bmatrix} \\ \text{FEAT}_4 \ \text{value}_4 & \end{bmatrix}$$

Linguists usually associate feature structures with AVMs. The most common way to think of feature structures more formally is in terms of deterministic automata, however.

Example 1
An automaton appropriate for the reconstruction of the AVM depicted here is $D = \langle Q, \mathsf{Lbls}, \delta, q_0, \mathsf{Atms} \rangle$ with:

$$\begin{aligned} Q &= \{q_0, q_1\} \cup F \\ \mathsf{Lbls} &= \{\text{FEAT}_1, \text{FEAT}_2, \text{FEAT}_3, \text{FEAT}_4\} \\ \mathsf{Atms} &= \{\text{value}_2, \text{value}_3, \text{value}_4\} \\ \delta(q_0, \text{FEAT}_1) &= q_1 \\ \delta(q_0, \text{FEAT}_4) &= \text{value}_4 \end{aligned}$$

$$\begin{array}{rcl} \delta(q_1, \text{FEAT}_2) & = & \text{value}_2 \\ \delta(q_1, \text{FEAT}_3) & = & \text{value}_3 \end{array}$$

An alternative formalization is in terms of Ψ-terms. In the simplest cases, the two approaches are equivalent, but Ψ-terms were designed to facilitate inheritance. A relevant class of Ψ-terms consists of a greatest element $\perp$ and complex terms $t = \langle P, \mu, l \rangle$, where P is a set of strings over Lbls (the term domain), an equivalence relation μ on P, and a labelling function $l : P/\mu \rightarrow \mathsf{Atms}$, where P/μ is a set of equivalence classes.

Example 2
Our example is represented by the Ψ-term:

$$P = \left\{ \lambda,\ \text{FEAT}_1,\ \text{FEAT}_2,\ \text{FEAT}_3,\ \text{FEAT}_4,\ \text{FEAT}_1.\text{FEAT}_2,\ \text{FEAT}_1.\text{FEAT}_3 \right\}$$

$$\mu = \left\{ \begin{array}{l} \langle \lambda, \lambda \rangle,\ \langle \text{FEAT}_1,\ \text{FEAT}_1 \rangle,\ \langle \text{FEAT}_2,\ \text{FEAT}_2 \rangle, \\ \langle \text{FEAT}_3,\ \text{FEAT}_3 \rangle,\ \langle \text{FEAT}_4,\ \text{FEAT}_4 \rangle,\ \langle \text{FEAT}_1.\text{FEAT}_2,\ \text{FEAT}_1.\text{FEAT}_2 \rangle, \\ \langle \text{FEAT}_1.\text{FEAT}_3,\ \text{FEAT}_1.\text{FEAT}_3 \rangle \end{array} \right\}$$

$$\begin{array}{rcl} l(\text{FEAT}_1.\text{FEAT}_2) & = & \text{value}_2 \\ l(\text{FEAT}_1.\text{FEAT}_3) & = & \text{value}_3 \\ l(\text{FEAT}_4) & = & \text{value}_4 \end{array}$$

Of course μ is trivial in the absence of reentrancies. For more details, see (Wedekind, 1997).

From a more logical perspective, a feature structure is just a tuple of nodes, binary and unary relations $\langle \mathbb{N}, \{R_\lambda | \lambda \in \mathsf{Lbls}\}, \{Q_\alpha | \alpha \in \mathsf{Atms}\} \rangle$. The unary relations indicate the "value" of terminal nodes in the graphs.

Example 3
The AVM depicted above is from a logical perspective a tuple $\langle \{n_1, n_2, n_3, n_4\}$, $\{R_{\text{FEAT}_1}(c_0, c_1), R_{\text{FEAT}_2}(c_1, c_2), R_{\text{FEAT}_3}(c_1, c_3), R_{\text{FEAT}_4}(c_0, c_4)\}$, $\{\text{value}_2(c_2)$, $\text{value}_3(c_3), \text{value}_4(c_4)\}\rangle$. If the AVM is tilted slightly, it is seen that it corresponds to a Kripke model $\langle \mathbb{W}, \mathbb{R}, \mathcal{V} \rangle$, where $\mathbb{W} = \mathbb{N}, \mathbb{R} = \{R_{\text{FEAT}_1}(c_0, c_1), R_{\text{FEAT}_2}(c_1, c_2)$, $R_{\text{FEAT}_3}(c_1, c_3), R_{\text{FEAT}_4}(c_0, c_4)\}$ and $\mathcal{V}$ is a valuation function such that

$$\begin{array}{rcl} \mathcal{V}(\text{value}_2) & = & c_2 \\ \mathcal{V}(\text{value}_3) & = & c_3 \\ \mathcal{V}(\text{value}_4) & = & c_4 \end{array}$$

Feature structures are governed by a number of axioms. Axiomatizations differ, but three axioms are conventional:

- Attributes or features are partial functions,
- terminals (atoms or constants) have no attributes themselves, and
- distinct unary relations have distinct denotations.

In addition, people often assume that feature structures are acyclic and connected.[1] Sometimes feature structures are also explicitly finite. A feature structure grammar is defined with respect to a signature $\langle \mathsf{Lbls}, \mathsf{Atms} \rangle$, and some appropriateness function $\rho : \mathsf{Lbls} \rightarrow \mathsf{Atms}$, roughly equivalent to δ in automata theory and the labelling function l in the theory of Ψ-terms.

TFSs are obtained from feature structures by removing the last two axioms. Consequently, no atomic values are singled out. Every value is said to be of some type, whether complex or not. A value is in other words labeled (or typed), and it is also of the types that subsumes its label. (In Ψ-terms, the domain of our labelling function l is extended to cover the entire set of equivalence classes P/μ.)

We now have a fully typed universe. Polymorphisms induce a structure on universes. Our concern is, as already mentioned, with universal finite polymorphims, and they are typically said to come in two flavors, namely inclusion polymorphisms and parametric polymorphisms. The reader of this introduction is likely to be best acquianted with inclusion polymorphisms, even if the name doesn't ring a bell. Inclusion polymorphisms are the kind of ISA relationships that organize information in many linguistic theories, including CG and the most common versions of HPSG.

More formally, a partial order is imposed on the types such that for any pair of types t_1, t_2 there exists a type t_3 such that $t_3 \sqsubseteq t_1$ and $t_3 \sqsubseteq t_2$. Each attribute is introduced in a greatest type that specifies its appropriate values, and all subtypes inherit these restrictions. $t \sqsubseteq t'$ conveys, intuitively, that $\mathsf{ISA}(t', t)$. Such partial orders are called (inclusion) type hierarchies. Technically, they are non-empty, countable, bounded complete, partially ordered sets.[2]

The mathematically inclined reader may wonder if there is some redundancy in using both features and a partial order. Features can be omitted, but only at the expense of the finiteness of the signature. The expressivity gain from the partial

1 An interesting counterexample is the analysis of mutual subcategorization of adjectives and nouns in (Pollard and Sag, 1994). Their analysis relies on the existence of cyclic feature structures.

2 The alternative, parametric type hierarchies, are slightly more complex: A parametric type hierarchy is a finite bounded-complete partial order $\langle \mathsf{ParTypes}, \sqsubseteq_{\mathsf{P}} \rangle$ in which:

- $\mathsf{ParTypes}$ consists of simple and parametric types and includes the most general type $\perp$, which is simple, i.e. $\rho(\perp) = 0$,
- for $t, t' \in \mathsf{ParTypes}$, $g(t, t', i)$ is defined iff $t \sqsubseteq_{\mathsf{P}} t'$ and $1 \leq i \leq \rho(t)$,
- $0 \leq g(t, t', i) \leq \rho(t)$, when it exists, and
- if $g(t, t', i) \neq 0$ and $g(t, t', i) = g(t, t', j)$, then $i = j$.

where $\rho : \mathsf{ParTypes} \rightarrow \mathbb{N}_0$ is an arity function and $g : \mathsf{ParTypes} \times \mathsf{ParTypes} \times \mathbb{N} \rightarrow \mathbb{N}_0$ a partial assignment function.

order is apparent in many of the contributions to this volume, e.g. (Haugereid, 2006).

What happens to appropriateness when we move to a fully typed universe? In fact, appropriateness for TFSs under inclusion polymorphism was informally discussed in the early HPSG literature (Pollard and Sag, 1987, 38), but a formal definition was first proposed by (Carpenter, 1992):

Definition 1 Appropriateness specification
An appropriateness specification over an inheritance hierarchy $\langle \mathsf{Types}, \sqsubseteq \rangle$ and labels Lbls is a partial function $\mathsf{AppAttr} : \mathsf{Lbls} \times \mathsf{Types} \rightarrow \mathsf{Types}$ that meets the following conditions:

- for every label $l \in \mathsf{Lbls}$, there is a most general type $\mathit{Intro}(f) \in \mathsf{Types}$ such that $\mathsf{AppAttr}(f, \mathit{Intro}(f))$ is defined, and
- if $\mathsf{AppAttr}(f, \sigma)$ is defined and $\sigma \sqsubseteq \tau$, then $\mathsf{AppAttr}(f, \tau)$ is also defined and $\mathsf{AppAttr}(f, \sigma) \sqsubseteq \mathsf{AppAttr}(f, \tau)$.

See (Penn and Hoetmer, 2003) for a similar definition of appropriateness for parametric hierarchies.

Remark 1
Parametric polymorphism is sometimes more convenient than inclusion morphism in linguistic applications. Here's an example: In theories such as CG and HPSG, different kinds of lists are employed. Linguistic structures may, for instance, include lists of phonemes, lists of complements and lists of semantic predicates. Under inclusion polymorphism, lists are defined Prolog-style in terms of HEAD and TAIL attributes, but under parametric polymorphism it is possible to define a parametric type *list*(α), where α is the type of the list members (phonemes, complements or predicates). For more linguistic arguments in favor of parametric polymorphism, see (Penn, 2004), for instance. (Penn and Hoetmer, 2003) claim that the English Resource Grammar (Flickinger, 2000) could be abbreviated considerably by introducing parametric types.

(Carpenter, 1992, 79), on the other hand, points out that parametric polymorphism and cyclicity may lead to trouble, if parametric types are not themselves allowed to be cyclic. Consider, for instance, the value for α in the list:

$$\begin{bmatrix} \boxed{1}\mathit{list}(\alpha) \\ \text{HEAD } \boxed{1} \\ \text{TAIL } \boxed{1} \end{bmatrix}$$

Most of the contributions in this volume rely on inclusion polymorphism rather than parametric polymorphism; as already mentioned, inclusion hierarchies are the more conventional today. (Richter and Kallmeyer, 2006) implicitly assume parametric types.

4 The history of TFSGs

Feature structure grammars are also called unification-based grammars. Feature structure grammars were introduced in response to the limited generative capacity of context-free grammar. Other alternatives include transformational and tree-adjoining grammars. The expressivity gain comes from the definition of parsing and the use of variables (reentrancy). Variables can, for instance, be used to stack information. Consequently, indexed language-style analyses of cross-serial dependencies can be directly implemented. Parsing is defined with respect to subsumption ($\sqsubseteq$ or $\sqsubseteq_{\mathsf{P}}$). In the absence of off-line parsability, this licenses infinite loops.

Call linguistic theories that rely on TFSs to some extent for typed feature structure grammars (TFSGs). Some TFSGs (CG and HPSG, for instance) adopt both extensions, a new definition of parsing and variables. It is interesting to note that TFSs are not only used for parsing, however. In this volume, TFSs are also used for lexical organization and semantic composition. In addition, two semantic composition languages associated with the HPSG formalism are discussed, namely Lexical and Minimal Recursion Semantics (LRS and MRS). TFSs have also been used in the context of phonology, pragmatics and cognitive science.

The linguistic use of TFSs is probably most worked-out in the context of HPSG. The obvious reason is that TFSs were first introduced in this context. In HPSG, a grammar is simply defined as a type hierarchy $\langle \mathsf{Types}, \sqsubseteq \rangle$ or $\langle \mathsf{ParTypes}, \sqsubseteq_{\mathsf{P}} \rangle$ and a set of linguistic principles. Other theories have more complex ontologies and concern also the interaction of hierarchies and other modules. Even if only linguistic theories that use hierarchies and principles are considered, there is substantial difference in how they use TFSs. One such difference was already mentioned, the difference between inclusion and parametric polymorphism. The expressivity of the underlying formal languages also differ considerably. Two poles serve to illustrate the differences:

- The LinGO consortium defined a conservative blend of (Carpenter, 1992) and related logics that omits disjunction, negation, set values and relational dependencies. The purely conjunctive language was motivated by both linguistic and computational concerns. See (Oepen et al., 2000) for background papers.

- The Reusability of Grammatical Resources Project, under EAGLES Working Group on Grammar Formalisms, see, for instance, (Erbach et al., 1995), defined a richer formal language. The language is even richer than the one envisioned in (Pollard and Sag, 1994).

Little more is said about the formal properties of such languages in this introduction. Instead we focus on the linguistic side of this story. Here's a nice example of typical linguistic use of TFSs, adopted from (Flickinger, 2000):

Example 4
Consider the two analyses of non-third-singular present-tense verbs in English. First the two feature structures, one that uses disjunction and one that doesn't:

$$\begin{bmatrix} \textit{non3sg-verb} \\ \text{AGR} \left\{ \begin{matrix} \begin{bmatrix} \text{NUM sing} \\ \text{PERS} \left\{\textit{first,second}\right\} \end{bmatrix} \\ \begin{bmatrix}\text{NUM plur}\end{bmatrix} \end{matrix} \right\} \end{bmatrix} \begin{bmatrix} \textit{non3sg-verb} \\ \text{AGR} \begin{bmatrix}\text{PERNUM } \textit{non3sg}\end{bmatrix} \end{bmatrix}$$

and the two (partial) inclusion hierarchies, respectively:

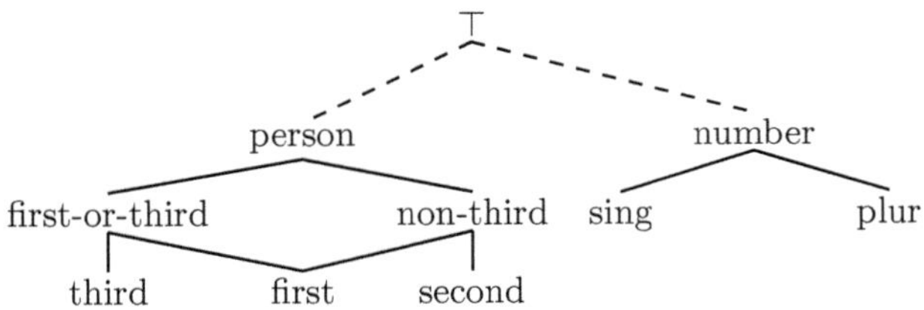

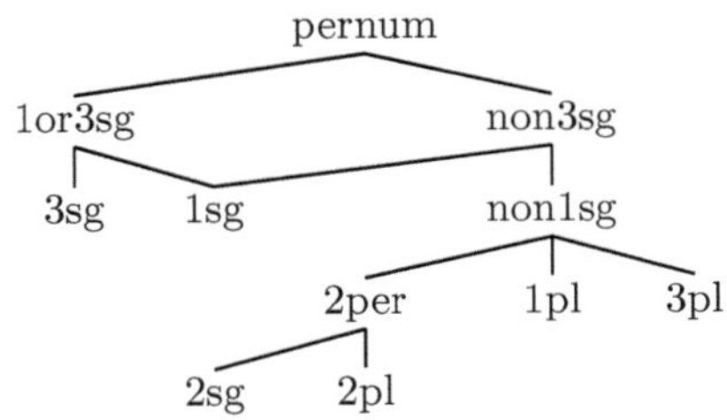

The second analysis makes heavier use of the hierarchy, and is more economic (viewed in isolation).

In fact, examples such as this motivated the choice of formal language in the LinGO consortium (Flickinger, 2000). The example is meant to illustrate the linguistic use of TFSs. Some papers in this volume make even heavier use of inheritance; see, for instance, (Haugereid, 2006).

It was mentioned in the first lines of this introduction that many linguistic theories count as TFSGs, or come in versions that rely on TFSs to some extent.

Here's a more complete list:

- HPSG (Pollard and Sag, 1987; Pollard and Sag, 1994)
- Definite Clause Grammar (Porter, 1987)
- Cognitive Grammar (Langacker, 1987)
- CUG (Kameyama, 1988; Moens et al., 1989)
- Word Grammar (Fraser and Hudson, 1992)
- Government and Binding (Meyers, 1994)
- LTAG (Evans, Gazdar, and Weir, 1995; Richter and Kallmeyer, 2006)
- CG (Kay, 2002)
- CCG (McConville, 2006)
- Discontinuous grammar (Buch-Kromann, 2006)

The hierarchies of one theory are usually comparable to hierarchies in other theories (to the extent they reflect similar linguistic generalizations). Some hierarchies have multiple inheritance, which is what licenses type *inference*, e.g. if a linguistic object is of type t_1 and t_2, it is of t_0 (where t_0 is the greatest lower bound of t_1 and t_2), a conclusion that may lead to further implications. Others have single inheritance. Compare, for instance, (46) in (Bjerre and Bjerre, 2006) with Figure 2 in (Flouraki, 2006) (both in this volume).

The first use of inheritance in linguistics is usually attributed to (Bobrow and Webber, 1980), but they didn't use feature structures. Of course TFSs serve different purposes in the various theories, even if they are quite similar from a formal point of view. The diversity of such purposes is displayed by the contributions of this volume. Some authors, as already mentioned, use TFSs for parsing, others for lexical organization or semantic composition.

5 The papers in this volume

5.1 Formalisms

It was pointed out in the introduction that TFSs are used in many formalisms. It is of interest to compare these uses and to study the effect of TFSs in different contexts. The papers in this section study complexity, compositionality and related design issues for different formalisms. Some of these formalisms are mildly context-sensitive (CCG, LTAG), while others are richer (HPSG).

Anders Søgaard: From unordered context-free grammar to polysize HPSG without moving The paper shows how an NP-complete TFSG can be obtained by "safe" extensions of unordered context-free grammar. It even suggests how a tractable fragment can be singled out. The bottom-up style of exposition clarifies how TFSG relates to many weaker formalisms.

Frank Richter and Laura Kallmeyer: Feature logic-based semantic composition: a comparison between LRS and LTAG Frank Richter and Laura Kallmeyer compare the use of TFSs in HPSG and LTAG. In particular, the semantic composition language LRS is compared to semantic composition in LTAG. Some illustratory linguistic analyses are provided, and the issue of compositionality is discussed. LTAG is shown to be compositional, while the compositionality of LRS remains an open question.

Mark McConville: Inheritance-based Combinatory Categorial Grammar Mark McConville puts TFSs to use in the context of CCG. His main motivation for this is to limit lexical redundancy and the complexity of lexical entries in CCG. McConville introduces two measures for lexical redundancy and lexical complexity, namely a functionality ratio ($\frac{e}{m}$) and an atomicity ratio ($\frac{s}{e}$), where e is the number of lexical entries, m the number of distinct morphemes, and s the number of category symbol tokens. The effect of using TFSs is illustrated by a small toy grammar. McConville integrates TFSs by reinterpreting CCG model-theoretically.

5.2 Syntactic and semantic analyses

Anne Bjerre and Tavs Bjerre: Sidder og ...: Constructional aspect in Danish The paper discusses syntactic and semantic aspects of the Danish *sidder og* V ('[sit]$_V$ and []$_V$') construction, an instance of what the authors call *pseudocoordination.* The construction seems to be restricted to a small class of similar verbs. One interesting aspect of this construction is its aspectual semantics. An implementation in the LKB system is presented.

The next paper is also about aspect:

Maria Flouraki: Aspectual composition in Minimal Recursion Semantics Aspectual composition, in the author's terminology, refers to the reinterpretation of verbs or nouns, when they combine with concepts that are incompatible in terms of eventuality type. The paper focuses on Modern Greek, a language with a particularly rich aspectual system. The proposal combines TFSs and insights from generative lexicon theory.

The last paper in this section is about one of the most talked-about linguistic constructions, but it presents a novel and, in the context of TFSs, very untraditional analysis:

Petter Haugereid: A constructional approach to syntax and the treatment of passive in Norwegian The paper presents a constructional approach to argument structure. All possible argument frames that verbs can occur in are assumed to be constellations of five syntactically realized sub-constructions. One of these sub-constructions can be realized as passive, in Norwegian either through the passive auxiliary *bli* or through the passive morpheme *-s*.

5.3 Language technology

TFSGs underlie many technological applications, as witnessed by the international Delph-In consortium (see `www.delph-in.net`), of which many authors of this volume are members. The paper in this section deals with one of the most challenging tasks in language technology, namely question answering. Other conventional applications of TFSGs include machine translation and email auto response.

Patrizia Paggio, Dorte Haltrup Hansen and Lene Offersgaard: Ontology-based question answering with feature structures The paper describes the use of TFSs in a major European ontology-based question-answering project. TFSs were used for parsing users' input, but also to inferface the grammar and an ontology. The authors focus on the semantics of questions, the interaction of grammar and ontology and the treatment of unknown words.

6 Acknowledgements

This publication is in part sponsored by Center for Language Technology at the University of Copenhagen and the Norwegian University of Science and Technology. Our thanks to the authors and the organizers of the 22nd Scandinavian Conference of Linguistics. Our most sincere thanks to the members of the workshop review committee:

- Lars Ahrenberg (Linköping University),
- Dan Flickinger (Stanford University),
- Lars Hellan (Norwegian University of Science and Technology),
- Lars G. Johnsen (University of Bergen),
- Stefan Müller (Universität Bremen and Universität Pottsdam),
- Stephan Oepen (University of Oslo and Stanford University),
- Jesse Tseng (CNRS Loria) and
- Jürgen Wedekind (University of Copenhagen).

The final papers were reviewed by the authors and

- Lars Ahrenberg (Linköping University),
- Carl Pollard (Ohio State University),
- Stefan Müller (Universität Bremen and Universität Pottsdam),
- Stephan Oepen (University of Oslo and CSLI, Stanford),
- Manfred Sailer (Universität Göttingen), and
- Jesse Tseng (CNRS Loria).

The value of their help cannot be overestimated. The 2nd International Workshop on Typed Feature Structure Grammars was held in Tartu, Estonia in May 2007 in conjunction with the 16th Nordic Conference of Computational Linguistics. The proceedings are available at

`cst.dk/anders/publ/tfsg/proceedings07.pdf.`

References

Bjerre, Anne and Tavs Bjerre. 2006. Sidder og .... In *this volume.*

Blackburn, Patrick. 1994. Structures, languages and translations: the structural approach to feature logic. In C. J. Rupp, Rod Johnson, and Michael Rosner, editors, *Constraints, language and computation.* Academic Press, London, pages 1–29.

Bobrow, Robert and Bonnie Webber. 1980. Knowledge representation for syntactic/semantic processing. In *Proceedings of the 1st National Conference on Artificial Intelligence*, pages 316–323, Stanford, California.

Buch-Kromann, Matthias. 2006. *Discontinuous grammar.* Copenhagen Business School, Copenhagen, Denmark: . Doctoral dissertation.

Carpenter, Bob. 1992. *The logic of typed feature structures.* Cambridge Tracts in Theoretical Computer Science, volume 32. Cambridge, England: Cambridge University Press.

Erbach, Gregor, Mark van der Kraan, Suresh Manandhar, Herbert Ruessink, Wojciech Skut, and Craig Thiersch. 1995. Extending unification formalisms. In *Second Language Engineering Convention*, London, England.

Evans, Roger, Gerald Gazdar, and David Weir. 1995. Encoding lexicalized tree adjoining grammars with a nonmonotonic inheritance hierarchy. In *Proceedings of the 33rd Annual Meeting of the Association for Computational Linguistics*, pages 77–84, Cambridge, Massachusetts.

Flickinger, Dan. 2000. On building a more efficient grammar by exploiting types. *Natural Language Engineering*, 6:15–28.

Flouraki, Maria. 2006. Aspectual composition in minimal recursion semantics. In *this volume.*

Fraser, Norman and Richard Hudson. 1992. Inheritance in word grammar. *Computational Linguistics*, 18(2):133–158.

Haugereid, Petter. 2006. A constructional approach to syntax and the treatment of passive in Norwegian. In *this volume.*

Kameyama, Megumi. 1988. Atomization in grammar sharing. In *Proceedings of the 26th Annual Meeting of the Association for Computational Linguistics*, pages 194–203, Buffalo, New York.

Kay, Paul. 2002. An informal sketch of a formal architecture for construction grammar. *Grammars*, 5(1):1–19.

Langacker, Ron. 1987. *Foundations of cognitive grammar.* Stanford, California: Stanford University Press.

McConville, Mark. 2006. Type-hierarchical combinatory categorial grammar. In *this volume.*

Meyers, Adam. 1994. *A unification-based approach to GB theory.* Ph.D. thesis, New York University, New York, New York.

Moens, Marc, Jo Calder, Ewan Klein, Mike Reape, and Henk Zeevat. 1989. Expressing generalizations in unification-based grammar formalisms. In *Proceedings of the 4th Conference of the European Chapter of the Association for Computational Linguistics*, Manchester, England.

Oepen, Stephan, Dan Flickinger, Hans Uszkoreit, and Jun-Ichi Tsujii. 2000. Introduction to this special issue. *Natural Language Engineering*, 6(1):1–14.

Penn, Gerald. 2004. Balancing clarity and efficiency in typed feature logic through delaying. In *Proceedings of the 20th Annual Meeting of the Association for Computational Linguistics*, pages 239–246, Barcelona, Spain.

Penn, Gerald and Kenneth Hoetmer. 2003. In search of epistemic primitives in the English Resource Grammar. In Stefan Müller, editor, *Proceedings of the 10th International Conference on Head-Driven Phrase Structure Grammar*, pages 318–337, Stanford, California. CSLI Publications.

Pollard, Carl and Ivan Sag. 1987. *Information-based syntax and semantics.* Chicago, Illinois: The University of Chicago Press.

Pollard, Carl and Ivan Sag. 1994. *Head-driven phrase structure grammar.* Chicago, Illinois: The University of Chicago Press.

Porter, Harry. 1987. Incorporating inheritance and feature structures into a logic grammar formalism. In *Proceedings of the 25th Annual Meeting of the Association for Computational Linguistics*, pages 228–234, Stanford, California.

Richter, Frank and Laura Kallmeyer. 2006. Feature logic-based semantic composition: a comparison between LRS and LTAG. In *this volume.*

Wedekind, Jürgen. 1997. Approaches to unification in grammar. In Patrick Blackburn and Maarten de Rijke, editors, *Specifying syntactic structure.* CSLI Publications, Stanford, California, pages 245–280.

Wintner, Shuly and Anoop Sarkar. 2002. A note on typing feature structures. *Computational Linguistics*, 28(3):389–397.

From unordered context-free grammar to polysize HPSG without moving

Anders Søgaard*
University of Copenhagen

1 Introduction

Complexity results are sometimes surprising. The story told in this paper, albeit a very simple one, is almost a mystery. It has been common knowledge ever since (Barton, Berwick, and Ristad, 1987) that the universal recognition problem of unordered context-free grammar (UCFG), a slight modification of context-free grammar specifically designed to encode free word order, is NP-complete, a result first proven in (Barton, 1985). On its own, it may surprise the reader that a context-free formalism has the same complexity as, for instance, off-line parsable lexical functional grammar (LFG); LFG has the capacity to generate some context-sensitive languages. Of course, the puzzle is only apparent. The literature includes a vast number of mildly context-sensitive formalisms, for which the universal recognition problem, by definition, is tractable. Of course the key to the NP-completeness of UCFG is the dissociation of dominance and precedence. It seems fair to conclude that, all things being equal, dissociation leads to intractability.

The correctness of this conjecture depends of course on what is meant by "all things being equal". Some indications are given in our final comments here. Back to our mystery: If "unordering", or dissociation of dominance and precedence, has this radical an effect on complexity, and since UCFG is actually NP-complete, one is lead to expect that even minor extensions of UCFG will take us beyond NPTIME. UCFG is, after all, as hard as any problem in NP, and the formalism is really simple, as indicated by its generative capacity. It is therefore of some surprise that UCFG can be extended in all sorts of ways without leaving the complexity class NP. In fact, it is possible to get very close to full-fletched (unordered or linearization-based) head-driven phrase structure grammar (HPSG), before universal recognition can no longer be encoded on a polynomial time bound nondeterministic Turing machine. The paper adds expressive power to UCFG step by step. Our point of departure is UCFG, but on our way we pass agreement grammar (AG) and unification categorial grammar (UCG) and common (albeit

* University of Copenhagen, Njalsgade 80, DK-2300 Copenhagen S, Denmark. Email: anders@cst.dk

rather poor) fragments of HPSG. Suddenly, we are there: a linguistically motivated fragment of HPSG suited in particular for the encoding of free word order. But wait a minute! It's a mystery! We realize at this late point of our journey that we never actually moved: We're still in NP.[1]

The structure of the paper is simple: Sect. 2 establishes the complexity of universal recognition of UCFG. A semantic proof technique is employed to establish an upper bound on complexity. The proof technique, which to the best of my knowledge is new in the context of linguistics, is introduced at this point for further reference. The proof is rather elaborate and relies on a translation of UCFG into dynamic logic, but its virtues become apparent later on. Sect. 3 concerns AG and UCG. First AG is formally defined. A translation of AG into dynamic logic is provided, similar to our translation of UCG, and the proof technique is again used to establish the upper bound on the complexity of the universal recognition problem for this theory. The lower bound is established by 3SAT reduction. The complexity of UCG, which is formally defined in the middle part of the section, is established in a similar way. In the last part of Sect. 3, our NP-completeness result is extended to cover an unordered and off-line parsable version of AG. Sect. 4 introduces a fragment of HPSG that extends this version of AG, but remains NP-complete. Sect. 5 considers the possibility of singling out tractable fragments, i.e. fragments whose universal recognition problems are decidable on polynomial time bound deterministic Turing machines. In this section, some results presented in a forthcoming journal article are briefly summarized. The last section, not surprisingly, summarizes our results.

2 Unordered context-free grammar

It should be apparent by now that this paper is about the complexity of universal recognition for various grammar formalisms. So we better define what we mean by universal recognition.

Definition 1
Universal recognition is the decision problem:

INSTANCE:	A grammar $\mathcal{G}$ and a string ω.
QUESTION:	Is ω in the language denoted by $\mathcal{G}$?

Our point of departure, we said, was UCFG. The definition is trivial for anyone who has seen the definition of context-free grammar before.

1 The tone is supposed to be a bit ironic here. The mystery is in a sense a trivial consequence of the way complexity classes are defined, but the observations are far from folklore in the linguistic community.

Definition 2
An unordered context-free grammar (UCFG) is a quadruple $\langle V_N, V_T, P, S\rangle$, where V_N is the set of nonterminals, V_T is the alphabet or terminals, P is a set of production rules, and $S \in V_N$. V_N, V_T, P are finite sets. Every rule $\rho \in P$ is written $\rho : A \rightarrow \omega$ where $A \in V_N$ and $\omega \in (V_N \cup V_T)^*$. If $\omega = x_1x_2x_3$, then $x_1x_2x_3$, $x_1x_3x_2$, $x_2x_1x_3$, $x_2x_3x_1$, $x_3x_1x_2$ and $x_3x_2x_1$ are derivable from A. If $\omega = x_1Bx_2$ is derivable from w and $B \rightarrow w' \in P$, then $x_1w'x_2$ is derivable from w too. The language denoted by $\mathcal{G} = \langle V_N, V_T, P, S\rangle$ is the set of strings $\{\omega \in V_T^* \mid S \stackrel{*}{\Longrightarrow} \omega\}$.

The lower bound on the complexity of the universal recognition problem was established in (Barton, Berwick, and Ristad, 1987) by reduction of the vertex cover problem. The proof is summarized below.

Lemma 1
Universal recognition of UCFG is NP-hard.

Proof
The vertex cover problem involves finding the smallest set V' of vertices in a graph $G = \langle V, E\rangle$ such that every edge has at least one endpoint in the set. Formally, $V' \subseteq V : \forall\{a,b\} \in E : a \in V' \vee b \in V'$. The problem is thus an optimization problem, formulated as a decision problem:

INSTANCE:	A graph G and a positive integer k.
QUESTION:	Is there a vertex cover of size k or less for G?

Say $k = 2, V = \{a,b,c,d\}, E = \{(a,c),(b,c),(b,d),(c,d)\}$. One way to obtain a vertex cover is to go through the edges and underline one endpoint of each edge. If you can do that and only underline two vertex symbols, a vertex cover has been found. Since $|V| = 4$, this is equivalent to leaving two vertex symbols untouched. Consequently, the vertex cover problem for this specific instance is encoded by the UCFG, where δ is a bookkeeping dummy symbol:

$$
\begin{array}{rcl}
S & \rightarrow & \rho_1\rho_2\rho_3\rho_4uu\delta\delta\delta\delta \\
\rho_1 & \rightarrow & a \mid c \\
\rho_2 & \rightarrow & b \mid c \\
\rho_3 & \rightarrow & b \mid d \\
\rho_4 & \rightarrow & c \mid d \\
u & \rightarrow & aaaa \mid bbbb \mid cccc \mid dddd \\
\delta & \rightarrow & a \mid b \mid c \mid d
\end{array}
$$

ρ_i captures the ith edge in E. The input string $\omega = aaaabbbbccccdddd$. One derivation structure in our example will have the form:

$$[[aaaa]_U[bbbb]_U[c]_{(b,c)}[c]_{(a,c)}[c]_{(c,d)}[c]_\delta[d]_{(b,d)}[d]_\delta[d]_\delta[d]_\delta]_S$$

Generally, the first production has as many ρ_i's as there are edges in the graph, $|V| - k$ many U's, and $|E| \times |V| - |E| - |E| \times (|V| - k)$ many δ's, i.e. the length of the string minus the number of edges and the extensions of $|V| - k$ many U's. The ρ_i productions are simple, U extends into $|E|$ many a's or b's and so on, and δ extends into all possible vertices. Since the grammar and input string can be constructed in polynomial time from an underlying vertex cover problem $\langle k, V, E\rangle$, universal recognition of UCFG must be at least as hard as solving the vertex cover problem. Since the vertex cover problem is NP-complete (Garey and Johnson, 1979), UCFG is accordingly NP-hard. ■

It should be trivial to see that UCFG is also *in* NP, and therefore NP-complete. The proof presented in (Barton, Berwick, and Ristad, 1987) is also relatively simple. Our proof, which is very different from the one presented in (Barton, Berwick, and Ristad, 1987), here will be rather elaborate, however. Why? Simply because a similar proof technique is used later on, and this is a good chance to familiarize yourself with it.

Lemma 2
Universal recognition of UCFG is in NP.

Proof
Let $\mathcal{G} = \langle V_N, V_T, P, S\rangle$ be a UCFG. τ translates G into a modal logic over models $\langle \mathcal{W}, \mathcal{R}, \mathcal{V}\rangle$, i.e. tuples of states (or worlds), relations and a valuation function $\mathcal{V} : \mathbb{PROP} \rightarrow 2^{\mathcal{W}}$, where $\mathbb{PROP}$ is the set of propositional variables:[2 3]

$$\begin{array}{r|rcl} a \in V_T : & \tau(a) & = & a(\in \mathbb{PROP}) \wedge t \\ \nu \in V_N : & \tau(\nu) & = & \nu(\in \mathbb{PROP}) \wedge n \\ A \rightarrow \omega \in P : & \tau(A \rightarrow \omega) & = & \tau(A) \rightarrow \langle \texttt{down}\rangle\sigma(\omega) \text{ where} \\ & & & \sigma(\epsilon) = \bot \text{ and } \sigma(X\omega') = \tau(X) \wedge \langle \texttt{down}\rangle\sigma(\omega') \end{array}$$

Of course τ needs to be total, and $\tau(V_N) \cap \tau(V_T) = \emptyset$, $\mathcal{W} \subseteq \tau(V_N) \cup \tau(V_T)$, and $\tau(S)$ is true in the initial state. One way to ensure the distinction between terminals and non-terminals, adopted here, is to introduce propositional variables t, n, and introduce axioms $\neg(t \wedge n)$ and $t \vee n$.

2 The reader for whom this is all new stuff, should probably consult an introductory textbook on modal logic, e.g. (Chellas, 1980). Briefly, modal logic is propositional logic plus a finite set of modalities quantifying over related states. Intuitively, $\langle\alpha\rangle\phi$ means that, from wherever you evaluate the formula, there is an α-transition to a state where ϕ holds true. If the $\langle\alpha\rangle$-operator is replaced with its dual, i.e. $[\alpha]\phi$, it means that ϕ holds true for all states reachable by an α-transition. UCFG trees are seen as Kripke models $\langle \mathcal{W}, R_{\texttt{down}}, R_{\texttt{right}}, \mathcal{V}\rangle$.

3 For convenience, disjunctive rules are omitted troughout the paper. Technically, the translation of such rules is trivial. Just assume to grammar to be in compact form and translate production rules into implications with $\tau(A)$ in the antecedent and disjunctive consequences.

Parsing then amounts to satisfiability of $S \wedge \langle \texttt{down}^* \rangle (w_1 \wedge \langle \texttt{right} \rangle w_2 \wedge \ldots)$.

Note that, ignoring our use of Kleene star, τ is not only a translation into modal logic, but into the modal logic D_c. Briefly, this modal logic is axiomatized by all propositional tautologies (**PROP**) and:

(K)	$\Box(p \rightarrow q) \rightarrow (\Box p \rightarrow \Box q)$
(Dual)	$\Box p \leftrightarrow \neg\Diamond\neg p$
(D$_c$)	$\Diamond p \rightarrow \Box p$

and the rules are substitution, detachment and generalization (Chellas, 1980). **(K)** ensures that all states are closed under logical consequence, **(Dual)** interrelates our modal operators, and **(D$_c$)** ensures that all relations are deterministic. (The axioms are copied for each relation, e.g. $R_{\texttt{down}}, R_{\texttt{right}}$ and so on.) Substitution and detachment are standard inference rules of propositional logic, detachment also known as modus ponens, and generalization allows you to infer that if ϕ is valid, then so is $\Box\phi$.

Example 1
$(\Diamond\neg q \wedge \Diamond(p \rightarrow q)) \rightarrow \Diamond\neg p$, which is not a theorem of standard modal systems such as K or $S5$, is a theorem of D_c, for instance:

1.	$\Diamond(p \rightarrow q) \rightarrow (\Box p \rightarrow \Box q)$	**(K)** + **(D$_c$)**
2.	$\Diamond(p \rightarrow q) \rightarrow (\neg\Box p \vee \Box q)$	1, **(PROP)**
3.	$(\neg\Box q \wedge \Diamond(p \rightarrow q)) \rightarrow \neg\Box p$	2, **(PROP)**
4.	$(\Diamond\neg q \wedge \Diamond(p \rightarrow q)) \rightarrow \Diamond\neg p$	3, **(Dual)**

D_c has an interesting property: The upper bound on the size of the domain of the satisfying models is $|\phi| + 1$, i.e. the length of the satisfied formula plus one. Consequently, satisfiability can be checked by an NP algorithm: Simply guess a model non-deterministically and evaluate it in polynomial time. Consider now D_c with Kleene star D_c^*. The satisfiability problem of this logic is EXPTIME-complete on arbitrary structures. Our use of D_c^* is restricted, however. Kleene star is only used over $R_{\texttt{down}}$. The maximum number of tuples in this relation is $(2n - 2)(n - 1)$ (the number of edges times the depth of the tree) if unary or non-branching productions are ignored. Unary productions are easily included, however; simply take the product of this number and $(u + 1)$, where u is the number of unary productions in the grammar. Since universal recognition turns into satisfiability on τ, this problem is no more complex than the satisfiability problem for D_c^* in this restricted use. ■

Remark 1
The property of interest of D_c is often called the polysize model property in the literature. This simply means that if a formula ϕ is satisfiable in some model then

there also exists a model whose size is polynomial in $|\phi|$ that satisfies ϕ. In other words, we don't need to worry about any bigger models to test satisfiability. Of course in the context of D_c, we don't even need to worry about all models of polynomial size, but to prove NP upper bounds, what is relevant is that models are polynomially bound. The reason is obvious: It is not possible to evaluate larger models in polynomial time (in the length of the input).

The theorem below is a direct consequence of the two lemmas just established:

Theorem
Universal recognition of UCFG is NP-complete.

3 Agreement grammar and unification categorial grammar

3.1 Agreement grammar

A UCFG is defined over a set of variables or non-terminals. Such variables represent syntactic categories. In agreement grammar (AG) (Barton, Berwick, and Ristad, 1987), categories are replaced by category structures. Informally, AGs are context-free grammars whose nonterminals are sets of attribute-value pairs. Category structures may be defined as:

Definition 3
A category structure of finite signature $\langle \mathsf{Attr}, \mathsf{Atms} \rangle$ is an ordered triple $\langle N, \{R_l\}_{l \in \mathsf{Attr}}, \{Q_\alpha\}_{\alpha \in \mathsf{Atms}} \rangle$, where N is a nonempty set of nodes; for each $l \in \mathsf{Attr}$, R_l is a binary relation on N that is a partial function; and for all $\alpha \in \mathsf{Atms}$, Q_α is a unary relation on N.

but the standard way of thinking about them is in terms of some specification $\rho : \mathsf{Attr} \rightarrow 2^{\mathsf{Atms}}$ from attributes into sets of values. Since $\mathsf{Attr}, \mathsf{Atms}$ are finite, ρ specifies a finite set of category structures $\mathcal{C}$. On this view, a category structure is a set of partial functions from attributes to values. Formally,

$$\mathcal{C} \quad = \quad \{\phi \in \mathsf{Attrs}^{\mathsf{Atms}} \mid \forall \alpha \in \mathtt{DOM}(\phi).\phi(\alpha) \in \rho(\alpha)\}$$

where $\mathsf{Attrs}^{\mathsf{Atms}}$ is the set of all partial functions from Attrs to Atms, $\mathtt{DOM}(\phi)$ is the domain of the function ϕ, and α is an element in this domain (an attribute).

Definition 4
Category structure σ extends σ' ($\sigma \sqsupseteq \sigma'$) iff $\forall \alpha \in \mathtt{DOM}(\sigma).\sigma'(\alpha) = \sigma(\alpha)$.

We single out a subset $\mathsf{AgrAttr}$ of Attr called the agreement attributes. It is universally required that the daughters of any rule in R bear the agreement features of the mother. In the next definition, this is captured by (1).

Definition 5
An agreement grammar is a five-tuple $\langle\langle \mathsf{Attr}, \mathsf{Atms}, \rho\rangle, \mathsf{AgrAttr}, V_T, P, S\rangle$, and $\mathsf{Attr} = \mathsf{AgrAttr} \cup \{\mathtt{cat}\}$, where **cat** is the attribute whose value is the syntactic category itself. Every category structure is specified for **cat**. Every production rule in P is of the form $C \to a$ or $C_0 \to C_1 \ldots C_n$ where

$$\forall f \in \mathtt{DOM}(C_0) \cap \mathsf{AgrAttr}.\forall 1 \leq i \leq n. f \in \mathtt{DOM}(C_i) \wedge C_i(f) = C_0(f) \qquad (1)$$

The language of an AG G is defined as

$$L(G) \quad = \quad \{x \in V_T^* : \exists S'.S' \sqsupseteq S \wedge S' \stackrel{*}{\Longrightarrow} x\}.$$

Lemma 3
The universal recognition problem for AG is in NP.

Proof
One typical proof of this is found in (Barton, Berwick, and Ristad, 1987). Instead we use the proof technique developed in the last section. Say τ is a translation of AGs into modal logic D_c.

$a \in V_T$:	$\tau(a)$	$=$	$a(\in \mathbb{PROP}) \wedge t$
$\nu \in \mathsf{Atms}$:	$\tau(\nu)$	$=$	$\nu(\in \mathbb{PROP}) \wedge a$
C :	$\tau(C)$	$=$	$\bigwedge_{\alpha \in \mathtt{DOM(C)}} \langle\alpha\rangle\tau(\phi(\alpha))$
$C_0 \to C_1 \ldots C_n$:	$\tau(C_0 \to C_1 \ldots C_n)$	$=$	$\tau(C_0) \to \langle\mathbf{down}\rangle\sigma(C_1 \ldots C_n)$ where $\sigma(\epsilon) = \bot$ and $\sigma(C_i C_{i+1} \ldots C_n) = \tau(C_i) \wedge \langle\mathbf{right}\rangle\sigma(C_{i+1} \ldots C_n)$

The axioms are obvious, except

$$\bigwedge_{\alpha \in \mathsf{AgrAttr}} \langle\alpha\rangle\phi \wedge \langle\mathbf{down}\rangle\top \to \langle\mathbf{down}\rangle\langle\alpha\rangle\phi \qquad (2)$$

This axiom captures the effect of the constraint in (1). Since our use of Kleene star is the same as for UCFG, the polysize model property can again be established, and universal recognition problem for AG is shown to be in NP. ■

It is not immediately obvious that AG is also NP-complete. D_c is obviously NP-complete, since it strictly extends propositional logic, whose satisfiability problem is NP-complete. The NP-completeness of AG is established in the next theorem:

Theorem
The universal recognition problem for AG is NP-complete.

Proof
It has already been established that the problem is in NP. Consequently, it is left for us to prove that the problem is also as hard as any problem in NP. One obvious strategy is 3SAT reduction (Garey and Johnson, 1979). The 3SAT problem is a variant of the satisfiability problem of propositional logic for conjunctions of clauses of three literals, e.g. $p \vee p \vee p \wedge \neg p \vee \neg p \vee \neg p$ is *not* satisfiable in any model. Its complexity is the same as its older sister's: It is NP-complete. It is relatively easy to code this problem up in AG. The details are left for the reader. *Hint:* Introduce agreement features for truth assignments and build ternary phrases that ensure at least one propositional variable in the original problem is true. Since agreement features must percolate by (1), you need four rules for each propositional variable (true and false for with and without negation). A proof is also found in (Barton, Berwick, and Ristad, 1987). ■

Consider a formalism AG_0, which is similar to AG, except the restriction that $\mathsf{Attr} = \mathsf{AgrAttr} \cup \{\mathtt{cat}\}$ is left out, and (1) is replaced by path equations. Somewhat surprisingly this leads to an undecidable formalism. The proof is reminiscent of (Johnson, 1988); it is not included here for brevity.

Theorem
The universal recognition problem for AG_0 is undecidable.

It teaches us an important lesson, however; namely the importance of off-line parsability in the context of category structures. It is necessary somehow to ensure that the derivation structure cannot be arbitrarily larger than the yield. For further reference, off-line parsability is formally defined here. Many alternative definitions are on the market, and most of them could probably replace this with no effect on subsequent results. See (Jaeger, Francez, and Wintner, 2005) for an overview. Of the definitions mentioned in that paper, ours is closest to "Kuhn's off-line parsability constraint".

Definition 6
A grammar G is off-line parsable, if for every $\omega \in L(G)$ there exists no derivation trees with cyclic branches.

3.2 Unification categorial grammar

In classical categorial grammar, the set of categories is defined recursively as:

Definition 7
The set of categories is the smallest set C such that $C_b \subset C$ where C_b is a finite set of basic categories, and $A/B, B\backslash A \in C$ if $A \in C$ and $B \in C$.

Informally, a UCG is a categorial grammar where the categories are replaced by category structures, and parsing is defined with respect to subsumption rather than exact matches. One way to encode functional application is in terms of reentrancy:

$$\begin{bmatrix} \text{CAT } \boxed{1} \\ \text{FUNCT} \begin{bmatrix} \text{FUNCT} \begin{bmatrix} \text{CAT } \boxed{1} \end{bmatrix} \\ \text{ARG} \begin{bmatrix} \text{CAT } \boxed{2} \end{bmatrix} \end{bmatrix} \\ \text{ARG} \begin{bmatrix} \text{CAT } \boxed{2} \end{bmatrix} \end{bmatrix}$$

The direction of application is ignored here, but is easily encoded. Since reentrant information is unbounded in these structures, i.e. the size of reentrant information is not fixed in advance, we need to step up our logics a bit; both D_c and D_c^* have the tree model property and are thus unable to encode unbounded reentrancies. We introduce intersection of modalities to accommodate this:

Definition 8
$D_c^{\cap}$ is the strict extension of D_c with the intersection operator defined on labels s.t $R_{\alpha\cap\beta} = R_\alpha \cap R_\beta$.

Our NP inclusion proof for UCG relies on the fact that the underlying derivation structures are polynomial in the input string length; in other words, UCG has the polysize model property. In fact, models (the ones we need to care about, that is) are linear and very small $(2n-1)$, since unary productions are absent in categorial grammar. Consequently, we only need to worry about our use of the intersection operator.

Lemma 4
UCG is in NP.

Proof
The number of reentrancies in a UCG derivation structure is linearly bound, since each functional application introduces two reentrancies, and no other reentrancies are introduced. The result follows immediately. ■

Theorem
UCG is NP-complete.

Proof
A 3SAT reduction is established in the same way as for AG. Simple ternary clauses are build such that one truth assignment percolates, and ternary clauses are conjoined by unification of semantic features. ■

3.3 Unordered and off-line parsable AG_0

It is easy to see that unordering a grammar doesn't have an effect on the maximum size of the smallest models that we need to consider. Consequently, the NP inclusion result for unordered and off-line parsable AG_0 can be established almost as a corollary of a similar result for off-line parsable AG_0. It is not obvious how such a result is established, however. One important assumption seems necessary to establish the result. Only attributes that are distributed in parallel with $R_{\mathtt{down}}$ (such as phonological and semantic difference lists) can be recursively defined. Formally,

Definition 9
An attribute $\alpha \in \mathsf{Attr}$ is distributed in parallel with some relation R_β iff $|R_\alpha| \leq |R_\beta|$.

This prevents us from forcing grids, for instance. If so, the maximum size of the smallest model we need to consider is $(2n-1)(u+1)p$ where p is the number of subpaths licensed by the non-recursive feature geometry. Of course, this is a rather brute force argument, and it is left for future research to come up with a logical characterization of this restriction. Off-line parsability, for instance, can be included in the axiom set, but the syntax somehow needs to be restricted to ensure the polysize model property. Our characterization is linguistic, but in the eyes of a logician, brute force is used. The lemma (and the subsequent theorem) follows anyway:

Lemma 5
Unordered and off-line parsable AG_0 is in NP if all attributes are in parallel distribution with $R_{\mathtt{down}}$ or non-recursively defined.

Theorem
Unordered and off-line parsable AG_0 is NP-complete if all attributes are in parallel distribution with $R_{\mathtt{down}}$ or non-recursively defined.

Proof
By strict inclusion of AG. ■

4 Head-driven phrase structure grammar

Some knowledge about the peculiarities of HPSG is helpful to read this section, but it shouldn't be necessary. Our exposition is somewhat "head-on", but a theory-neutral definition of the linguistic theory of interest is provided in a minute. Compared to the standard version of HPSG, presented in (Pollard and Sag, 1994), the theory presented here is a bit limited. Certain prominent features of standard HPSG are ignored: lexical rules, set values and explicit relational dependencies. This is for expository reasons as well as technical ones.[4] The fragment of HPSG that our theory corresponds to is comparable, but *not* equivalent to LKB-style HPSG (Copestake, 2001). For one thing, LKB-style HPSG employs lexical rules. In addition, there is no dissociation of dominance and linear precedence in this version of HPSG. It is an interesting challenge to formalize the more complex standard version of HPSG in extensions of modal logic; this line of research is currently pursued in joint work with Martin Lange. In this work, it is also shown how to single out a rather subtle fragment of HPSG that includes set values and relational dependencies, but remains NP-complete. In this section, the fragment considered is a bit poorer, but expressivity is still considerable, compared to UCFG, AG, and so on.

How is the version of HPSG described here different from unordered and off-line parsable AG_0? Only in two respects, actually:

- It uses propositional variables ($\mathbb{PROP}$) to decorate non-terminals in the feature geometry, and
- it arranges propositional variables in an inheritance hierarchy.

The last point is, as the reader is likely to know (having read the introduction to this volume, if not from previous encounters with similar theories), an important characteristic of HPSG. It allows us to talk about subsets of sets of linguistic structures and declare properties of such structures in an economic fashion. Under certain circumstances, this means a gain in expressive power. It is important to note, however, that the arrangement of propositional variables itself can be coded up in full in propositional logic. Consider our extension of our translation function τ to see how this works:

$$t \sqsubseteq t' : \mid \tau'(t \sqsubseteq t') \quad \Rightarrow \quad \tau(t) \leftarrow t'$$

Extension is, in other words, translated into implication. Of course this is not enough (as indicated by our use of $\Rightarrow$). It is necessary to say that (with some abuse of notation)

4 The reason for ignoring lexical rules, set values and relations are, respectively: (i) Lexical rules, on their most orthodox interpretation, leads to undecidability, immediately (Carpenter, 1991), (ii) Kripke structures that present sets of unbounded size, say linear in the length of the input string, are themselves exponential in this number, and (iii) explicit operators for relational dependencies complicate our logic considerable, at the cost of clarity.

$$\tau'(t \sqsubseteq t_1 \wedge \ldots \wedge t \sqsubseteq t_n) \quad \Rightarrow \quad t \rightarrow t_1 \vee \ldots \vee t_n$$

This condition says that any linguistic object of some type must be in the denotation of one its subtypes. Of course types that are not vertically related (one dominates the other), have disjoint denotations. Type hierarchies are usually said to satisfy a number of extra conditions, that is, they must be finite and complete. The relevant axioms are ignored here.

Call our fragment of HPSG HPSG$^-$. It is defined, briefly (informally):

Definition 10
An HPSG$^-$ grammar is a tuple $\langle\langle \mathsf{Types}, \sqsubseteq\rangle, P, S\rangle$. Every production rule in P is of the form $t \rightarrow a$ or $t \rightarrow t_1 \ldots t_n$ and unordered, and the grammar itself is off-line parsable. The appropriate attributes of a type are determined by $\mathsf{AppAttr} : \langle \mathsf{Type}, \sqsubseteq\rangle \rightarrow \mathsf{Attr}$, and if $\mathsf{AppAttr}(t, \alpha)$ and $t \sqsubseteq t'$, then $\mathsf{AppAttr}(t', \alpha)$. The appropriate values of attributes are determined by a specification function ρ that specifies the most general value of every attribute.

While Atms is not singled out from Types in the definition of HPSG$^-$ grammars, the distinction is maintained in the translation for easier comparison. The last clauses of our new definition of τ:

$t \in \mathsf{Atms}$:	$\tau'(t)$	$=$	$t(\in \mathbb{PROP})$
$t \sqsubseteq t'$:	$\tau'(t \sqsubseteq t')$	$\Rightarrow$	$\tau(t) \leftarrow t'$
$t \in \mathsf{Types} - \mathsf{Atms}$:	$\tau'(t)$	$=$	$t(\in \mathbb{PROP}) \wedge \forall \alpha \in \mathsf{AppAttr}(t).\langle\alpha\rangle\alpha'(t)$

Briefly, this amounts to translating all atomic types into propositional variables and complex types into attribute-value structures. $\mathsf{AppAttr} : \langle \mathsf{Type}, \sqsubseteq\rangle \rightarrow \mathsf{Attr}$, and $\alpha'(t)$ is the value of α in the declaration of t.

HPSG$^-$ is richer than AG_0 in a linguistic sense, since inheritance can be used to capture linguistic generalizations, but also in a mathematical sense, since a great number of ambiguities can now be underspecified by introduction of supertypes that encode the intersection of linguistic types. The complexity is immediate, however:

Lemma 6
HPSG$^-$ is in NP.

Proof
The propositional theory of linguistic types has no effect on the size of the models and does not require additional logical power. ■

Our fragment is also richer than a similar fragment of HPSG introduced by (Trautwein, 1995) and proven therein to be NP-complete, for one particular reason: Unordered interpretation of phrases (rules) is permitted. Such an extension is not immediate in (Trautwein, 1995), but is entirely obvious at this point of our journey. The reason is, of course, that our proof technique relies on the size of the smallest models we need to consider.

Theorem
$HPSG^-$ is NP-complete.

Proof
By strict inclusion of the NP-complete fragment of AG_0 and Trautwein's fragment of HPSG. ■

5 Can we walk backwards without cutting off our legs?

We've come a long way, but surprisingly, our theorems remind us that we're still in NP. This is of course a pleasant surprise. No sane linguist would hope for his theory to turn out undecidable. Unfortunately, NP-hard theories are sometimes not efficient enough. In real life, linguists find *ad hoc* ways of avoiding the complexities of NP-hard theories, but everyone prefers truly tractable theories. It thus makes sense to ask if there is a way to walk backwards, from NP to P? In other words, is there a way to single out a tractable fragment of $HPSG^-$?

This section is a small summary of a (Søgaard and Haugereid, 2007) and related work. In this article, a tractable theory is developed which maintains a number of nice properties at the expense of ambiguity in parse charts. The properties include:

- unordered rules (and local and global constraints on linear precedence),
- LFG-style functional uncertainty over grammatical attributes,
- HPSG-style inheritance, and
- unrestricted reentrancies.

Such a grammar is easily encoded in D_c^* with intersection, but on arbitrary structures this logic has an undecidable satisfiability problem (Harel, 1985). What to do?

Our strategy is to restrict ambiguity. A rigid lexicon is the first constraint to be imposed. In a rigid lexicon every phonological string is associated with at most one lexical entry. If this sounds odd to the reader, remember that since HPSG-style inheritance is adopted, we are free to underspecify lexical ambiguities. In the case of open class items, this is unproblematic. In the case of closed class items, which are typically used to further specify the open class ones, it may be more problematic. If the number of closed class items and lexical ambiguity is fixed, ambiguous closed class items are tolerated. The next step is to restrict ambiguity in parsing.

Definition 11
A sign is horizontally k-ambiguous if it only combines with k signs in a sentence. A grammar is horizontally k-ambiguous if all signs are k-ambiguous. A grammar is vertically k-ambiguous if signs are combined unambiguously after k steps.

It is important to remember that our unordered grammars allow signs to combine non-locally. The notion of k-ambiguity can be illustrated by an example from Icelandic:

Example 2
Icelandic has nominative objects. Consider, for instance:

(3) *Hún* *spurði* *hvort* *sá* *grunaði* *væri*
she asked whether the.NOM suspected.NOM was.3SG.SUBJ
örugglega *þú.*
surely you.SG.NOM
'She asked whether the suspect surely was you.'

In addition, both SVO and OVS constructions occur. So in many cases, a verb that seeks to combine with an object has more than one candidate for doing so, even in sentences with only three constituents:

The V constituent is said to be horizontally 2-ambiguous in this case.

The results below are obtained in the forthcoming paper:

Theorem
Vertically k-ambiguous HPSG$^-$ is in P.

Theorem
Horizontally 1-ambiguous HPSG$^-$ is in $\mathcal{O}(n^3)$.

The proofs can be found in (Søgaard and Haugereid, 2007) and related work. In addition, it turns out that the k-ambiguous languages cross-cut the Chomsky Hierarchy in an interesting way. They include context-sensitive languages, but not all the context-free ones. Horizontally 1-ambiguous HPSG$^-$ also turns out to be learnable under relatively uncontroversial circumstances.

6 Conclusions

It was shown that somewhat surprisingly, a reasonably interesting fragment of HPSG is no more complex than UCFG. Both theories are NP-complete. The results were obtained under a semantic proof-technique that relied heavily on the notion of polysize model property. Some suggestions as to how a tractable fragment is singled out, were presented.

References

Barton, Edward. 1985. The computational difficulty of ID/LP parsing. In *Proceedings of the 23th Annual Meeting of the Association for Computational Linguistics*, pages 76–81, Chicago, Illinois.

Barton, Edward, Robert Berwick, and Erik Ristad. 1987. *Computational complexity and natural language*. Cambridge, Massachusetts: MIT Press.

Carpenter, Bob. 1991. The generative power of categorial grammars and head-driven phrase structure grammars with lexical rules. *Computational Linguistics*, 17(3):301–313.

Chellas, Brian. 1980. *Modal logic*. Cambridge, England: Cambridge University Press.

Copestake, Ann. 2001. *Implementing typed feature structure grammars*. Stanford, California: CSLI Publications.

Garey, Michael and David Johnson. 1979. *Computers and intractability*. New York, New York: W. H. Freeman & Co.

Harel, David. 1985. Recurring dominoes: making the highly undecidable highly understandable. *Annals of Discrete Mathematics*, 24:51–72.

Jaeger, Efrat, Nissim Francez, and Shuly Wintner. 2005. Unification grammars and off-line parsability. *Journal of Logic, Language and Information*, 14:199–234.

Johnson, Mark. 1988. *Attribute-value logic and the theory of grammar*. Stanford, California: CSLI Publications.

Pollard, Carl and Ivan Sag. 1994. *Head-driven phrase structure grammar*. Chicago, Illinois: The University of Chicago Press.

Søgaard, Anders and Petter Haugereid. 2007. A tractable typed feature structure grammar for Mainland Scandinavian. *Nordic Journal of Linguistics*, 30(1):87–128.

Trautwein, Maarten. 1995. *Computational pitfalls in tractable grammar formalisms*. Ph.D. thesis, University of Amsterdam, Amsterdam, the Netherlands. ILLC Dissertation Series DS-1995-15.

Feature logic-based semantic composition: a comparison between LRS and LTAG

Frank Richter*
University of Tübingen

Laura Kallmeyer†
University of Tübingen

In this paper we will explore the similarities and differences between two feature logic-based approaches to the composition of semantic representations. The first approach is formulated for Lexicalized Tree Adjoining Grammar (LTAG, (Joshi and Schabes, 1997)), the second is Lexical Resource Semantics (LRS, (Richter and Sailer, 2004)) and was first defined in Head-driven Phrase Structure Grammar. The two frameworks have several common characteristics that make them easy to compare: 1. They use languages of two-sorted type theory for semantic representations. 2. They allow underspecification: LTAG uses scope constraints $\geq$ while LRS provides component-of constraints $\triangleleft$. 3. They use feature logics for computing semantic representations. 4. They are designed for computational applications. By comparing the two frameworks we will also point out some characteristics and advantages of feature logic-based semantic computation in general.

1 Introduction

Except for a few early and largely informal explorations of the relationship between semantic representations in unification-based frameworks using typed feature logics (TFLs) and the lambda calculus-based Montague Grammar of mainstream research on semantics in linguistics (c.f. (Moore, 1989; Nerbonne, 1992)), for a long time there was little or no explicit connection between these two techniques for semantic representations. (Sailer, 2003) finally proved that a feature logic for Head-driven Phrase Structure Grammar (HPSG, (Pollard and Sag, 1994)) such as Relational Speciate Re-entrant Language (RSRL, (Richter, 2004b)) is sufficiently expressive to encode a higher-order logic such as Intensional Logic or two-sorted type theory (Ty2, (Gallin, 1975)), and the combinatorial system of the lambda calculus. This means that it is mathematically possible to completely embed a categorial semantics such as Flexible Montague Grammar (Hendriks, 1993)

* University of Tübingen, Seminar für Sprachwissenschaft, Wilhelmstraße 19, D-72074 Tübingen, Germany. Email: fr@sfs.uni-tuebingen.de
† University of Tübingen, Collaborative Research Center 441, Nauklerstr. 35, D-72074 Tübingen, Germany. Email: lk@sfs.uni-tuebingen.de

within a TFL grammar. However, undecidability results make it unattractive to integrate RSRL or alternative feature logics that are expressive enough for a direct logical specification of HPSG grammars wholesale in grammar development environments. On the other hand, reducing the expressivity of the feature logic prevents a logical specification in the feature logic of the syntax of Ty2 and basic operations of the lambda calculus such as beta reduction. In addition, it should be noted that it is at least an open question whether the assumption is justified that semantic composition in natural languages can be adequately described by the techniques provided by the lambda calculus. Other means of semantic composition might turn out to be better suited to analyze the relationship between the semantics of syntactically complex expressions and their constituents in natural languages.

To prevent misunderstandings it should be stressed very clearly that we do not mean to say that the lambda calculus is in any sense insufficient for specifying the composition of meanings along the syntactic structures of natural languages. Due to the universal nature of the lambda calculus as an abstract characterization of computation it is likely that this goal could be achieved. The question that we want to raise is whether the lambda calculus is a linguistically *adequate* tool for expressing as directly as possible the most important linguistic generalizations over the mechanisms of semantic composition in natural languages. One of the prime purposes of this paper is to present key concepts of an attractive alternative to the lambda calculus. These key concepts will appear in two mathematical implementations. The two views on the same concepts that our comparison of two frameworks offers are meant to highlight what belongs to the abstract ideas behind what we essentially view as one single alternative, and what is due to particular realizations of the basic concepts in terms of different mathematical structures in two grammar frameworks.

Unification-based LTAG semantics (Kallmeyer and Romero, 2007) and LRS (Richter and Sailer, 2004) draw different conclusions from the tension between the expressivity needed in a feature logic for the specification of the combinatorics and representations of Ty2, and the requirements of effective computation. As one of the consequences, they use feature logics of different expressivity for similar purposes in semantic composition. Like Minimal Recursion Semantics (MRS, (Copestake et al., 2005)) they do not use the lambda calculus but the feature logic for the semantic combinatorics. In contrast to MRS, however, which focuses almost entirely on the design of semantic representations for large-coverage grammars without saying much about the interpretation of the derived representations, LTAG semantics and LRS subscribe to model-theoretic semantics and truth conditions specified in terms of Ty2. To overcome the tension between the demands on the expressivity of the feature logic and on the computational properties of the system, LTAG semantics and LRS choose different options. LTAG semantics combines a restricted feature logic with other mathematical structures that provide semantic representations and take over computational tasks. LRS relies on a uniform logical specification and a re-implementation of the LRS module of grammars in a computationally tractable constraint language. Important features of these two options of implementing constraint-based semantic composition will be worked out in the course of our discussion below.

In this paper we will investigate the two solutions which our two frameworks provide for integrating a model-theoretic semantics with syntactic structures using typed feature logics. We will focus on the technical choice points, identifying those properties of the two syntax-semantics interfaces which the two approaches have in common despite the technical differences, and those which differ due to different means of combining the syntactic and semantic module of grammar. This will also help distinguish fundamental properties of a feature logic-based syntax-semantics interface from accidental properties of a single system which are due to particular grammar architectures.

The paper is structured as follows: Sections 2 and 3 will lay the mathematical foundations for the comparison of the two frameworks. Section 2 will briefly introduce the most important logical properties of the HPSG framework, indicate how LRS can be specified in the same TFL as an HPSG grammar, and present the most important principles of LRS together with the analysis of a simple sentence. Section 3 is the counterpart of Section 2 for LTAG: A short summary of the mathematical architecture of LTAG is followed by an overview of the framework for LTAG with semantic unification and the role of TFL in this framework. The analysis of our simple example illustrates how the components of the theory interact. The next two sections are concerned with a direct comparison of specific crucial aspects of LRS and LTAG semantics. Section 4 focuses on the treatment of scope ambiguities and the role which TFL plays in their description. Section 5 shows how the differences in the application of semantic underspecification techniques in LRS and LTAG lead to different analyses of negative concord, an interesting linguistic phenomenon at the syntax-semantics interface. Section 6 turns to the conceptually important question of whether semantic systems whose combinatorics is based on feature logic are compositional. Although received opinion has it that they are not, Section 6 sketches a construction for LTAG that indicates that this might not be true. Section 7 concludes our investigation by a summary of the differences between the two systems and of the common properties of TFL-based semantic computation.

2 Lexical Resource Semantics

In the LRS architecture the feature logic may be used to specify the entire grammar, including well-formed Ty2 terms as semantic representations, and their mode of composition. This idea is particularly straightforward to implement in HPSG, since HPSG assumes an expressive feature logic as the single means of stating the entire grammar. While HPSG is by no means the only grammar architecture which can be combined with an LRS component, combining them is particularly simple, because the HPSG constraint language itself can be employed to specify the LRS structures. In this section we will explain how this can be achieved and what it means for an HPSG grammar with LRS semantics.

2.1 HPSG: Grammars as Logical Theories

From a mathematical point of view, an HPSG grammar is a logical theory consisting of a signature and a set of axioms. The purpose of the logical theory is to characterize all and only the grammatical linguistic structures of a natural language. The signature declares the non-logical symbols which the grammar writer may use, and it imposes certain structural conditions on interpretations of the grammar. Non-logical symbols of this kind of feature logic are sorts, attributes and relation symbols. The set of sorts is organized in a partial order, which is called the *sort hierarchy*. Examples of sorts are *sign*, *word* and *phrase*, and the HPSG sort hierarchy puts *word* and *phrase* below *sign*. HPSG's *signs* must have a SYNSEM attribute with values of sort *synsem*, *category* objects (which are found as values of the attribute CATEGORY) must have a HEAD attribute with a small set of possible values while they do not have a SYNSEM attribute, and so on. Typical HPSG relations are the binary relation `member` (for stating that some entity is on a list or in a set) and the ternary relation **append**, which is often used to state that the list-value of an attribute is obtained by appending the list-value of a second attribute to the list-value of a third attribute. The structural restrictions on interpretations that we have described above come from appropriateness conditions which declare certain attributes (such as SYNSEM) appropriate to certain sorts (such as *sign*) and prescribe the possible sort-values of these pairs (e.g., *synsem*).[1]

The statements of the logical theory (the axioms) are known to linguists as the principles of grammar. Their syntax uses the standard boolean logical connectives (conjunction, disjunction, negation, etc.), existential and universal quantification, and the attributes, sorts and relation symbols of the signature. The syntactic component of an HPSG grammar uses these symbols to state principles such as the HEAD FEATURE PRINCIPLE (the head value of a phrase and its head daughter are identical), the SUBCATEGORIZATION PRINCIPLE (regulating the discharge of arguments of a syntactic functor) or the IMMEDIATE DOMINANCE PRINCIPLE (playing the role of phrase structure rules of generative frameworks). We will not repeat any of these principles but illustrate HPSG's typed feature logic with a brief sketch of a TFL specification of LRS.

2.2 HPSG with an LRS Semantics

In a TFL specification of LRS, two components can be distinguished. First, we need to specify the syntax of the language of semantic representations, i.e., the

1 Readers more familiar with algebraic specifications might note that sorts here are like their types, and attributes are like unary term constructors. There are no counterparts of constants in algebraic signatures. Thanks are due to an anonymous reviewer for pointing this out.

language which we want to use to specify the meaning of linguistic signs. In previous work on LRS, this has always been Ty2 for compatibility with the semantics literature in linguistics, but many other logical languages are conceivable candidates without major changes to the overall architecture of LRS. Second, the combinatoric system must be specified. The combinatorics determines how the restrictions on semantic representations provided by syntactic daughters and their mode of combination as well as the nature of their syntactic mother determine the restrictions on the meaning of the phrase. It is this combinatoric system and the kind of structural information in syntax and semantic representations that it refers to which form the core of the LRS theory. In principle, any logical language strong enough to express these principles, and any syntactic theory which comprises the relevant syntactic structures can be used to specify a grammar with an LRS module.

The TFL specification of the syntax of Ty2 is very technical, and we do not need all of its details in the present context. To provide a general impression of how it works, Fig. 1 shows a fragment of a signature for Ty2.

```
ty2
  me  TYPE  type
    variable  NUM-INDEX  integer
    constant  NUM-INDEX  integer
    application  FUNCTOR  me
                 ARG      me
    abstraction  VAR   variable
                 BODY  me
    equation  ARG1  me
              ARG2  me
    negation  ARG  me
    generalized-quantifier  VAR    var
                            RESTR  me
                            SCOPE  me
      every
      some
      three
    logical-constant  ARG1  me
                      ARG2  me
      disjunction
      conjunction
      implication
      bi-implication
    ...
```

Figure 1
Fragment of the signature for a grammar of Ty2 expressions

The sort *ty2* subsumes all other sorts in the hierarchy, as indicated by indentation. Its most important subsort is *me (meaningful expression)*, with maximally specific subsorts for the logical constructs needed in the language. All expressions are typed, with the types encoded as values of an attribute TYPE. Variables and constants bear a natural number as their index, since our semantic representation language provides a countably infinite set of variables and constants of each type. For example, the 127th constant of type e is designated $\mathsf{const}_{\langle 126,e\rangle}$. In linguistic grammars, these constants are usually given more intuitive names. The constant $\mathsf{const}_{\langle 126,e\rangle}$ might thus be referred to by the symbol john', and $\mathsf{const}_{\langle 126,\langle e,t\rangle\rangle}$ by laugh'. Our signature fragment also includes sorts for three generalized quantifiers, *every*, *some* and *three*, which we will need in our linguistic examples. These generalized quantifiers can of course already be expressed with other basic constructions in our syntax for semantic representations, *viz.* variables, application, lambda abstraction and equations. Including them explicitly in our syntactic constraint language for Ty2 expressions will, however, turn out more than just a simple convenience when we formulate restrictions on the occurrence of (subsets of) quantificational expressions within certain structural domains. Further details of the signature of Ty2 such as the sort symbols for the encoding of integers and the type system are omitted from Fig. 1.

Of course, the signature alone does not guarantee the well-formedness of the expressions in the denotation of the grammar. To obtain this, we need a theory of the set of well-formed expressions of Ty2. (1) shows two of the necessary principles:[2]

(1) a. $$\textit{application} \rightarrow \begin{bmatrix} \text{TYPE} & \boxed{2} \\ \text{FUNCTOR TYPE} & \begin{bmatrix} \text{IN} & \boxed{1} \\ \text{OUT} & \boxed{2} \end{bmatrix} \\ \text{ARG TYPE} & \boxed{1} \end{bmatrix}$$

b. $$\textit{equation} \rightarrow \begin{bmatrix} \text{TYPE} & \textit{truth} \\ \text{ARG1 TYPE} & \boxed{1} \\ \text{ARG2 TYPE} & \boxed{1} \end{bmatrix}$$

(1a) requires that in an application, the argument be of a type that the functor can combine with, and the resulting type is determined by the functor. For example, if the functor is of type $\langle e,t\rangle$, it takes an argument of type $\langle e\rangle$ and yields an expression of type $\langle t\rangle$. (1b) says that an equation is of a truth type (i.e., true or false), and the two arguments of an equation are of the same type. More restrictions of this kind are needed for all logical connectives, as well as restrictions which guarantee the finiteness of Ty2 structures and the existence of a bijection of Ty2 expressions and the Ty2 structures in the denotation of the TFL specification

2 In RSRL, tags are treated as variables, and all variables in grammar principles must be bound by a quantifier. By convention, if no quantifier binds a tag in a given principle, this tag is understood to be bound by an existential quantifier taking wide scope over the entire expression.

of Ty2.[3] The full set of axioms needed in a TFL encoding of Ty2 can be found in (Penn and Richter, 2004, pp. 426–429). In order to avoid cumbersome notation, TFL descriptions of Ty2 expressions are typically avoided in specifications of LRS grammars. Instead it is common practice to write (partial) Ty2 expressions in TFL descriptions. It is important to keep in mind that this notation actually abbreviates descriptions of Ty2 expressions, and one such meta-expression may in fact describe an infinite number of Ty2 expressions. This should become clearer in our examples below.

For our comparison with semantics in LTAG the specification of the combinatorial system of LRS is even more important than the exact details of a TFL encoding of Ty2. The main idea here is as follows: Signs refer to various aspects of their meaning in various feature values. The values of their LRS features restrict the meaning contribution to the utterances in which the signs may occur. Although it is very tempting at the beginning, the Ty2 values of LRS attributes such as EXCONT, INCONT and PARTS should thus not be understood as describing separate Ty2 expressions. It is more useful to think of the descriptions of these feature values in a sign as separate but interacting constraints on the possible meanings of the utterance to which the sign belongs. Metaphorically speaking, these restrictions are collected as we go up the syntactic tree until we have collected them all as restrictions on the EXCONT value of the overall utterance. LRS grammars are written in such a way that the EXCONT value of an utterance is a Ty2 expression which specifies the meaning of the utterance. When looking at each utterance in the denotation of an LRS grammar one discovers that in fact all LRS attributes of all signs in the utterance have values which are components of this EXCONT value. In other words, the descriptions of these feature values in the grammar turn out to be restrictions on the EXCONT value of the utterances predicted by the grammar.

The schematic description of signs in Fig. 2 reveals the main distinctions made in the feature geometry. LRS distinguishes between local (lexically oriented) and non-local (combinatorial) aspects of the semantics of signs. The local aspects can be selected by syntactic functors and are located under SYNSEM. More precisely, they are under the attributes VAR and MAIN, which are both located at the traditional place for semantic representations in HPSG, the CONTENT value.

The attributes which are responsible for building the semantic representations of phrases from the semantics of their daughters are under a new attribute LOGICAL-FORM (LF), which is not accessible for selectional restrictions since it is appropriate to the sort *sign*. Three combinatorial aspects of the semantic representation of a sign are identified: The external content (under EXCONT) is the semantic contribution which a sign makes at its highest syntactic projection to

3 This means that Ty2 expressions are encoded by the grammar in such a way that for each Ty2 expression there is one class of isomorphic structures in the denotation of the grammar such that these structures correspond to the expression.

$$\begin{bmatrix} \textit{sign} & & \\ \text{PHONOLOGY} & \textbf{phonological structure} & \\ \text{SYNSEM} & \begin{bmatrix} \text{LOCAL} & \begin{bmatrix} \text{CATEGORY} & \textbf{(local) syntactic structure} \\ \text{CONTENT} & \begin{bmatrix} \textit{content} & \\ \text{INDEX} & \begin{bmatrix} \textit{ext-index} & \\ \text{VAR} & \textit{me} \\ \text{PHI} & \textit{index} \end{bmatrix} \\ \text{MAIN} & \textit{me} \end{bmatrix} \end{bmatrix} \end{bmatrix} & \\ \text{LF} & \begin{bmatrix} \textit{lrs} & \\ \text{EXCONT} & \textit{me} \\ \text{INCONT} & \textit{me} \\ \text{PARTS} & \textit{list(me)} \end{bmatrix} & \end{bmatrix}$$

Figure 2
Feature geometry of signs

the overall utterance in which it occurs; the internal content (under INCONT) is that part of the semantic representation of a sign which is within the scope of any operator the sign combines with; the PARTS list marks those pieces of the semantic representations connected to words which count as being contributed to the utterance in which the word occurs.[4] We observe that every subterm of the meaning representation of an utterance must be introduced as an element on the PARTS list of (at least) one word in the utterance.[5] Conversely, the meaning representation of an utterance must contain all elements on all PARTS lists of all words in the utterance. Intuitively speaking, the meaning of an utterance consists precisely of those sub-expressions which come from the words in it. Nothing can be added from outside, and nothing gets lost.

The function of the new attributes is best understood by considering the semantic analysis of a few words in LRS as in Fig. 3.

The analysis of proper names such as *John* (2a) is particularly simple. Since proper names are analyzed as contributing only a non-logical constant (john') to the semantic representation, the INDEX VAR value, the MAIN value, the internal content and their semantic contribution (on PARTS) are all identical. Note that the four attributes refer to the very same symbol in the denotation of the TFL specification, as indicated by the tag $\boxed{1}$. The external content of the word *John* is not lexically determined. The EXCONT value *me* (meaningful expression) indicates

4 Readers familiar with the development of HPSG might recall that (Kasper, 1997) used attributes called ECONT and ICONT in an analysis of recursive modification which solved certain problems with Pollard and Sag's original proposal for analyzing the semantics of modifiers in HPSG. The attribute names are adapted from Kasper by LRS to acknowledge the inspiration Kasper's paper gave for distinguishing between constituent-internal and external content. However, the two approaches differ significantly in detail, and this is not the place for a comparison.

5 As we will see in Section 5, there are special cases in which at least one of the meaning contributions of two (or more) words may be identical. In particular, the single sentential negation in negative concord constructions may come from several n-words and the negative marker in a sentence.

(2) a. John:

$$\begin{bmatrix} \text{PHON} & \langle \textit{john} \rangle \\ \text{SS LOC} & \begin{bmatrix} \text{CAT} & \begin{bmatrix} \text{HEAD} & \textit{noun} \\ \text{SUBCAT} & \langle \rangle \end{bmatrix} \\ \text{CONT} & \begin{bmatrix} \text{INDEX VAR} & \boxed{1}\ \mathsf{john}' \\ \text{MAIN} & \boxed{1}\ \mathsf{john}' \end{bmatrix} \end{bmatrix} \\ \text{LF} & \begin{bmatrix} \text{EXCONT} & \textit{me} \\ \text{INCONT} & \boxed{1}\ \mathsf{john}' \\ \text{PARTS} & \langle \boxed{1}\ \mathsf{john}' \rangle \end{bmatrix} \end{bmatrix}$$

b. laughs:

$$\begin{bmatrix} \text{PHON} & \langle \textit{laughs} \rangle \\ \text{SS LOC} & \begin{bmatrix} \text{CAT} & \begin{bmatrix} \text{HEAD} & \textit{verb} \\ \text{SUBCAT} & \left\langle \text{NP}_{\boxed{1}} \right\rangle \end{bmatrix} \\ \text{CONT MAIN} & \boxed{2a}\ \mathsf{laugh}' \end{bmatrix} \\ \text{LF} & \begin{bmatrix} \text{EXCONT} & \textit{me} \\ \text{INCONT} & \boxed{2}\ \mathsf{laugh}'(\boxed{1}) \\ \text{PARTS} & \langle \boxed{2}\ \mathsf{laugh}'(\boxed{1}),\ \boxed{2a}\ \mathsf{laugh}' \rangle \end{bmatrix} \end{bmatrix}$$

c. always:

$$\begin{bmatrix} \text{PHON} & \langle \textit{always} \rangle \\ \text{SS LOC} & \begin{bmatrix} \text{CAT} & \begin{bmatrix} \text{HEAD} & \begin{bmatrix} \textit{adv} \\ \text{MOD} & \text{V}[\text{LOC CONT MAIN } \boxed{2a}\ ] \end{bmatrix} \\ \text{SUBCAT} & \textit{elist} \end{bmatrix} \\ \text{CONT MAIN} & \boxed{5a}\ \mathsf{always}' \end{bmatrix} \\ \text{LF} & \begin{bmatrix} \text{EXCONT} & \textit{me} \\ \text{INCONT} & \boxed{5}\ \mathsf{always}'(\boxed{3}) \\ \text{PARTS} & \langle \boxed{5}\ \mathsf{always}'(\boxed{3}),\ \boxed{5a}\ \mathsf{always}' \rangle \end{bmatrix} \end{bmatrix}$$

$$\&\ \boxed{2a} \triangleleft \boxed{3}$$

Figure 3
Three fragments of lexical entries

that any Ty2 expression is permitted. Only when the word is combined with a functor will other principles fix the EXCONT value (which will also be john').

Verbs such as *laughs* are more interesting. Its local MAIN value is laugh', indicating the lexical meaning of the word. Its internal content is the application of the predicate laugh' to a lexically underspecified constant or variable of the appropriate type. Which constant or variable it is will be determined by the subject NP, whose VAR value, [1], contributes the relevant logical argument.[6] From the perspective of semantic contributions to the utterance in which it occurs, *laughs* provides the application which we already saw as the INCONT value, and the non-logical constant laugh'.[7] The PARTS list of *laughs* does not contain [1], since the verb does not contribute the relevant expression of type e to the meaning of the utterance in which it occurs. This expression is contributed by the subject.

The subject NP of *laughs* is syntactically selected by the verb as the first element on its SUBCAT list. The notation 'NP', employed here to describe the first element on the SUBCAT list of *laughs*, is a frequent abbreviation in the attribute-value matrix (AVM) notation of HPSG descriptions. It describes *synsem* objects with a saturated (empty) SUBCAT lists and HEAD value *noun*. Elsewhere we will use similar standard abbreviations for verbal *synsems* (V, VP) and adjunct *synsems* (A).

The description of the adverb *always*, (2c), introduces another important type of constraint on semantic representations, component-of constraints. The analysis of *always* resembles the analysis of *laughs*, except that *always* as an adverb selects its argument via the MOD attribute instead of a SUBCAT list. The selected argument, [2a], of the operator always' is, however, not analyzed as an immediate argument. Instead the lexical entry requires that [2a] be a component of the argument, [3], of *always*. If nothing else intervenes and the type of the MAIN value of the selected argument were appropriate, [2a] could be identical to [3] in a given sentence as far as the component-of constraint is concerned. As this example shows, component-of constraints are used for saying that (i) one expression belongs in an argument slot, or (ii) is in the scope of another expression. However, we usually do not know whether the first expression combines with something else before it fits into the relevant argument slot in (i), or whether we face a relationship of immediate scope in (ii). Moreover, type clashes might force the first expression to be combined with something else first before it fits into the alloted slot.

Two things deserve to be pointed out about the lexical entry in (2c): The typing of the always' operator as a predicate taking a truth value is, of course, an oversimplification and only meant as an illustration of the guiding ideas.[8]

6 The identity requirement between the VAR value of the syntactically selected argument and the logical argument of laugh' must in fact be relaxed when we extend the analysis to arguments that are definite descriptions of type e such as *the student*, and semantically similar constructions. See (Sailer, 2004) for the relevant generalization in terms of a component-of constraint. For our present purposes, the simpler identity requirement will suffice.

7 For the purposes of the present paper, we ignore the INDEX VAR value of verbs, for which (Richter and Sailer, 2004) proposes event variables.

8 For a real semantic analysis compatible with the present LRS framework, one could follow the LTAG

(2) a. John:

$$\left[\begin{array}{ll} \text{PHON} & \langle \textit{john} \rangle \\ \text{SS LOC} & \left[\begin{array}{ll} \text{CAT} & \left[\begin{array}{ll} \text{HEAD} & \textit{noun} \\ \text{SUBCAT} & \langle\rangle \end{array}\right] \\ \text{CONT} & \left[\begin{array}{ll} \text{INDEX VAR} & \boxed{1}\ \mathsf{john'} \\ \text{MAIN} & \boxed{1}\ \mathsf{john'} \end{array}\right] \end{array}\right] \\ \text{LF} & \left[\begin{array}{ll} \text{EXCONT} & \textit{me} \\ \text{INCONT} & \boxed{1}\ \mathsf{john'} \\ \text{PARTS} & \langle \boxed{1}\ \mathsf{john'} \rangle \end{array}\right] \end{array}\right]$$

b. laughs:

$$\left[\begin{array}{ll} \text{PHON} & \langle \textit{laughs} \rangle \\ \text{SS LOC} & \left[\begin{array}{ll} \text{CAT} & \left[\begin{array}{ll} \text{HEAD} & \textit{verb} \\ \text{SUBCAT} & \left\langle \text{NP}_{\boxed{1}} \right\rangle \end{array}\right] \\ \multicolumn{2}{l}{\text{CONT MAIN } \boxed{2a}\ \mathsf{laugh'}} \end{array}\right] \\ \text{LF} & \left[\begin{array}{ll} \text{EXCONT} & \textit{me} \\ \text{INCONT} & \boxed{2}\ \mathsf{laugh'}(\boxed{1}) \\ \text{PARTS} & \langle \boxed{2}\ \mathsf{laugh'}(\boxed{1}),\ \boxed{2a}\ \mathsf{laugh'} \rangle \end{array}\right] \end{array}\right]$$

c. always:

$$\left[\begin{array}{ll} \text{PHON} & \langle \textit{always} \rangle \\ \text{SS LOC} & \left[\begin{array}{ll} \text{CAT} & \left[\begin{array}{ll} \text{HEAD} & \left[\begin{array}{l} \textit{adv} \\ \text{MOD V}[\text{LOC CONT MAIN } \boxed{2a}\ ] \end{array}\right] \\ \text{SUBCAT} & \textit{elist} \end{array}\right] \\ \multicolumn{2}{l}{\text{CONT MAIN } \boxed{5a}\ \mathsf{always'}} \end{array}\right] \\ \text{LF} & \left[\begin{array}{ll} \text{EXCONT} & \textit{me} \\ \text{INCONT} & \boxed{5}\ \mathsf{always'}(\boxed{3}) \\ \text{PARTS} & \langle \boxed{5}\ \mathsf{always'}(\boxed{3}),\ \boxed{5a}\ \mathsf{always'} \rangle \end{array}\right] \end{array}\right]$$

$\&\ \boxed{2a} \triangleleft \boxed{3}$

Figure 3
Three fragments of lexical entries

that any Ty2 expression is permitted. Only when the word is combined with a functor will other principles fix the EXCONT value (which will also be john').

Verbs such as *laughs* are more interesting. Its local MAIN value is laugh', indicating the lexical meaning of the word. Its internal content is the application of the predicate laugh' to a lexically underspecified constant or variable of the appropriate type. Which constant or variable it is will be determined by the subject NP, whose VAR value, [1], contributes the relevant logical argument.[6] From the perspective of semantic contributions to the utterance in which it occurs, *laughs* provides the application which we already saw as the INCONT value, and the non-logical constant laugh'.[7] The PARTS list of *laughs* does not contain [1], since the verb does not contribute the relevant expression of type *e* to the meaning of the utterance in which it occurs. This expression is contributed by the subject.

The subject NP of *laughs* is syntactically selected by the verb as the first element on its SUBCAT list. The notation 'NP', employed here to describe the first element on the SUBCAT list of *laughs*, is a frequent abbreviation in the attribute-value matrix (AVM) notation of HPSG descriptions. It describes *synsem* objects with a saturated (empty) SUBCAT lists and HEAD value *noun*. Elsewhere we will use similar standard abbreviations for verbal *synsems* (V, VP) and adjunct *synsems* (A).

The description of the adverb *always*, (2c), introduces another important type of constraint on semantic representations, component-of constraints. The analysis of *always* resembles the analysis of *laughs*, except that *always* as an adverb selects its argument via the MOD attribute instead of a SUBCAT list. The selected argument, [2a], of the operator always' is, however, not analyzed as an immediate argument. Instead the lexical entry requires that [2a] be a component of the argument, [3], of *always*. If nothing else intervenes and the type of the MAIN value of the selected argument were appropriate, [2a] could be identical to [3] in a given sentence as far as the component-of constraint is concerned. As this example shows, component-of constraints are used for saying that (i) one expression belongs in an argument slot, or (ii) is in the scope of another expression. However, we usually do not know whether the first expression combines with something else before it fits into the relevant argument slot in (i), or whether we face a relationship of immediate scope in (ii). Moreover, type clashes might force the first expression to be combined with something else first before it fits into the alloted slot.

Two things deserve to be pointed out about the lexical entry in (2c): The typing of the always' operator as a predicate taking a truth value is, of course, an oversimplification and only meant as an illustration of the guiding ideas.[8]

6 The identity requirement between the VAR value of the syntactically selected argument and the logical argument of laugh' must in fact be relaxed when we extend the analysis to arguments that are definite descriptions of type *e* such as *the student*, and semantically similar constructions. See (Sailer, 2004) for the relevant generalization in terms of a component-of constraint. For our present purposes, the simpler identity requirement will suffice.

7 For the purposes of the present paper, we ignore the INDEX VAR value of verbs, for which (Richter and Sailer, 2004) proposes event variables.

8 For a real semantic analysis compatible with the present LRS framework, one could follow the LTAG

Secondly, note that the type of laugh' ($\langle e,t\rangle$) and the subterm requirement of (2c) suffice to guarantee that laugh' has to apply to its argument first so as to fit into the argument slot of always'. Type restrictions of this kind play a very important role in the use of underspecification in LRS.

Before we can analyze sentences, we need to introduce the most important LRS principles, the INCONT PRINCIPLE, the EXCONT PRINCIPLE and the LRS PROJECTION PRINCIPLE. They are listed in (3). For simplicity, we assume binary branching structures throughout this paper.

(3) a. The INCONT PRINCIPLE:
In each *lrs*, the INCONT value is an element of the PARTS list and a component of the EXCONT value.

$$lrs \rightarrow \left(\begin{bmatrix} \text{EXCONT} & \boxed{1} \\ \text{INCONT} & \boxed{2} \\ \text{PARTS} & \boxed{3} \end{bmatrix} \wedge \texttt{member}(\boxed{2},\boxed{3}) \wedge \boxed{2} \triangleleft \boxed{1} \right)$$

b. The EXCONT PRINCIPLE:

Clause (a):
In every phrase, the EXCONT value of the non-head daughter is an element of the non-head daughter's PARTS list.

$$phrase \rightarrow \left(\left[\text{NH-DTR LF} \begin{bmatrix} \text{EXCONT} & \boxed{1} \\ \text{PARTS} & \boxed{2} \end{bmatrix} \right] \wedge \texttt{member}(\boxed{1},\boxed{2}) \right)$$

Clause (b):
In every utterance, every subexpression of the EXCONT value of the utterance is an element of its PARTS list, and every element of the utterance's PARTS list is a subexpression of the EXCONT value.

$$u\text{-}sign \rightarrow$$

$$\forall\boxed{1}\ \forall\boxed{2}\ \forall\boxed{3}\ \forall\boxed{4} \left(\begin{array}{l} \left(\left[\text{LF} \begin{bmatrix} \text{EXCONT} & \boxed{1} \\ \text{PARTS} & \boxed{2} \end{bmatrix} \right] \wedge \boxed{3} \triangleleft \boxed{1} \wedge \texttt{member}(\boxed{4},\boxed{2}) \right) \rightarrow \\ (\texttt{member}(\boxed{3},\boxed{2}) \wedge \boxed{4} \triangleleft \boxed{1}) \end{array} \right)$$

c. LRS PROJECTION PRINCIPLE:

In each *phrase*,
1. the EXCONT values of the head and the mother are identical,

$$phrase \rightarrow \begin{bmatrix} \text{LF EXCONT } \boxed{1} \\ \text{H-DTR LF EXCONT } \boxed{1} \end{bmatrix}$$

proposal of (Kallmeyer and Romero, 2007).

2. the INCONT values of the head and the mother are identical,

$$phrase \rightarrow \begin{bmatrix} \text{LF INCONT} & \boxed{1} \\ \text{H-DTR LF INCONT} & \boxed{1} \end{bmatrix}$$

3. the PARTS value contains all and only the elements of the PARTS values of the daughters.

$$phrase \rightarrow \left(\begin{bmatrix} \text{LF PARTS} & \boxed{1} \\ \text{H-DTR LF PARTS} & \boxed{2} \\ \text{NH-DTR LF PARTS} & \boxed{3} \end{bmatrix} \wedge \ \mathbf{append}(\boxed{2}, \boxed{3}, \boxed{1}) \right)$$

(3a) requires that the part of the meaning of a sign which is outscoped by everything else (the internal content) is actually contributed by the sign itself and is a subterm of its external content. The external content is governed by two principles which have to do with maximal projections. According to ((3b), Clause a) the maximal projection of a sign (identified as the non-head daughter of an embedding sign) must be a contributor of its external content. In other words, the external content must originate from within a maximal projection, it cannot come from outside. ((3b), Clause b) is a closure principle. Every sign in the language is a daughter of one unique unembedded sign or utterance. The closure principle says that the meaning of an utterance (its external content) consists of all and only those symbols and ways of combining symbols (by application and abstraction) which are contributed by the signs in the utterance. The projection principle (3c) makes sure that internal and external contents are identical along syntactic head projections and the contributions to the semantic representations of all daughters are collected in the PARTS lists of the mother nodes.

With the lexical entries and the core LRS principles we can already derive the semantic representation of a simple sentence. The analysis of (4) is shown in Fig. 4.

(4) John always laughs.

Each word specifies its contribution to the overall meaning of the sentence (PARTS), the part of its semantics which is outscoped by all signs it combines with (INCONT), and the overall semantic contribution of its maximal projection (EXCONT). The feature percolation mechanism introduced by the LRS PROJECTION PRINCIPLE identifies INCONT and EXCONT along head projections and collects the elements of the PARTS lists of the daughters at each phrase. The combination of the adjunct with a verbal projection induces a number of restrictions: Since each non-head daughter's EXCONT must be on its PARTS list (EXCONT PRINCIPLE, Clause a) and the INCONT must be a component of the EXCONT (INCONT PRINCIPLE), the EXCONT of *always* must equal the INCONT of *always*. Moreover, the EXCONT of *always* must be within the EXCONT of *laughs* (EXCONT PRINCIPLE, Clause

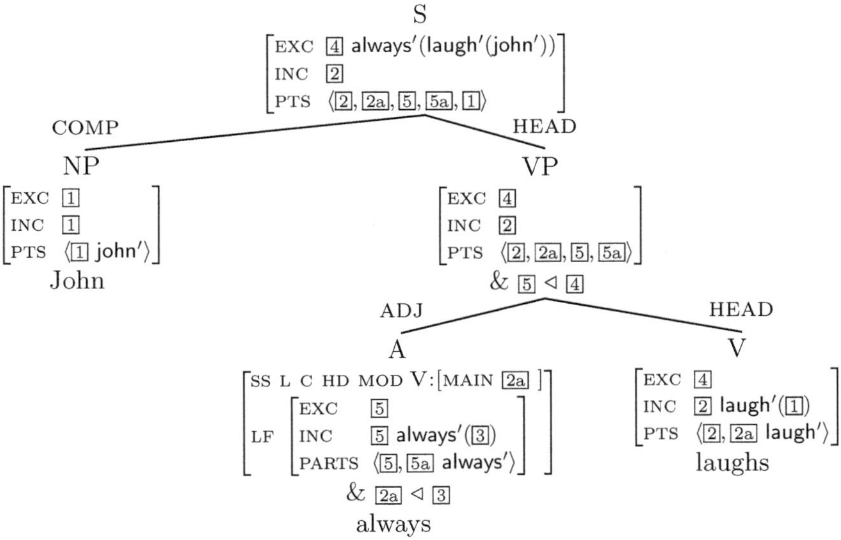

Figure 4
LRS analysis of *John always laughs*

b). Next, the INCONT of *laughs* must be in the scope of *always* according to the component-of constraint in the lexical entry of *always*, (2c). The semantic argument of *laughs*, john', is identified by subcategorization, as indicated in the lexical entry of *laughs* ((2b), tag [1]). The closure condition of the EXCONT PRINCIPLE ((3b), Clause b)) requires that the semantic representation of an utterance use up all and only the PARTS contributions of all signs, which finally yields the semantic representation spelled out as the EXCONT description of the S node in Fig. 4. As the reader may verify, this expression is the only solution of the combined constraints on the semantic representation of the overall sentence. These constraints come from the lexical entries as well as from syntactic properties of the sentence.

2.3 Summary: The Architecture

In this section, we showed that LRS can be integrated seamlessly with the logical architecture of HPSG. There is no distinction between the TFL specification of syntactic structures and the TFL specification of semantic representations which carry the truth conditional meaning of the entire structure. Syntactic and semantic constraints can interact freely.

It is an important feature of this architecture that underspecification is a matter of the TFL level of grammatical descriptions. The structures in the denotation of the grammar are complete structures, including the semantic representations.

This means that there is no semantic underspecification in the denotation of the grammar.

It is not necessary for a grammar with an LRS semantics that its constraints are expressed in the same language as the rest of the grammar. An example of a system which uses distinct languages is the computational implementation of LRS in the TRALE system described in (Penn and Richter, 2004). The *Constraint Language for Lexical Resource Semantics* (CLLRS) is a specialized constraint language designed to facilitate the notation of the constraints and to eliminate the technical overhead caused by the TFL encoding of the syntax of Ty2. In CLLRS the well-formedness of the semantic representations is guaranteed by an independently implemented set of well-formedness axioms that the user does not have to declare or even know (Penn and Richter, 2005). Despite the different approaches in CLLRS and the LRS architecture presented in Subsection 2.2, CLLRS maintains the tight connection to syntactic structures. It supports constraints in which semantic inferences are grounded in syntactic structure, and semantic structure may trigger syntactic constraints. All properties of LRS relevant in our comparison between LTAG semantics and LRS are preserved in CLLRS. However, the comparison of LTAG semantics and LRS is more transparent when we can refer to a single typed feature logic with a uniform model theory which is responsible for semantic representations and for syntactic structure simultaneously.

3 Lexicalized Tree Adjoining Grammars and Semantic Unification

In contrast to the LRS integration with HPSG using one single TFL, LTAG is characterized by a modular architecture, where the feature logic is used solely for semantic computation and nothing else. The basis is a syntactic tree-generating formalism with a limited generative capacity. The trees from the grammar are linked to semantic representations that are sets of Ty2 formulas that need to be put together. The way these formulas are combined in order to obtain the meaning of natural language expressions involves two further characteristics of the grammar architecture of LTAG semantics: First, the semantic representations are linked to feature structure descriptions, which encode 1. the arguments needed to complete the formulas and 2. the values provided as possible arguments for other formulas. Depending on the tree combination operations performed in the syntax, feature value equations are computed between the different feature structure descriptions, at which point some of the open argument slots in the semantic formulas are filled. Second, the result of this process is still an underspecified representation, similar to the ones proposed in Hole Semantics (Bos, 1995) and Minimal Recursion Semantics (MRS, (Copestake et al., 2005)). In order to obtain the final meanings of a sentence one has to compute the different disambiguations of this representation.

In the next sections we will describe the components of this system.

Substitution in TAG:

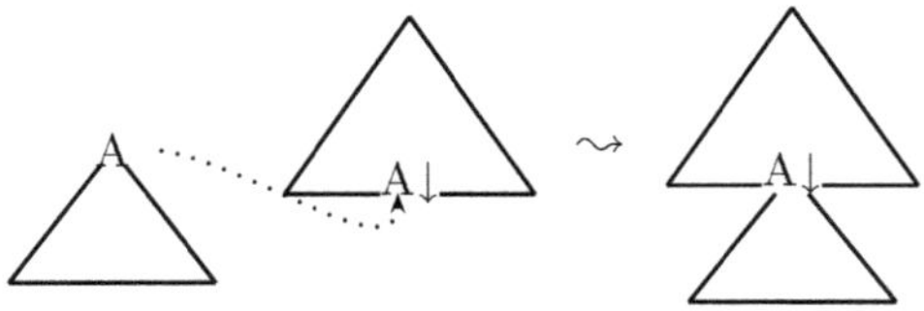

Adjunction in TAG:

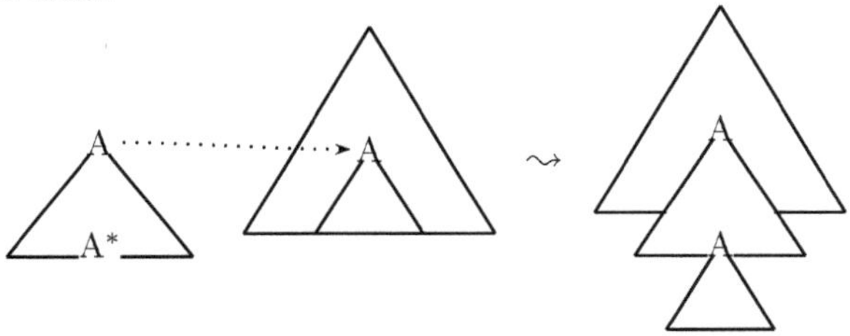

Figure 5
Substitution and adjunction in TAG

3.1 Lexicalized Tree Adjoining Grammars

LTAG (Joshi and Schabes, 1997) is a tree-rewriting formalism. An LTAG consists of a finite set of *elementary* trees associated with lexical items. From these trees, larger trees are derived by substitution (replacing a leaf with a new tree) and adjunction (replacing an internal node with a new tree). The two operations are depicted in Fig. 5. In case of an adjunction, the new tree, called an *auxiliary* tree, has a special leaf node, the *foot node* (marked with an asterisk). LTAG requires the nodes involved in these operations to be labelled with the same non-terminal symbols (A in Fig. 5). When adjoining a tree to a node μ, in the resulting tree, the subtree with root μ from the old tree is put below the foot node of the auxiliary tree. Non-auxiliary elementary trees are called *initial* trees. Each derivation starts with an initial tree.

The elementary trees of an LTAG represent extended projections of lexical items and encapsulate all syntactic/semantic arguments of the lexical anchor. They are minimal in the sense that only the arguments of the anchor are encapsulated, all recursion is factored out. These linguistic properties are formulated in the *Condition on Elementary Tree Minimality (CETM)* in (Frank, 2002).

A crucial property of LTAG is its *extended domain of locality*. The recursive material that is factored out is put in separate auxiliary trees that can be adjoined. As a consequence, in the final derived tree, the contribution of an elementary tree can be separated into different parts that might be far away from each other. For example, in a long-distance dependency such as (5), the slot for the wh-word and

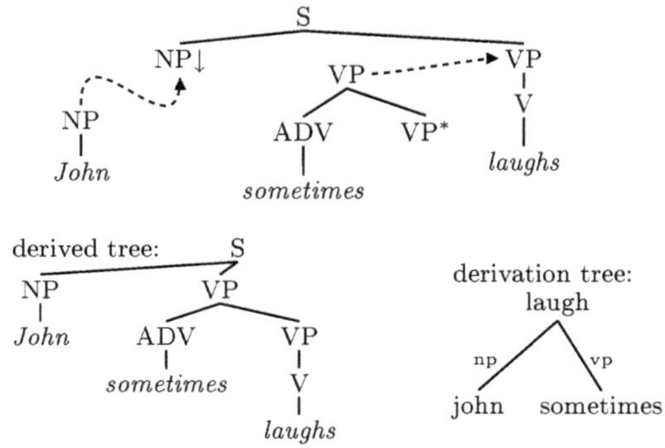

Figure 6
TAG derivation for (6)

the verb *marry* are in the same elementary tree while the trees for *wants*, *said* and *think* all adjoin to the S node in the middle.

(5) Who does John think Bill said Mary wants to marry?

LTAG derivations are represented by derivation trees that record the way the elementary trees are put together. A derived tree is the result of carrying out the substitutions and adjunctions. Each edge in the derivation tree stands for an adjunction or a substitution. The edges are equipped with addresses of the nodes where the substitutions/adjunctions take place. The derivation of (6) in Fig. 6 illustrates this: Starting from the elementary tree of *laugh*, the tree for *John* is substituted for the node at position *np* and *sometimes* is adjoined at position *vp*.

(6) John sometimes laughs.

In contrast to the logical foundations underlying HPSG, LTAG has very limited generative capacity; it belongs to the class of mildly context-sensitive grammar formalisms (Joshi, 1985) and only slightly extends the generative capacity of context-free grammars (CFG). This explains why LTAG has attractive formal properties; it is polynomially parsable (see among others (Schabes and Joshi, 1988; Vijay-Shanker and Weir, 1993; Nederhof, 1997)), tree adjoining languages (TAL) have desirable closure properties (Vijay-Shanker and Joshi, 1985; Vijay-Shanker, 1987), there is a pumping lemma for TALs (Vijay-Shanker, 1987), and there is an extension of pushdown-automata that accepts TALs (Vijay-Shanker, 1987). In general, the use of LTAG for natural languages is motivated on the one hand by the fact that CFGs are not powerful enough to describe all natural language phenomena (Shieber, 1985) and on the other hand by the desire to stay as close as possible to CFG in terms of complexity and generative capacity.

3.2 LTAG Semantics with Semantic Unification

In the LTAG semantics approach we consider here (see (Kallmeyer and Romero, 2007)), each elementary tree in the Tree Adjoining Grammar (TAG) is linked to a pair consisting of a semantic representation and a semantic feature structure description. These feature structure descriptions are used to compute assignments for variables in the representations using conjunction and additional equations introduced depending on the derivation tree.

3.2.1 Semantic Representations and Semantic Feature Structure Descriptions As in (Kallmeyer and Joshi, 2003), we use flat semantic representations in the style of MRS (Copestake et al., 2005): Semantic representations consist of a set of labelled Ty2 formulas and a set of scope constraints. A scope constraint is an expression $x \geq y$ where x and y are propositional labels or propositional meta-variables (these correspond roughly to holes in (Bos, 1995)).

The formulas in a semantic representation contain meta-variables – depicted as boxed Arabic numbers, e.g. $\boxed{1}$ – of type e (individuals), s (situations) and $\langle s, t \rangle$ (propositions).[9] Each semantic representation is linked to a semantic feature structure description which can include the meta-variables from the formulas. Between the descriptions, feature value equations are computed depending on the derivation tree. From the descriptions and these additional feature equations, which are interpreted conjunctively, assignments can be inferred for some of the meta-variables in the semantic representations.

As an example consider the semantic representation and the semantic feature structure of *laughs* in Fig. 7. The fact that the meta-variable of the argument of laugh' appears in the top (T) feature of the subject NP node position NP indicates that this argument will be obtained from the semantics of the tree substituted at the subject node. The label of the laugh' proposition, l_1, is linked to the bottom of the VP node. This signifies that the proposition l_1 is the minimal proposition corresponding to this node. If an adverb adjoins at the VP node, l_1 will be embedded under that adverb, and the larger proposition $\boxed{4}$ will be provided by the adverb. Note that the variables in the description, e.g., $\boxed{4}$ in this example, need not occur in the semantic representation.

$$\boxed{l_1 : \mathsf{laugh}'(\boxed{1})} \qquad \begin{bmatrix} \text{NP} & \begin{bmatrix} \text{T} & \begin{bmatrix} \text{I} & \boxed{1} \end{bmatrix} \end{bmatrix} \\ \text{VP} & \begin{bmatrix} \text{T} & \begin{bmatrix} \text{P} & \boxed{4} \end{bmatrix} \\ \text{B} & \begin{bmatrix} \text{P} & l_1 \end{bmatrix} \end{bmatrix} \end{bmatrix}$$

Figure 7
Semantic representation and semantic feature structure description of *laughs*

9 We take the term "situation" to be more general than "worlds": worlds are considered to be special kinds of situations, namely maximally specified situations.

Since the focus of this paper is on the use of feature logics for computational semantics, let us say a little more about the semantic feature structure descriptions in LTAG. The feature logic descriptions serve the sole purpose of putting semantic representations together; they are a kind of glue. In principle, they could be defined either as partial feature structures with unification or as feature structure descriptions with conjunctions and equalities. We chose the latter option since this allows us to use a simple inference mechanism for calculating assignments for the meta-variables in our semantic representations.

Our semantic feature structures as well as the corresponding terms of the feature logic are typed. We will call the feature structure types *fs-types* to distinguish them from the types of the terms in the semantic representations. The whole feature structure that goes with an elementary tree is of fs-type *sem* and has attributes NP, VP, etc. for all node positions occurring in the elementary trees of the TAG (finite for each TAG) whose values are of fs-type *tb* (for "top-bottom"). These in turn have attributes T and B whose values are of fs-type *bindings* and have attributes I, P, S (for "individual", "proposition" and "situation") with values of fs-types var_e (these are the variables of type e from our Ty2 language), $var_{\langle s,t \rangle}$ (the labels of propositional type), and var_s (the variables of type s from our Ty2 language) respectively.

The fs-types do not have a hierarchical structure. In other words, there are no sub-types (no sort hierarchy) as in the feature logic of HPSG (including LRS).[10]

The intuition behind our typed feature structures is the following: A semantic feature structure description links individuals, situations and propositions to syntactic positions, i.e., to nodes in the (syntactic) elementary tree. Each node has a top and a bottom feature structure. If no substitution or adjunction occurs at a node, top and bottom get identified. Otherwise, they can have different values.

The feature structure descriptions linked to the semantic representations are simple first order formulas with attributes and with constants for values of atomic fs-type, similar to those introduced by (Johnson, 1988; Johnson, 1990). The main difference is that our logic is typed, thus we do not need a symbol $\perp$ for undefined values. We avoid computing potentially undefined values by typing our feature terms and defining terms in such a way that attributes are applied only to terms of appropriate fs-types. The logic we are using is only a fragment of first order logic since we need neither negation nor disjunction or universal quantification.

We will use fs-variables $\boxed{0}, \boxed{1}, \ldots$. Feature structure descriptions will be given in the usual AVM notation. An example is provided in Fig. 8, where all conjuncts have a complex fs-term of the form $a(u)$ equated with a simple fs-variable or fs-constant.

10 Actually, one might do without fs-types. Attributes will then denote partial functions and, in the terms of our feature logic, they might occur in places where they do not make sense because their value is undefined. In our logic, the typing disallows building such terms.

Feature structure description:
$\text{I}(\text{T}(\text{NP}(\boxed{0}))) = \boxed{1} \wedge$
$\text{P}(\text{T}(\text{VP}(\boxed{0}))) = \boxed{4} \wedge$
$\text{P}(\text{B}(\text{VP}(\boxed{0}))) = l_1$

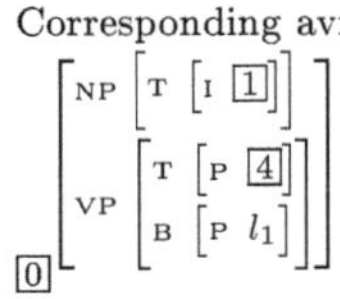

Figure 8
Feature structure description in AVM notation

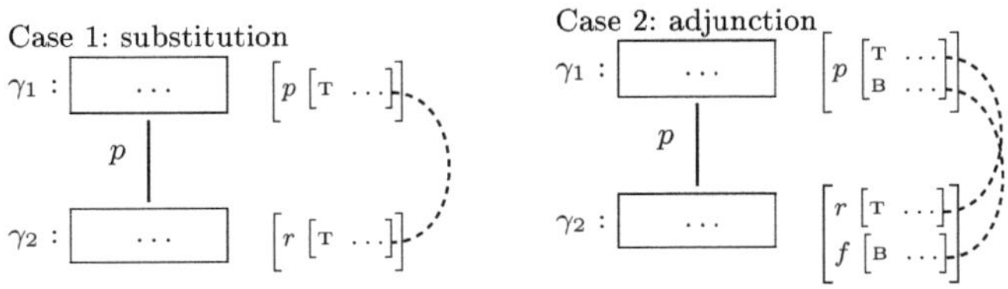

Figure 9
Feature identifications depending on substitutions and adjunctions

3.2.2 Semantic Composition Semantic composition consists of conjoining feature structure descriptions while adding further feature value equations. It corresponds to the feature unifications in the syntax in Feature Structure-based TAG (FTAG, (Vijay-Shanker and Joshi, 1988)) that are performed during substitutions, adjunctions and the final top-bottom unifications in the derived tree.

In the derivation tree, elementary trees are replaced by their semantic representations plus the corresponding semantic feature structure description. (See the derivation tree on the left and the structure for computing semantics on the right in Fig. 10.) We assume that each time a new elementary semantic entry is chosen from the grammar, it contains fresh instances of labels, individual and situation variables and meta-variables. This way, the sets of labels and variables occurring in different nodes of the derivation tree are pairwise disjoint.

The additional feature equations added at substitution or adjunction edges in the derivation tree are depicted schematically in Fig. 9. They are specified as follows: For each edge in the derivation tree from γ_1 to γ_2 with position p:

- The top feature of position p in γ_1 and the top feature of the root position in γ_2, i.e., the features $\gamma_1.p.\text{T}$ and $\gamma_2.r.\text{T}$ are equated (where r is the root node position),
- and if γ_2 is an auxiliary tree, then the bottom feature of the foot node of γ_2 and the bottom feature of position p in γ_1, i.e., the features $\gamma_1.p.\text{B}$ and $\gamma_2.f.\text{B}$ are equated (where f is the position of the foot node in γ_2).

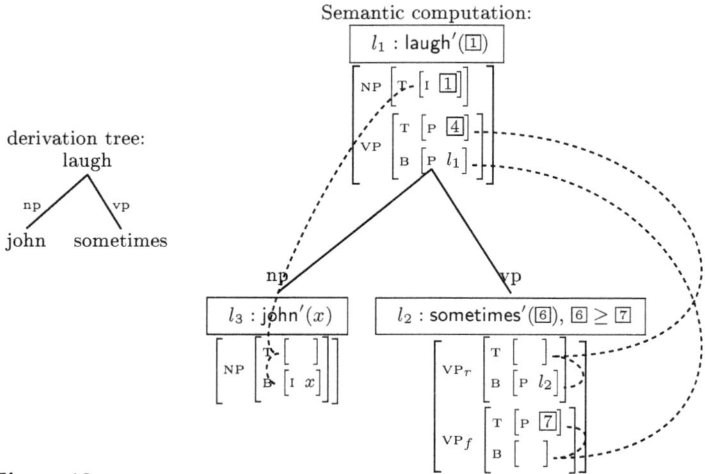

Figure 10
Semantic representations and semantic identifications for (6) *John sometimes laughs*

Furthermore, for all γ in the derivation tree and for all positions p in γ such that there is no edge from γ to some other tree with position p, the T and B features of $\gamma.p$ are equated.

As an example consider the analysis of (6): Fig. 10 shows the derivation tree with the semantic representations and the semantic feature structure descriptions of the three elementary trees involved in the derivation. The formula john′(x) is interpreted as meaning "there is a unique individual *John* and x is this individual".[11] *Sometimes* scopes over a proposition $\boxed{6}$ containing at least $\boxed{7}$ and contributes a new proposition l_2.

The feature value identifications lead to the identities marked in Fig. 10 with dotted lines. The top of the subject NP of *laughs* is identified with the top of the root NP of *John* (substitution) and with the bottom of the root of *John* (final top-bottom unification). Consequently $\boxed{1} = x$. The bottom of the VP in *laughs* is identified with the bottom and top of the foot VP_f of *sometimes* (adjunction and final top-bottom unification), yielding $\boxed{7} = l_1$. Finally, the top of the VP in *laughs* is identified with the top and bottom of the root VP_r of *sometimes* (again, adjunction and final top-bottom unification), with the result $\boxed{4} = l_2$.

11 This is similar to the treatment of proper nouns in DRT of (Kamp and Reyle, 1993).

Equality between fs-terms is reflexive, symmetric and transitive, and it extends to the different attributes allowed for the fs-type of the term. This permits us to derive further conjuncts using corresponding inference rules. Conjoining the different feature descriptions on the derivation tree, the new feature equations and the further conjuncts one can derive yields a large description δ.

If δ is satisfiable, we can continue computing an assignment function from δ. In order to check for satisfiability, we have to check whether for all fs-constants c_1, c_2 with $\delta \vdash c_1 = c_2$, c_1 is indeed equal to c_2. Then, from δ an assignment function g can be obtained for some of the meta-variables occurring in the semantic representations. We assume that the meta-variables are alphabetically ordered. Then g is defined as follows:

- for all fs-variables $\boxed{n}$ such that there is a fs-constant c with $\delta \vdash \boxed{n} = c$: $g(\boxed{n}) = c$,
- for all fs-variables $\boxed{n_1}$ such that there is no fs-constant c with $\delta \vdash \boxed{n_1} = c$: if $\boxed{n_2}$ is the alphabetically first fs-variable such that $\delta \vdash \boxed{n_1} = \boxed{n_2}$, then $g(\boxed{n_1}) = \boxed{n_2}$.

This assignment is then applied to the semantic representation and the union of the representations is built. In our example this leads to (7):

(7) $\boxed{l_1 : \mathsf{laugh}'(x), l_2 : \mathsf{sometimes}'(\boxed{6}), l_3 : \mathsf{john}'(x), \boxed{6} \geq l_1}$

3.2.3 Disambiguation The semantic representation obtained in the way described above is usually underspecified and cannot be interpreted yet. First, appropriate disambiguations must be found. These are assignments for the remaining meta-variables, i.e., functions that assign propositional labels to propositional meta-variables respecting the scope constraints. The definition of these disambiguations roughly corresponds to the possible pluggings in (Bos, 1995). The disambiguated representation is then interpreted conjunctively.

(7) has only one disambiguation, $\boxed{6} \rightarrow l_1$, since $\boxed{6}$ cannot possibly equal l_2 ($\boxed{6}$ must be in the scope of l_2) and $\boxed{6}$ cannot possibly equal l_3 (otherwise there would be no meta-variable left below $\boxed{6}$ to be equated with l_1 in order to satisfy the constraint $\boxed{6} \geq l_1$).

(8) $\mathsf{john}'(x) \wedge \mathsf{sometimes}'(\mathsf{laugh}'(x))$

3.3 Computational aspects

The computation of the underspecified semantic representation via feature identification on the derivation tree uses the same mechanisms as ordinary LTAG parsing in a feature structure-based TAG (FTAG, (Vijay-Shanker and Joshi, 1988)). The only difference is that the set of possible feature values is not finite in general (e.g., possible values for features of propositional type are $l_1, l_2, l_3, \ldots$). However,

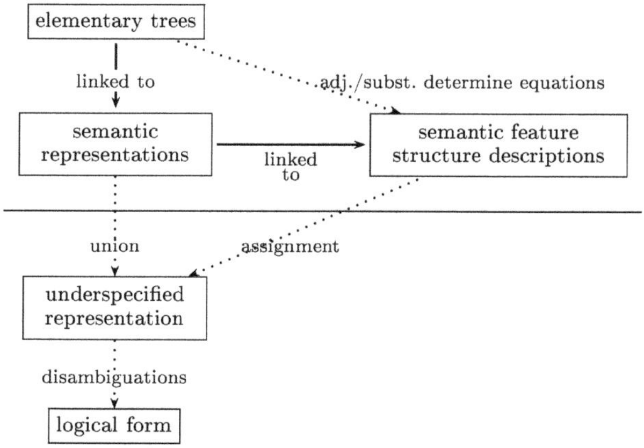

Figure 11
Components of the LTAG system

in practical applications, the feature value set can always be limited. Then the complexity of syntactic FTAG parsing (which is $O(n^6)$) and FTAG parsing including semantics is the same except for some constant factors. There exists already an extension of an LTAG parser that takes into consideration semantics, assuming a syntax-semantics interface very similar to the one presented here. It outputs the TAG derivation trees and the underspecified semantic representations computed on these derivation trees (SemConst, (Gardent and Parmentier, 2005)).

The second aspect to consider is the complexity of the disambiguation, i.e., the computation of the different readings that an underspecified representation yields. In general, the complexity of disambiguating expressions with scope constraints of the form $x \geq y$ is NP-complete (Koller, Niehren, and Treinen, 2001). But the semantic representations we actually use are close to so-called *normal dominance constraints* (Koller, Niehren, and Thater, 2003; Fuchss et al., 2004). For this type of constraints an efficient polynomial solver has been developed.

3.4 Summary: The Overall Architecture of LTAG

As already mentioned, in contrast to LRS, LTAG is a very modular system. The different components and their relations are summarized in Fig. 11. The parts above the horizontal line are components of the lexicon while the parts below this line are generated in the course of the derivation. The interface structure between syntax and semantics is the derivation tree; it determines locally both the compositions of elementary trees and the equations between feature structure descriptions.

Let us emphasize once again the difference in the use of feature logics: In LRS, a powerful feature logic is used to specify the whole grammar. In LTAG, a simple feature logic (a fragment of first order logic) is used to specify the argument requirements/contributions of semantic representations and, as we will see later, also to specify scope boundaries. In LRS the identities between feature values stemming from the feature value equations of different lexical entries arise from general principles which of course are also defined using the feature logic. In LTAG even these equations are not part of the TFL descriptions of the grammar writer. Rather, they arise from an extra feature identification mechanism defined on the derivation tree.

4 Expressing Scope Boundaries with Features

In this section we will compare the ways in which the two frameworks model the scopal behavior of quantificational NPs, adverbs and modal verbs. We focus on the similarities arising from the use of feature logics to encode scope boundaries, and we ignore a number of subtle differences in the linguistic theory between LTAG and LRS grammars. These differences primarily concern assumptions the nature and grammatical characterization of scope boundaries in complex NP constructions or with propositional attitude verbs. We will be interested in constructions like those in (9)–(12):

(9) Exactly one student admires every professor.
$\exists > \forall, \forall > \exists$

(10) Two policemen spy on someone from every city.
$\forall > \exists > \mathit{two}$ (among others)

(11) John seems to have visited everybody.
$\mathit{seem} > \forall, \forall > \mathit{seem}$

(12) Three girls are likely to come.
$\mathit{three} > \mathit{likely}, \mathit{likely} > \mathit{three}$

As illustrated in the examples (9)–(12), in principle quantificational NPs in English can scope freely. An analysis of quantifier scope must minimally guarantee two things: 1) The proposition to which a quantifier attaches must be in the nuclear scope of the quantifier, and 2) A quantifier cannot scope over the next higher finite clause.[12] One way to model this is to define a scope window delimited by a maximal scope boundary and a minimal scope boundary for a quantifier. This

12 The linguistic theory of scope in LRS is in fact constructed to accommodate the assumption that in certain syntactic environments a limited class of quantifiers may scope out of the finite clause where they syntactically originate. We will henceforth ignore this genuinely linguistic difference from the theory formulated in LTAG.

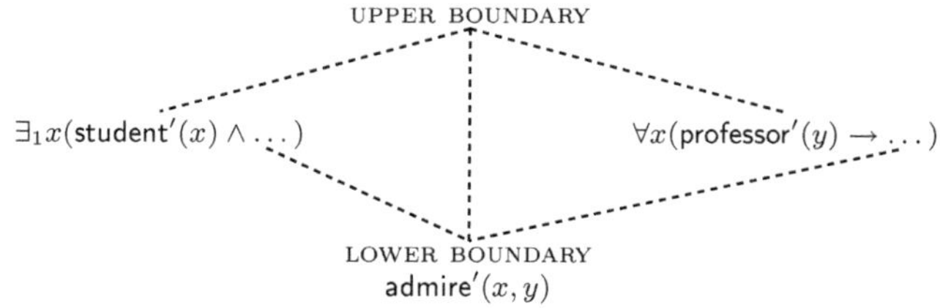

Figure 12
Depiction of the scope window accounting for the ambiguity in (9)

idea is illustrated in Fig. 12. A dotted edge from x (higher node) to y (lower node) signifies that y is in the scope of (i.e., is a component of) x. Both LTAG and LRS specify such scope windows for quantifiers. We will now outline the two analyses.

4.1 Specifying a Scope Window for Quantifiers: LTAG

(Kallmeyer and Romero, 2007) assumes that each verb specifies a scope window for attaching quantifiers. The lower boundary is the label of the proposition introduced by the verb. The upper boundary is a meta-variable. The boundaries are encoded by features MAXS and MINS (corresponding to UPPER BOUNDARY and LOWER BOUNDARY in Fig. 12). Since these two features represent a property of the verb that is not linked to a specific node position, they are defined as global features.[13]

(13) Everybody laughs.

Let us go through the analysis of (13), shown in Fig. 13. The lexical entry of *laugh* (the root node of the derivation tree in Fig. 13) provides an upper boundary MAXS $= \boxed{2}$ and a lower boundary MINS $= l_1$ delimiting the scope window for any quantifier attaching to *laughs*. These boundaries mean that a quantifier that attaches to *laughs* has to minimally scope over the laugh′ proposition (label l_1), and it cannot scope higher than $\boxed{2}$.[14]

13 Global features are grouped under a feature GLOBAL that is linked to the elementary tree as a whole and not to single node positions. Each semantic representation can look into the global features of the mother node in the derivation tree (by putting a request on its root node position or its foot node position) or into the global features of a daughter (by putting a request on the node position to which the daughter attaches).

14 In this simple case, there are no further constraints on the MAXS value $\boxed{2}$, i.e., this upper limit does not have any effect. However, an attitude verb embedding *laugh* as in (14) would embed the *laugh* MAXS feature in its propositional argument and thereby prevent the quantifiers occurring in the embedded clause from taking scope outside of the embedded clause.

(14) Mary fears that everybody laughs.

Note that existential quantifiers such as *someone* always allow for a referential wide scope reading, even when being embedded under an attitude verb. In LTAG we assume that this reading is not a proper scope reading but it is obtained by a different mechanism.

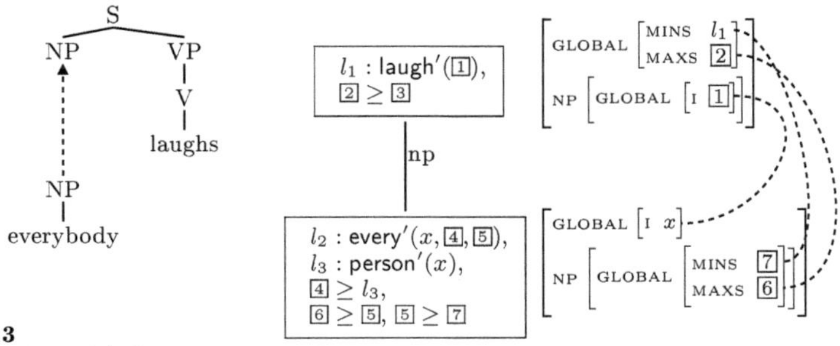

Figure 13
LTAG analysis of (13) *Everybody laughs*

The semantics of *everybody* has two parts: The generalized quantifier every′[15] with its restriction $\boxed{4}$ and its nuclear scope $\boxed{5}$, and a proposition person′(x) that is part of the restriction (constraint $\boxed{4} \geq l_3$). The quantifier looks for the global MAXS and MINS features of the verb it attaches to in order to find the upper and lower boundaries for its nuclear scope. In the semantic representation, the nuclear scope $\boxed{5}$ is situated between the variables $\boxed{6}$ and $\boxed{7}$ (constraints $\boxed{6} \geq \boxed{5}$, $\boxed{5} \geq \boxed{7}$). In order to equate these with the MAXS and MINS values of the verb, a request for these features is put on the root node (position NP) of *everybody*. The mechanism of adding feature equations for global features guarantees that this request gets identified with the global feature of *laughs*.

The feature identifications (indicated by dotted lines) lead to the constraints $\boxed{2} \geq \boxed{5}, \boxed{5} \geq l_1$. With the assignments following from the feature identifications ($\boxed{1} \rightarrow x, \boxed{6} \rightarrow \boxed{2}, \boxed{7} \rightarrow l_1$), we obtain the semantic representation (15):

(15)

l_1 : laugh′(x),
l_2 : every′(x,$\boxed{4}$,$\boxed{5}$), l_3 : person′(x)
$\boxed{2} \geq l_1$,
$\boxed{4} \geq l_3, \boxed{2} \geq \boxed{5}, \boxed{5} \geq l_1$

There is one possible disambiguation consistent with the scope constraints, namely $\boxed{2} \rightarrow l_2$, $\boxed{4} \rightarrow l_3, \boxed{5} \rightarrow l_1$. This leads to the semantics (16):

(16) every′(x, person′(x), laugh′(x))

15 Note that in LTAG, generalized quantifiers are treated as constants of a specific type in the underlying Ty2 logic. For a generalized quantifier q, $q(x, p_1, p_2)$ can be read as $q(\lambda x.p_1, \lambda x.p_2)$. In this sense, q is a constant of type $\langle\langle e, \langle s, t\rangle\rangle, \langle\langle e, \langle s, t\rangle\rangle, \langle s, t\rangle\rangle\rangle$. In particular, generalized quantifiers are not treated as syncategorematic in LTAG and cannot be identified as a special class of symbols. This is different in LRS where a sort hierarchy of subsorts of ***generalized-quantifier*** is employed in formulating principles of (immediate) scope constraints and quantifier islands (see Section 4.2 for simple principles referring to the relevant sorts).

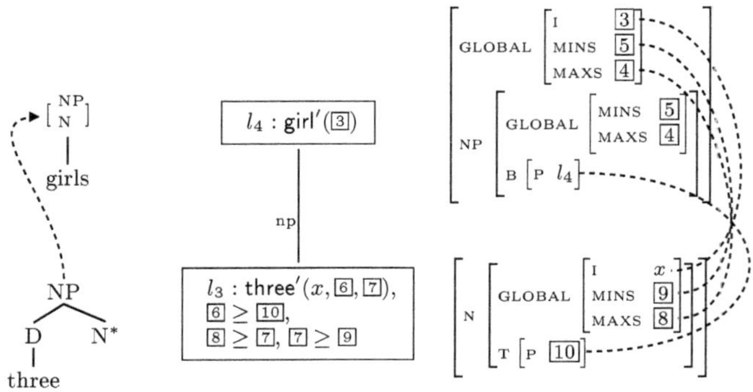

Figure 14
Analysis of NP *three girls* in LTAG

In order to illustrate the way quantifiers interact with other scope taking operators, let us consider the analysis of (12) *Three girls are likely to come.* The combination of the determiner and the noun into the NP *three girls* is shown in Fig. 14. The generalized quantifier *three* carries a request for the global features MAXS (variable 8) and MINS (variable 9) of the tree it attaches to, which is the *girls* tree. This tree, in turn, identifies its own global features MAXS (variable 4) and MINS (variable 5) with the global features obtained by requesting the global features of the verb. This means that the request for the global MAXS and MINS of the verb at the root of the *girls* tree ultimately concerns the upper and lower scope boundaries of *three.* The P feature provided by *girls* (label l_4) provides the restriction of *three.*

The syntactic analysis of (12) in LTAG is shown in Fig. 15. The raising predicate *be likely* is analyzed like adverbs, using a VP auxiliary tree that adjoins to the verbal spine of the infinitive.
The semantic analysis on the derivation tree is shown in Fig. 16. (The node positions VP_1 and VP_2 stand for the root and foot node positions of the *likely* tree.) The scope properties of the raising verb do not depend on the MAXS–MINS scope window. Instead, its scope depends on its attachment site. It is in a sense inserted between the top and the bottom part of the VP node to which it adjoins, embedding the proposition it finds at the bottom (here l_1) and providing a new proposition (label l_2) at the top. This new proposition is then passed up the verbal spine. This analysis is motivated by the empirical observation that in cases where more than one operator attaches to the verbal spine, the order on the spine determines the scope order:

(17) John tries to seem to be a nice boy.
tries > seem > be a nice boy, **seem > tries > be a nice boy*

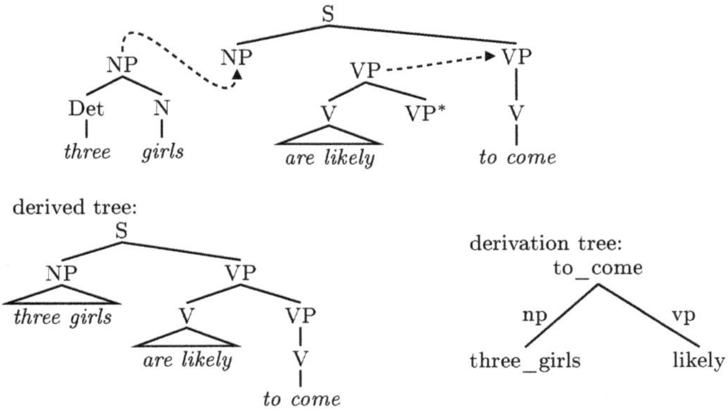

Figure 15
Syntactic analysis of (12) *Three girls are likely to come* in LTAG

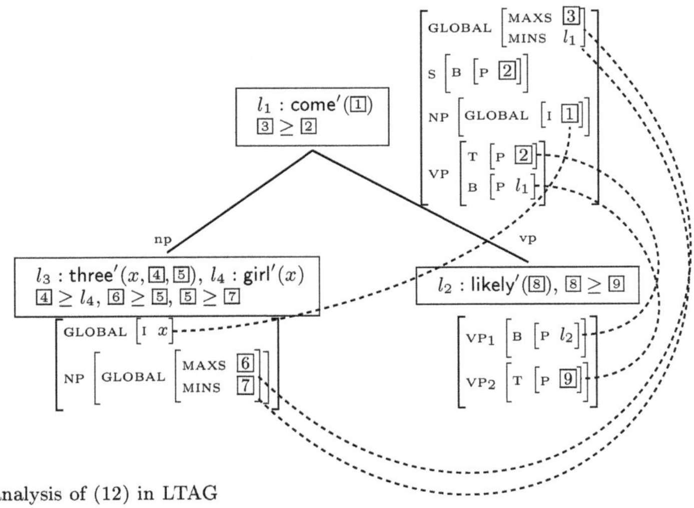

Figure 16
Semantic analysis of (12) in LTAG

The scope constraints for the raising verb interact with the quantifier scope window: The larger proposition on the verbal spine, $\boxed{2}$, is below the MAXS boundary (constraint $\boxed{3} \geq \boxed{2}$), and the proposition l_1 contained in the scope of the raising verb is the MINS boundary. As a consequence, *likely* also scopes within the quantifier scope window.

From the additional feature equations in Fig. 16, we obtain the assignments $\boxed{1} \rightarrow x, \boxed{2} \rightarrow l_2, \boxed{6} \rightarrow \boxed{3}, \boxed{7} \rightarrow l_1, \boxed{9} \rightarrow l_1$, which lead to the semantic representation

(20) everybody:

$$\begin{bmatrix} \text{PHON} & \langle \textit{everybody} \rangle \\ \text{SS LOC} & \begin{bmatrix} \text{CAT} & \begin{bmatrix}\text{HEAD} & \textit{noun}\\ \text{SUBCAT} & \langle\rangle\end{bmatrix} \\ \text{CONT} & \begin{bmatrix}\text{INDEX VAR} & x \\ \text{MAIN} & \mathsf{every}(x,\alpha,\beta)\end{bmatrix}\end{bmatrix} \\ \text{LF} & \begin{bmatrix} \text{EXCONT} & \textit{me} \\ \text{INCONT} & \boxed{2}\ \mathsf{person}'(x) \\ \text{PARTS} & \langle x,\ \boxed{2},\ \boxed{2a}\mathsf{person}',\ \boxed{4}\ \mathsf{every}(x,\alpha,\beta)\rangle \end{bmatrix}\end{bmatrix}$$

$$\& \boxed{2} \triangleleft \alpha \ \&\ x \triangleleft \alpha \ \&\ x \triangleleft \beta$$

Figure 17
Lexical entry of *everybody* in LRS

in (18):

$$(18)\quad \boxed{\begin{array}{l} l_1 : \mathsf{come}'(x) \\ l_3 : \mathsf{three}'(x,\boxed{4},\boxed{5}),\ l_4 : \mathsf{girl}'(x) \\ l_2 : \mathsf{likely}'(\boxed{8}) \\ \boxed{3} \geq l_2, \\ \boxed{4} \geq l_4,\ \boxed{3} \geq \boxed{5},\ \boxed{5} \geq l_1 \\ \boxed{8} \geq l_1 \end{array}}$$

This underspecified representation has the two disambiguations and scope orders in (19):

(19) a. $\boxed{3} \rightarrow l_3, \boxed{5} \rightarrow l_2, \boxed{8} \rightarrow l_1, \boxed{4} \rightarrow l_4$.
$l_3 : \mathsf{three}'(x, l_4 : \mathsf{girl}'(x), l_2 : \mathsf{likely}'(l_1 : \mathsf{come}'(x)))$

b. $\boxed{3} \rightarrow l_2, \boxed{8} \rightarrow l_3, \boxed{5} \rightarrow l_1, \boxed{4} \rightarrow l_4$.
$l_2 : \mathsf{likely}'(l_3 : \mathsf{three}'(x, l_4 : \mathsf{girl}'(x), l_1 : \mathsf{come}'(x)))$

4.2 Specifying a Scope Window for Quantifiers: LRS

To analyze the sentences (12) and (13) in LRS, we need to introduce the lexical entries for the quantificational expressions and a new principle, the SEMANTICS PRINCIPLE. The SEMANTICS PRINCIPLE of LRS consists of construction-specific clauses which put restrictions on the possible ways in which the semantic representations of syntactic daughters can be combined. Let us start with the lexical entry of *everybody* in Fig. 17.
From a syntactic point of view, *everybody* is a quantified noun phrase like *every girl* and *many boys in my class*. The combination of quantified noun phrases with a verbal projection is subject to a restriction by the SEMANTICS PRINCIPLE,

given in (21). We introduce two clauses of this fundamental principle.[16] The first one, (21a), applies when a quantificational determiner combines with a nominal projection; the second, (21b), governs the combination of a quantified noun phrase with a verbal projection.

(21) SEMANTICS PRINCIPLE:

In each *headed-phrase*, the following conditions hold:

a. if the non-head is a quantificational determiner then its INCONT value is of the form *gen-quantifier*(x, ρ, ν), the INCONT value of the head is a component of ρ, and the INCONT value of the non-head daughter is identical with the EXCONT value of the head daughter,

$$\begin{bmatrix}\text{NH-DTR SS LOC}\begin{bmatrix}\text{CAT HEAD} & \textit{det}\\ \text{CONT MAIN} & \textit{gen-quantifier}\end{bmatrix}\end{bmatrix} \rightarrow$$

$$\left(\begin{bmatrix}\text{H-DTR LF} & \begin{bmatrix}\text{EXCONT} & \boxed{1}\\ \text{INCONT} & \boxed{2}\end{bmatrix}\\ \text{NH-DTR LF} & \begin{bmatrix}\text{INCONT } \boxed{1}\begin{bmatrix}\textit{gen-quantifier}\\ \text{RESTR } \boxed{3}\end{bmatrix}\end{bmatrix}\end{bmatrix} \wedge \boxed{2} \triangleleft \boxed{3}\right)$$

b. if the non-head is a quantified NP with an EXCONT value of the form *gen-quantifier*(x, ρ, ν), then the INCONT value of the head is a component of ν,

$$\forall\boxed{1}\left(\begin{bmatrix}\text{NH-DTR}\begin{bmatrix}\text{SS LOC CAT} & \begin{bmatrix}\text{HEAD} & \textit{noun}\\ \text{SUBCAT} & \langle\rangle\end{bmatrix}\\ \text{LF EXCONT} & \begin{bmatrix}\textit{gen-quantifier}\\ \text{SCOPE } \boxed{1}\end{bmatrix}\end{bmatrix}\end{bmatrix} \rightarrow \exists\boxed{2}\left(\begin{array}{l}\begin{bmatrix}\text{H-DTR LF INCONT } \boxed{2}\end{bmatrix}\\ \wedge\ \boxed{2}\triangleleft\boxed{1}\end{array}\right)\right)$$

According to (21a), when a quantificational determiner is combined with a nominal head, the internal content of the nominal goes into the restrictor of the generalized quantifier. Note that this is a true 'component-of' constraint. There might be more in the restrictor of the generalized quantifier than just the internal content of the nominal projection. This is the case if the nominal is modified by a restrictive relative clause or by an intersective adjectival modifier. Their representations will also be part of the restrictor of the generalized quantifier (with the possible exception of certain quantificational operators).

16 The SEMANTICS PRINCIPLE for LRS was first formulated with more sub-clauses in (Richter and Sailer, 2001, p. 283), where it still included the LRS principles in (3a)–(3c). Additional clauses of an extended SEMANTICS PRINCIPLE introduce combinatoric restrictions on head-marker phrases, different kinds of head-adjunct phrases, and head-filler phrases. In general, these clauses contribute semantic restrictions on phrases obtained by certain modes of syntactic combination and often take the semantic types or syntactic and semantic class of the immediate daughters of the phrase into account.

In LRS, the EXCONT value of the utterance is the upper scope boundary while the INCONT value of the syntactic head which selects a quantifier is the lower boundary for scope. This can be seen in the analysis of (13), which is depicted in Fig. 18. The upper boundary is obtained through the interaction of 1) the LRS PROJECTION PRINCIPLE, (3c), stating that the PARTS list of a phrase contains all elements on the PARTS lists of its daughters, and 2) the EXCONT PRINCIPLE, (3b), which states that a) the PARTS list of each non-head contains its own EXCONT, and b) in an utterance, everything on the PARTS list is a component of the EXCONT. This leads to the constraint [4] $\triangleleft$ [6] in Fig. 18, among others. The lower boundary is obtained from the SEMANTICS PRINCIPLE, (21b), which states that if the non-head of a headed phrase is a quantifier, then the INCONT of the head is a component of its nuclear scope. This yields [1] $\triangleleft\ \beta$ in Fig. 18.

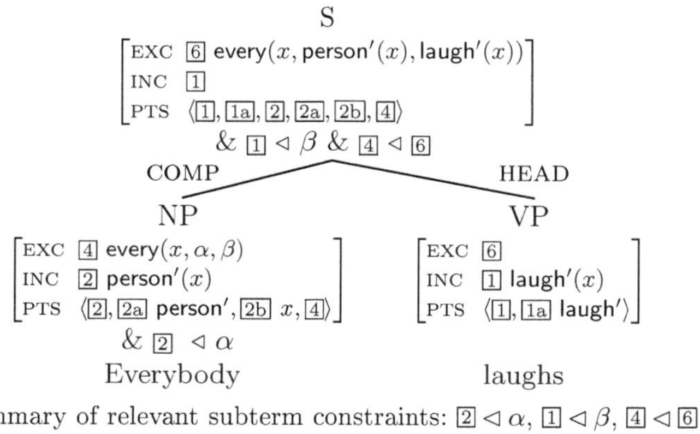

Figure 18
LRS analysis of (13) *Everybody laughs*

The situation becomes more complex when several scope taking elements interact, as in the ambiguous sentence (12), repeated in (22).

(22) Three girls are likely to come.

In order to analyze this sentence, we first need to explain how LRS handles the combination of a quantificational determiner with a count noun. (23a) and (23b) in Fig. 19 introduce the relevant parts of the lexical entries for *three* and *girls*.

Using the first clause of the SEMANTICS PRINCIPLE, we obtain the structure shown in Fig. 20. The nominal head of the noun phrase gains access to the variable x introduced by the determiner by selecting the determiner as the first element on the SUBCAT list and identifying the argument of the predicate girl′ with the variable found under INDEX VAR ([4a]). A comparison of the semantic representation of the quantified noun phrase *three girls* at the NP node with the semantic

(23) a. three:

$$\begin{bmatrix} \text{PHON} & \langle \textit{three} \rangle \\ \text{SS LOC} & \begin{bmatrix} \text{CAT} & \begin{bmatrix} \text{HEAD} & \textit{det} \\ \text{SUBCAT} & \langle\rangle \end{bmatrix} \\ \text{CONT} & \begin{bmatrix} \text{INDEX VAR} & \boxed{4a} x \\ \text{MAIN} & \boxed{4}\ \mathsf{three}(x, \alpha, \beta) \end{bmatrix} \end{bmatrix} \\ \text{LF} & \begin{bmatrix} \text{EXCONT} & \textit{me} \\ \text{INCONT} & \boxed{4}\ \mathsf{three}(x, \alpha, \beta) \\ \text{PARTS} & \langle \boxed{4}, \boxed{4a} \rangle \end{bmatrix} \end{bmatrix}$$

$$\&\ x \triangleleft \alpha\ \&\ x \triangleleft \beta$$

b. girls:

$$\begin{bmatrix} \text{PHON} & \langle \textit{girls} \rangle \\ \text{SS LOC} & \begin{bmatrix} \text{CAT} & \begin{bmatrix} \text{HEAD} & \textit{noun} \\ \text{SUBCAT} & \left\langle \text{DetP}_{\boxed{4a}} \right\rangle \end{bmatrix} \\ \text{CONT} & \begin{bmatrix} \text{INDEX VAR} & \boxed{4a} \\ \text{MAIN} & \mathsf{girl}' \end{bmatrix} \end{bmatrix} \\ \text{LF} & \begin{bmatrix} \text{EXCONT} & \begin{bmatrix} \textit{gen-quantifier} \\ \text{VAR}\ \boxed{4a} \end{bmatrix} \\ \text{INCONT} & \boxed{2}\ \mathsf{girl}'(\boxed{4a}) \\ \text{PARTS} & \langle \boxed{2}\ \mathsf{girl}'(\boxed{4a}), \boxed{2a}\ \mathsf{girl}' \rangle \end{bmatrix} \end{bmatrix}$$

Figure 19
Lexical entries for *three* and *girls* in LRS

representation of the quantifier *everybody* (20) immediately reveals their parallel structure.

Before we can analyze (22) we need to provide the semantics of the predicative adjective *likely*. According to (24) in Fig. 21, it embeds its own INCONT value in the argument α of the operator likely'. The INCONT value is assumed to be raised from its verbal complement. Since the INCONT of the complement is not part of the selected *synsem* structure of the complement, this INCONT raising cannot be lexically specified in the lexical entry of *likely*. Following (Sailer, 2006) we assume that a general INC RAISING PRINCIPLE takes care of INCONT raising and identifies the INCONT values of the appropriate predicates and their complements. The semantic constraints of the lexical entry of *come* are parallel to the lexical entry of *laugh* (2b); the auxiliaries *to* and *are* are analyzed as INC raising predicates similar to *likely* but without contributing any constant to the semantic representations.

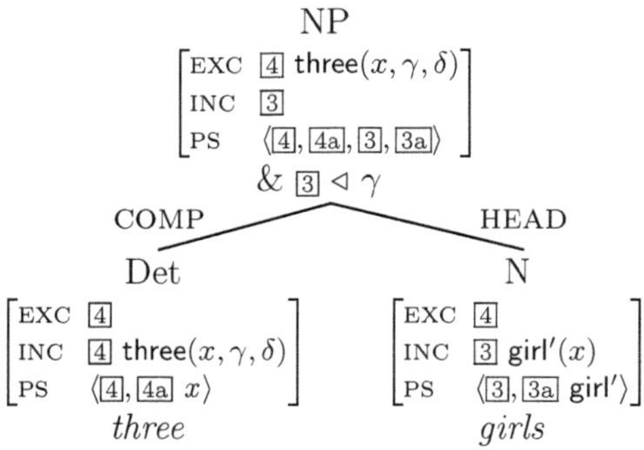

Figure 20
LRS analysis of *three girls*

(24) likely:

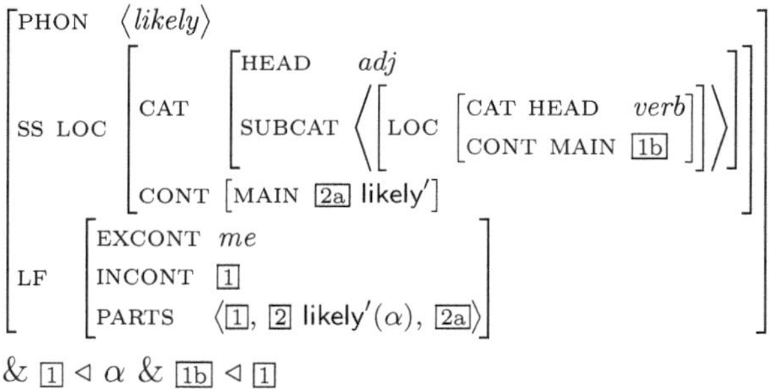

Figure 21
Lexical entry for *likely*

Fig. 22 shows the structure of (22) which follows from the lexical entries and the LRS principles above. The figure repeats only those subterm constraints which are essential to see the treatment of scope windows and the way the two readings of the sentence are derived.

The restrictions in Fig. 22 (in combination with the grammar of well-formed expressions of Ty2 presented in Section 2.2) leaves two possibilities for the EXCONT value [5]:

(25) a. [5] = three(x, girl′(x), likely′(come′(x)))

b. [5] = likely′(three(x, girl′(x), come′(x)))

The scope window for the operators in (22) is delineated by the internal content of *come*, [1], and the external content of the complete utterance, [5]. By definition,

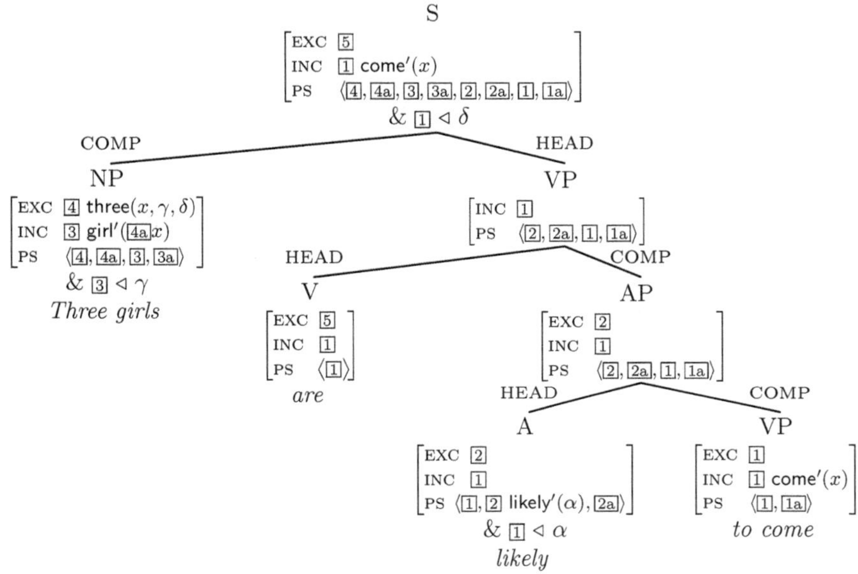

Figure 22
LRS analysis of *Three girls are likely to come*

the internal content of each sign *s* is outscoped by all scope-taking elements of the signs with which *s* combines. The equality of the INCONT of the sentence with the INCONT of *come* is mediated by the fact that *to*, *likely* and *are* are analyzed as INCONT raisers which identify their own INCONT with the INCONT of their VP (or AP) argument. Two subterm constraints interact with the internal content of *come*. The predicative adjective *likely* outscopes $\boxed{1}$ according to its lexical restrictions ($\boxed{1} \triangleleft \alpha$). Clause b of the SEMANTICS PRINCIPLE, (21), adds the restriction that $\boxed{1}$ be in the nuclear scope of the quantifier *three girls* ($\boxed{1} \triangleleft \delta$). In essence, these component constraints demand that both the quantifier and likely′ outscope come′(x), their relative scope is not determined. Adding the fact that girl′(x) must be in the restrictor of *three girls* ($\boxed{3} \triangleleft \gamma$), the two expressions in (25) are the only Ty2 terms satisfying all restrictions of the grammar.[17]

For a complete understanding of underspecification in the HPSG-LRS architecture, it is important to consider the (exhaustive) models in the denotation of the grammar. These models contain two structures for the sentence (22), one for each reading. The two structures are syntactically identical, but one has the EXCONT value in (25a) whereas the other has the EXCONT value in (25b). This

17 Note that the reading in (25b) implies $\boxed{5} = \boxed{2}$, which is not the case in reading (25a).

means that there is no underspecification at the level of semantic representations. Underspecification is only a matter of the TFL specification of the grammar.[18]

4.3 Summary: Features and Scope Constraints

The two quantifier scope analyses in LTAG and LRS illustrate two points. The first concerns the comparison of LTAG and LRS. As we have shown, both approaches use a feature architecture for a quantifier scope window to capture the freedom of quantifier scope within certain syntactically defined domains. LTAG semantics and LRS use a level of underspecification involving 'component-of'-constraints, although the status of the underspecification layer of grammar is different in the two frameworks. In finite sentences, there is a clear correspondence between LTAG's attributes MAXS and MINS and the attributes EXCONT and INCONT in LRS. The striking similarity between the two analyses shows that, despite the mathematical differences between the frameworks, central insights can be modelled in parallel. Interesting differences are expected to emerge in detailed analyses of subtle linguistic facts and possibly in the computational behavior of implementations of LTAG semantics and CLLRS.[19] An area in which differences between the two architectures matter will be discussed in the next section. As for computational differences, it is still too early to draw conclusions.

The second point concerns a contrast between feature logic-based computational semantics and the tradition of logical form semantics as an extension of generative syntax in the style of (Heim and Kratzer, 1998). As we have demonstrated, the use of feature logics with feature value identifications in combination with underspecification techniques allows us to avoid syntactic movement operations such as quantifier raising for the representation of scope. In other words, features are not only used to establish predicate-argument relations but they also serve to determine scope boundaries. This is possible because of the mechanisms for percolating feature values on the derived tree provided in LRS and LTAG and, in addition, because of LTAG's extended domain of locality.

5 Consequences of Encoding Semantic Formulas in a Feature Logic: The Case of Negative Concord

Negative concord can be characterized as a type of construction in which the occurrence of several negation-bearing elements such as negative quantifiers (*no one, nothing*) and negative particles (*not*) lead to an interpretation with only one negation. The analysis of negative concord in Polish in LTAG and LRS described in this section highlights differences in the theories' implementation of underspecification techniques. They are of particular interest to our discussion because they

18 Underspecification is also a crucial ingredient of the CLLRS implementation. Computation with CLLRS can thus be viewed as computation using underspecification techniques.

19 See the remarks in Section 2.3 on CLLRS.

go along with the different functions of the feature logics in the two frameworks. Both LTAG and LRS use component-of constraints, but they are used in different ways in the two grammar architectures. In LTAG, these constraints link underspecified Ty2 terms that are augmented with holes and labels of Hole Semantics, while in LRS, they belong to the descriptions of fully specified Ty2 terms. The possibility in LRS of referring to the same Ty2 expressions multiple times and at different points in the constituent structure of a sentence permits an interesting treatment of negative concord which cannot be mirrored directly in LTAG.

5.1 Negative Concord in Polish

Polish is a classical negative concord language. The basic facts of sentential negation and negative concord in Polish are illustrated in (26)–(28):

(26) Janek nie pomaga ojcu.
Janek NM helps father
'Janek doesn't help his father.'

(27) a. Janek nie pomaga nikomu.
Janek NM helps nobody
'Janek doesn't help anybody.'

b. *Janek pomaga nikomu.

(28) Nikt nie przyszedł.
nobody NM came
'Nobody came.'

The verbal prefix *nie* is obligatory for expressing sentential negation, and it can co-occur with any number of n-words (such as *nikt*, 'nobody/anybody') without ever leading to a double negation reading. As a consequence, (28) expresses only one logical sentential negation, although both the negation prefix *nie* on the verb and the n-word *nikt* can carry logical negation alone in other contexts. We will now present analyses in LTAG and LRS of negative concord in Polish, taking sentence (28) as our example.

5.2 Concord Phenomena in LRS

LRS takes advantage of the fact that its specifications of semantic representations are descriptions of logical expressions which can, in principle, mention the same parts of the expressions several times. (29) in Fig. 23 shows the relevant part of the lexical entries of *nikt (nobody)* and *nie przyszedł* which we need in the analysis of (28). Following (Kupść, 2000) we assume that *nie* is a verbal prefix and forms a morphological unit with the verb. The lexical entry of *nikt (nobody)* in (29a) is similar to the relevant parts of English *everybody* in (20). However, as

(29) a. nikt (*nobody*):

$$\left[\begin{array}{ll} \textit{word} & \\ \text{PHON} & \langle \textit{nikt} \rangle \\ \text{SS LOC CONT} & \left[\begin{array}{ll} \text{INDEX VAR} & \boxed{3b}\ x \\ \text{MAIN} & \boxed{5}\ \mathsf{some}(x,\gamma,\delta) \end{array}\right] \\ \text{LF} & \left[\begin{array}{ll} \textit{lrs} & \\ \text{EXCONT} & \boxed{5}\ \mathsf{some}(x,\gamma,\delta) \\ \text{INCONT} & \boxed{3}\ \mathsf{person'}(\boxed{3b}x) \\ \text{PARTS} & \langle \boxed{3}, \boxed{3a}\mathsf{person'}, \boxed{3b}, \boxed{4}\neg\beta, \boxed{5} \rangle \end{array}\right] \end{array}\right]$$

$$\&\ \boxed{5} \triangleleft \beta\ \&\ \boxed{3} \triangleleft \gamma\ \&\ x \triangleleft\ \gamma\ \&\ x \triangleleft\ \delta$$

b. nie przyszedł (*NM came*):

$$\left[\begin{array}{ll} \textit{word} & \\ \text{PHON} & \langle \textit{nie przyszedł} \rangle \\ \text{SS LOC} & \left[\begin{array}{l} \text{CAT SUBCAT } \left\langle \left[\text{LOC CONT INDEX VAR } \boxed{3b}\right] \right\rangle \\ \text{CONT MAIN } \mathsf{come'} \end{array}\right] \\ \text{LF} & \left[\begin{array}{ll} \textit{lrs} & \\ \text{EXCONT} & \boxed{0} \\ \text{INCONT} & \boxed{1}\ \mathsf{come'}(\boxed{3b}) \\ \text{PARTS} & \langle \boxed{1}, \boxed{1a}\mathsf{come'}, \boxed{2}\neg\alpha, \rangle \end{array}\right] \end{array}\right]$$

$$\&\ \boxed{1} \triangleleft \alpha\ \&\ \boxed{2} \triangleleft \boxed{0}$$

Figure 23
Lexical entries of *nikt* and *nie przyszedł* in LRS

a negative quantifier it also introduces a negation into the semantic representation. This negation receives a special treatment. According to (29a), the negation component, $\boxed{4}$, of *nikt* is not a component of its external content, which looks like an existential quantifier. Instead, the condition $\boxed{5} \triangleleft \beta$ only demands that the existential quantifier in the external content be in the scope of the negation.

In contrast to the specifications for *nikt*, the verb *nie przyszedł* realizes the negation within its external content. The lexical entry (29b) does this by stating that the negation, $\boxed{2}$, must be a subterm of the external content, $\boxed{0}$.

Without additional principles these lexical specifications are not sufficient to guarantee the only available reading of the sentence (28), i.e., the reading with a single sentential negation. First of all, nothing enforces the obligatory presence of the negation prefix with the finite verb in the presence of *nikt*. Second, a double negation reading may result from not identifying the negation contributed by *nikt* and by the verb. To overcome these shortcomings, (Richter and Sailer, 2004) introduces two language-specific principles which determine the behavior of negative concord in Polish.

We restate these two principles informally in (30a) and (30b).

(30) a. The NEG CRITERION:
For every finite verb, if there is a negation in the external content of the verb that has scope over the verb's MAIN value, then the negation must be an element of the verb's PARTS list.

b. The NEGATION COMPLEXITY CONSTRAINT:
For each sign, there may be at most one negation which is a component of the external content and has the MAIN value as its component.

According to the NEG CRITERION for Polish a (finite) verb in the scope of negation must contribute negation itself. The NEGATION COMPLEXITY CONSTRAINT limits to one the number of negations taking scope over a MAIN value within the projection domain of an external content. With these additional restrictions in place, we can now derive the meaning of (28) in LRS. Fig. 24 shows that both *nikt* and the verb *nie przyszedł* introduce descriptions of negations ($\boxed{4}$ and $\boxed{2}$, respectively). The constraints on negative concord in Polish conspire to force the negations contributed by the two words to be the same in the overall logical representation $\boxed{0}$ of the sentence ($\boxed{2} = \boxed{4}$ ($= \boxed{0}$)). Moreover, the negation must outscope the existential quantifier introduced by *nikt* due to the lexical scope constraint $\boxed{5} \triangleleft \beta$ of *nikt*. The restriction $\boxed{1} \triangleleft \delta$ comes from the second clause of the SEMANTICS PRINCIPLE, (21).

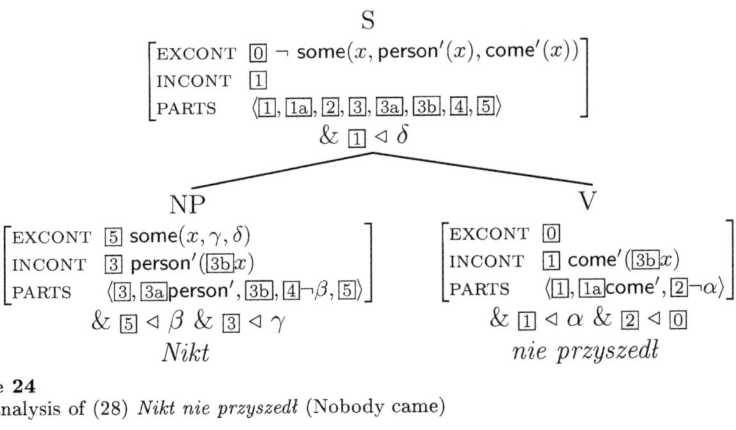

Figure 24
LRS analysis of (28) *Nikt nie przyszedł* (Nobody came)

5.3 Concord Phenomena in LTAG

An LRS-style analysis of negative concord is not possible in LTAG. Recall that the feature logic is not used to encode the Ty2 formulas as is the case in LRS. In LTAG, the formulas in the semantic representations are considered different objects, i.e., different subformulas of the final semantic representations we obtain after disambiguating the underspecified representation. Therefore, each negation in the interpretation corresponds to exactly one negated term introduced in the semantic representations from the lexicon.

Since the interpretation of (28) contains only one negation, there can be only one negation in the lexical entries involved in the derivation. As there can be several n-words in a sentence without resulting in multiple negation and the presence of the negative marker *nie* is obligatory, *nie* necessarily introduces the negation. The n-word *nikt* can then be analyzed as an existential quantifier that requires 1. the presence of a negation and 2. being in the scope of this negation.

An LTAG analysis along these lines is sketched in Fig. 25. It resembles in many respects the NPI analysis proposed in (Lichte and Kallmeyer, 2006). Let us explain its different aspects.

Verbs have two more global features, besides MAXS and MINS that were already introduced in Section 4: a feature NEG indicating the presence of a negation and a feature N-SCOPE containing the scope of this negation. If the verb is negated (as it is the case in Fig. 25), the global NEG should be set to *yes*, otherwise it should be set to *no*. (In the latter case, the feature N-SCOPE is irrelevant.) To achieve this, we introduce an additional local feature NEG on the V node. At the bottom, this feature has the value *no*. If no negative marker adjoins, this will be identified with the top (variable $\boxed{3}$) and passed from there to the global NEG. The negative marker adjoins to the V node and switches this local NEG feature to *yes* by specifying NEG= *yes* at the top of its root node. This *yes* gets identified with $\boxed{3}$ because of the adjunction. In addition, the negation *nie* identifies its scope (variable $\boxed{9}$) with the global N-SCOPE of the verb it attaches to (here $\boxed{1} = \boxed{9}$) and scopes over the proposition of the verb (the MINS feature, constraint $\boxed{9} \geq \boxed{10}$).

The n-word is an existential quantifier. It requires the global feature NEG of the verb it attaches to to be *yes* thereby checking the presence of a negation. Furthermore, its maximal scope boundary (constraint $\boxed{7} \geq \boxed{6}$) is not the MAXS value of the verb but the N-SCOPE value (identification $\boxed{1} = \boxed{7}$). This ensures that the existential quantifier is in the scope of the negation.
As a result, building the union of the semantic representations and applying the assignment obtained from the feature identification, we obtain the semantic representation in (31) for Fig. 25:

(31)
$$\begin{array}{|l|}\hline l_2 : \mathsf{come}'(x),\ l_3 : \mathsf{some}'(x, \boxed{5}, \boxed{6}),\ l_4 : \mathsf{person}'(x),\ l_1 : \neg\boxed{1} \\ \boxed{4} \geq l_2,\ \boxed{5} \geq l_4,\ \boxed{1} \geq \boxed{6},\ \boxed{6} \geq l_2,\ \boxed{1} \geq l_2 \\ \hline\end{array}$$

5.4 Summary: Underspecification in LRS and in LTAG

The analysis of negative concord demonstrates that the two frameworks differ substantially in their treatment of underspecification: 1. LRS employs partial descriptions of fully specified models, whereas LTAG generates underspecified representations in the style of (Bos, 1995) that require the definition of a disam-

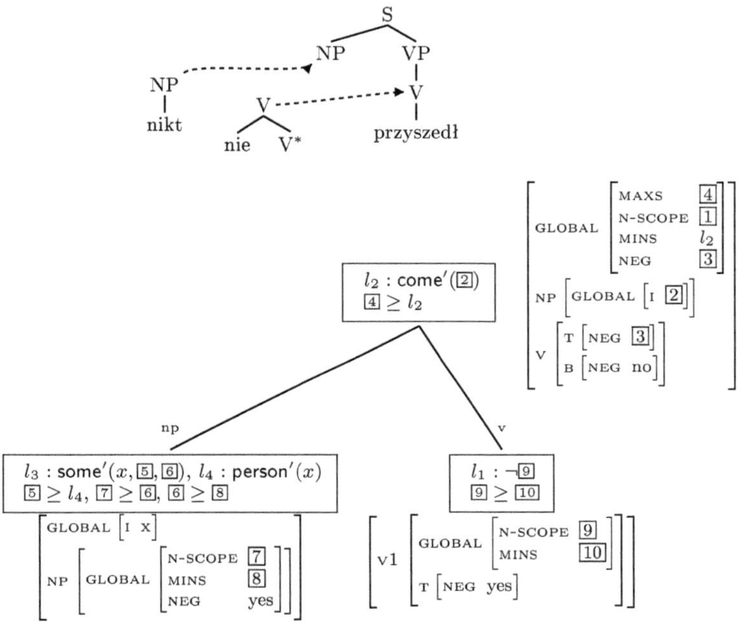

Figure 25
LTAG analysis of (28) *Nikt nie przyszedł*

biguation (a "plugging" in the terminology of Bos). 2. LRS constraints contain descriptions of Ty2 terms rather than Ty2 terms. Therefore, unlike in LTAG, two descriptions can denote the same formula. Because of this, the analysis of negative concord in LRS described above can introduce several negations at the TFL description level that get identified in the models of the constraint system. This is not possible in LTAG, where the feature logic only mediates between pieces of underspecified Ty2 expressions. As a result, LTAG is more limited than LRS. On the other hand, the way semantic representations are defined in LTAG guarantees that they almost correspond to *normal dominance constraints*, which are known to be polynomially parsable (see (Althaus et al., 2003)).

The difference in the use of underspecification techniques reflects the more general difference between the two types of mathematical systems: In a generative linear rewriting system such as LTAG the elements of the grammar are objects (here: elementary trees paired with sets of Ty2 terms), and copying or erasing is disallowed during derivations. By contrast, in a purely description-based formalism such as HPSG token identities between different components of linguistic structures are natural and frequently employed.

6 Feature Logic-Based Semantic Computation and Compositionality

At first sight, feature logic-based computational semantics systems such as LTAG and LRS do not seem compatible with a notion of compositionality. Clearly, in these frameworks the derived trees do not determine the meaning of a phrase in such a way that it is the result of applying the meaning of one daughter to the meaning of another (in binary branching structures). In order to show that these systems are still compositional, we have to identify a different structure that determines syntax and semantics. In this section we will sketch some ideas for LTAG concerning this question.

The key to answering the question about the compositionality of LTAG semantics is the fact that LTAG is a mildly context-sensitive grammar: The derivation process (i.e., the process of syntactic combination) can be described by a context-free structure, the derivation tree. In this section we will demonstrate that this context-free structure also specifies the process of semantic combination in a way that corresponds to Hodges' definition of a compositional semantics (Hodges, 2001).

6.1 TAG as a Linear Context-free Rewriting System

TAGs are mildly context-sensitive; they belong to the class of linear context-free rewriting systems (LCFRS, (Weir, 1988)). Consequently, they have an underlying context-free backbone – the derivation trees – that denotes the trees that can be derived. In this section we will outline how to define a context-free grammar describing the derivation trees. We can then define syntactic and semantic denotations for this grammar: The syntactic denotations are the derived trees while the semantic denotations are the resulting semantic representations plus the feature structure descriptions one obtains from the conjunction of the different descriptions involved and the equations arising from the substitutions and adjunctions.

An LCFRS consists of

- a generalized context-free grammar (GCFG) generating terms in a term algebra that correspond, in our case, to the derivation trees,
- the (syntactic) denotations of these terms (the derived trees), and
- functions specifying how to compute the strings they yield.

In the following, we will ignore the strings produced by the terms of the GCFG. Instead, we will focus on defining the semantic denotations of the terms.

6.1.1 The Generalized Context-free Grammar A Generalized Context-free Grammar (GCFG) is a context-free grammar that generates terms. It consists of

- disjoint alphabets N and F, the nonterminals and the function symbols,

- a start symbol $S \in N$, and
- a finite set of productions P of the form $A \to f(A_1, \ldots, A_n)$ where $n \geq 0, f \in F$ and $A, A_1, \ldots, A_n \in N$.

A GCFG derives a set of terms in the following way:

- $A \Rightarrow f()$ if $A \to f()$ is a production.
- $A \stackrel{*}{\Rightarrow} f(t_1, \ldots, t_n)$ if there is a production $A \to f(A_1, \ldots, A_n)$ and $A_i \stackrel{*}{\Rightarrow} t_i$ for $1 \leq i \leq n$.

The idea of the GCFG specifying the derivations of a TAG is as follows: The GCFG productions specify possible adjunctions and substitutions for each elementary tree. The elementary trees are the nonterminal symbols of the GCFG. The set of terms one can derive from some elementary γ specifies all the derivation trees with root symbol γ. In particular, the γ-productions specify the different possibilities for the daughters of γ in the derivation tree, i.e., the different combinations of adjunctions and substitutions possible for γ. More concretely, the productions have the form $\gamma \to f_{\gamma:p_1,\ldots,p_n}(\gamma_1, \ldots, \gamma_n)$ with $\gamma, \gamma_1, \ldots, \gamma_n$ being elementary trees and $p_1, \ldots, p_n$ being node addresses in γ. This production indicates that $\gamma_1, \ldots, \gamma_n$ can be attached (by substitution or adjunction) to γ at node addresses $p_1, \ldots, p_n$.

Consider for example the TAG in Fig. 26 with the corresponding GCFG that characterizes the derivation trees.[20] With this grammar, for (32) we obtain the derivation tree and corresponding term tree in (33).[21] (The term itself is $f_{\alpha_l:1,2,22}(f_{\alpha_j}(), f_{\beta:\epsilon}(f_\beta()), f_{\alpha_m}())$. Interpreted as a bracketed tree, this gives the second tree in (33).)

(32) John sometimes sometimes loves Mary

(33)
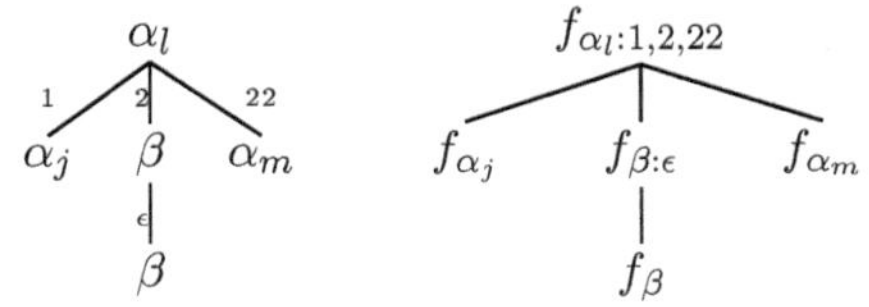

The general construction of the GCFG G for a given TAG is as follows:

- The nonterminal symbols of G are the elementary trees.

20 Here, we use Gorn addresses for the positions of the nodes: The root has the address ϵ and the jth child of a node with address p has address $p \cdot j$.

21 We are aware that (32) is not really an English sentence. But for the examples in this section, we try to keep our grammar as small as possible and thus provide only one VP modifier. This is why we chose this odd example.

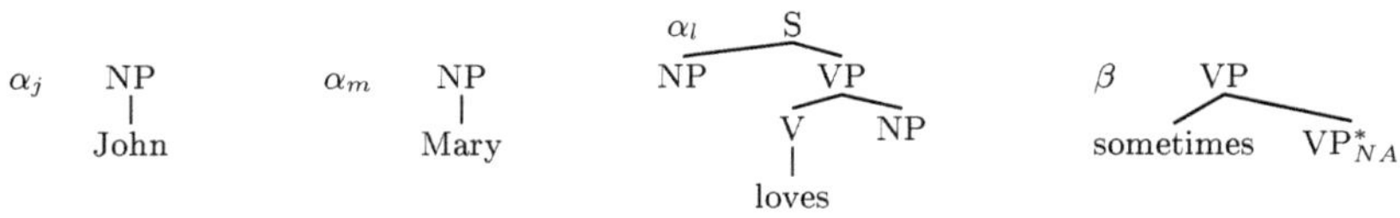

Corresponding GCFG:

$\alpha_j \rightarrow f_{\alpha_j}()$	no subst./adj. to α_j
$\alpha_m \rightarrow f_{\alpha_m}()$	no subst./adj. to α_m
$\beta \rightarrow f_\beta()$	no subst./adj. to β
$\beta \rightarrow f_{\beta:\epsilon}(\beta)$	adjunction of β to the root of β
$\alpha_l \rightarrow f_{\alpha_l:1,22}(\alpha_j, \alpha_m)$	substitutions of α_j and α_m at addr. 1 and 22 resp. in α_l
$\alpha_l \rightarrow f_{\alpha_l:1,22}(\alpha_j, \alpha_j)$	...
$\alpha_l \rightarrow f_{\alpha_l:1,22}(\alpha_m, \alpha_j)$	...
$\alpha_l \rightarrow f_{\alpha_l:1,22}(\alpha_m, \alpha_m)$	...
$\alpha_l \rightarrow f_{\alpha_l:1,2,22}(\alpha_j, \beta, \alpha_m)$	subst./adj. of α_j, β and α_m at addr. 1, 2 and 22 resp. in α_l
$\alpha_l \rightarrow f_{\alpha_l:1,2,22}(\alpha_j, \beta, \alpha_j)$	...
$\alpha_l \rightarrow f_{\alpha_l:1,2,22}(\alpha_m, \beta, \alpha_j)$	...
$\alpha_l \rightarrow f_{\alpha_l:1,2,22}(\alpha_m, \beta, \alpha_m)$	...

Figure 26
Sample LTAG and corresponding GCFG

- For each elementary γ without OA constraints[22] and without substitution nodes: there is a zero arity function f_γ and a production $\gamma \rightarrow f_\gamma()$.
- For each γ and positions $p_1, \ldots, p_n$ in γ comprising all OA nodes and all substitution nodes and $\gamma_1, \ldots, \gamma_n$ that can be adjoined/substituted at positions $p_1, \ldots, p_n$ respectively: There is a n-ary function $f_{\gamma:p_1,\ldots p_n}$ and a production $\gamma \rightarrow f_{\gamma:p_1,\ldots p_n}(\gamma_1, \ldots, \gamma_n)$

6.1.2 The syntactic denotation The term trees denote derived trees in the same way as derivation trees determine derived trees:

- For all productions of the form $\gamma \rightarrow f_\gamma()$: $[\![f_\gamma()]\!]_{syn} := \gamma$.
- For all productions of the form $\gamma \rightarrow f_{\gamma:p_1,\ldots p_n}(\gamma_1, \ldots, \gamma_n)$: $[\![f_{\gamma:p_1,\ldots p_n}(t_1, \ldots, t_n)]\!]_{syn} := \gamma[p_1, [\![t_1]\!]_{syn}] \ldots [p_n, [\![t_n]\!]_{syn}]$.[23]

For our sample LTAG we obtain:

22 OA stands for "obligatory adjunction". TAG allows one to specify for each node whether adjunction at that node is obligatory or not. If it is obligatory, the node is said to have an OA constraint.

23 $\gamma[p, \gamma']$ is defined as follows: if γ' is (derived from) an initial tree and the node at position p in γ is a substitution node, then $\gamma[p, \gamma']$ is the tree one obtains by substituting γ' into γ at node position p. If γ' is (derived from) an auxiliary tree and the node at position p in γ is an internal node, then $\gamma[p, \gamma']$ is the tree one obtains by adjoining γ' to γ at node position p. Otherwise $\gamma[p, \gamma']$ is undefined. (Note that the undefined case cannot happen here due to the construction of the GCFG.)

(34)
$$\begin{array}{lll} [\![f_{\alpha_j}()]\!]_{syn} = \alpha_j & [\![f_{\alpha_m}()]\!]_{syn} = \alpha_m & [\![f_{\beta}()]\!]_{syn} = \beta \\ \multicolumn{3}{l}{[\![f_{\beta:\epsilon}(X)]\!]_{syn} = \beta[\epsilon, [\![X]\!]_{syn}]} \\ \multicolumn{3}{l}{[\![f_{\alpha_l:1,22}(X,Y)]\!]_{syn} = \alpha_l[1, [\![X]\!]_{syn}][22, [\![Y]\!]_{syn}]} \\ \multicolumn{3}{l}{[\![f_{\alpha_l:1,2,22}(X,Y,Z)]\!]_{syn} = \alpha_l[1, [\![X]\!]_{syn}][2, [\![Y]\!]_{syn}][22, [\![Z]\!]_{syn}]} \end{array}$$

The syntactic denotation of the term tree (33) for (32) is then (35):

(35) $[\![f_{\alpha_l:1,2,22}(f_{\alpha_j}(), f_{\beta:\epsilon}(f_{\beta}()), f_{\alpha_m}())]\!]_{syn} = \alpha_l[1, \alpha_j][2, \beta[\epsilon, \beta]][22, \alpha_m]$

The expression $\alpha_l[1, \alpha_j][2, \beta[\epsilon, \beta]][22, \alpha_m]$ in (35) denotes the derived tree one obtains by starting with α_l (the *likes* tree), substituting the node at position 1 for a tree t_1, adjoining a tree t_2 at position 2 and substituting the node at position 22 for a tree t_3 where t_1, t_2, t_3 are as follows: t_1 is the tree α_j of *John* without any further adjunctions or substitutions, t_3 is the tree α_m of *Mary* without any further adjunctions or substitutions, and t_2 ($\beta[\epsilon, \beta]$) can be obtained by taking the *sometimes* tree β and adjoining to its root (position ϵ) again the *sometimes* tree β.

6.2 Semantic Denotation of the GCFG Terms

The crucial question now is whether the GCFG productions also specify semantic composition. In the following we will show that this is the case.

Let σ be a function assigning to each elementary tree a pair consisting of a semantic representation and a feature structure description. The function σ for our sample grammar is shown in Fig. 27.

$$\sigma(\alpha_j) = \langle \sigma_{\alpha_j}, \delta_{\alpha_j} \rangle := \langle \; \boxed{\mathsf{john}'(x)} \;,\; \boxed{0}\begin{bmatrix} \epsilon \; \begin{bmatrix} \mathrm{B} \; \begin{bmatrix} \mathrm{I} \; x \end{bmatrix} \end{bmatrix} \end{bmatrix} \; \rangle$$

$$\sigma(\alpha_m) = \langle \sigma_{\alpha_m}, \delta_{\alpha_m} \rangle := \langle \; \boxed{\mathsf{mary}'(y)} \;,\; \boxed{1}\begin{bmatrix} \epsilon \; \begin{bmatrix} \mathrm{B} \; \begin{bmatrix} \mathrm{I} \; y \end{bmatrix} \end{bmatrix} \end{bmatrix} \; \rangle$$

$$\sigma(\alpha_l) = \langle \sigma_{\alpha_l}, \delta_{\alpha_l} \rangle := \langle \; \boxed{l_1 : \mathsf{love}'(\boxed{2}, \boxed{3})} \;,\; \boxed{4}\begin{bmatrix} 1 & \begin{bmatrix} \mathrm{T} \; \begin{bmatrix} \mathrm{I} \; \boxed{2} \end{bmatrix} \end{bmatrix} \\ 22 & \begin{bmatrix} \mathrm{T} \; \begin{bmatrix} \mathrm{I} \; \boxed{3} \end{bmatrix} \end{bmatrix} \\ 2 & \begin{bmatrix} \mathrm{T} \; \begin{bmatrix} \mathrm{P} \; \boxed{5} \end{bmatrix} \\ \mathrm{B} \; \begin{bmatrix} \mathrm{P} \; l_1 \end{bmatrix} \end{bmatrix} \end{bmatrix} \; \rangle$$

$$\sigma(\beta) = \langle \sigma_{\beta}, \delta_{\beta} \rangle := \langle \; \boxed{\begin{array}{l} l_2 : \mathsf{sometimes}'(\boxed{6}) \\ \boxed{6} \geq \boxed{7} \end{array}} \;,\; \boxed{8}\begin{bmatrix} \epsilon & \begin{bmatrix} \mathrm{B} \; \begin{bmatrix} \mathrm{P} \; l_2 \end{bmatrix} \end{bmatrix} \\ 2 & \begin{bmatrix} \mathrm{T} \; \begin{bmatrix} \mathrm{P} \; \boxed{7} \end{bmatrix} \end{bmatrix} \end{bmatrix} \; \rangle$$

Figure 27
Function σ for LTAG from Fig. 26

We assume that each time a syntactic category (an elementary tree γ) occurs in a term, σ assigns a fresh instance of $\sigma(\gamma)$ (i.e., an instance with fresh labels, variables and meta-variables).

Now we have to define the semantic functions corresponding to the $f_{\gamma\ldots}$, i.e., the semantic denotations of the terms in our term algebra.[24] In order to compute the semantics of a node in the term tree, we need to know a) the unions of the semantic representations from the subtrees, b) the feature structure descriptions computed from the different subtrees, and c) the top fs-variables of the feature structure descriptions of the daughters. For a feature structure description δ linked to the semantic representation of an elementary tree, let $top(\delta)$ be the unique top variable. (E.g., in Fig. 27, $top(\delta_{\alpha_j}) = \boxed{0}, top(\delta_{\alpha_m}) = \boxed{1}\ldots$) We then define our semantic denotations as triples $\langle\overline{\sigma_\gamma}, \delta'_\gamma, top(\delta_\gamma)\rangle$ where the three components correspond to a)–c) above.

For a pair $\langle\sigma, \delta\rangle$ let $\overline{\sigma}$ be the result of applying to σ the meta-assignments following from δ.

Let us first illustrate the idea of the semantic denotations looking at some terms from our sample grammar.

(36) $[\![f_{\alpha_j}()]\!]_{sem} := \langle\overline{\sigma_{\alpha_j}}, \delta'_{\alpha_j}, top(\delta_{\alpha_j})\rangle$ with

$$\delta'_{\alpha_j} \quad = \quad \delta_{\alpha_j} \bigwedge\{\mathrm{T}(p(top(\delta_{\alpha_j}))) = \mathrm{B}(p(top(\delta_{\alpha_j}))) \,|\, p \text{ position in } \alpha_j\}$$

This means that the semantic denotation of the tree α_j with no other trees attaching to it consists of the top variable of the feature structure description δ_{α_j} (third component), the description δ_{α_j} conjoined with top-bottom equations for all nodes (second component), and the semantic representation obtained from applying the assignment arising from δ_{α_j} and the new equations to σ_{α_j}. The denotations for $f_{\alpha_m}()$ and $f_\beta()$ look similar.

(37) $[\![f_{\beta:\epsilon}(X)]\!]_{sem} := \langle\overline{\sigma_\beta \cup \sigma_X}, \delta', top(\delta_\beta)\rangle$ where $[\![X]\!]_{sem} = \langle\sigma_X, \delta_X, top_X\rangle$ with

$$\begin{aligned}\delta' \quad = \quad & \delta_\beta \wedge \delta_X \\ & \wedge\mathrm{T}(\epsilon(top(\delta_\beta))) = \mathrm{T}(\epsilon(top_X)) \wedge \mathrm{B}(\epsilon(top(\delta_\beta))) = \mathrm{B}(f_X(top_X)) \\ & \bigwedge\{\mathrm{T}(p(top(\delta_\beta))) = \mathrm{B}(p(top(\delta_\beta))) \,|\, p \neq \epsilon, p \text{ position in } \beta\}\end{aligned}$$

f_X gives the foot node position of the tree γ such that the term X has the form $f_{\gamma\ldots}(\ldots)$.

For terms denoting adjunctions or substitutions, things are more complex: The new description is the conjunction of the daughter descriptions plus additional equations corresponding to the adjunctions/substitutions and the final top-bottom identifications. In (37) these new equations identify the top of the adjunction site (address ϵ) in β with the top of the root of the adjoined tree, and the bottom of the adjunction site (address ϵ) in β with the bottom of the foot node of the adjoined tree. Furthermore, for all positions in β other than the adjunction site,

24 For simplicity we do not consider global features (an extension to global features is straightforward).

top and bottom are identified. The new semantic representation is of course the union of the representations from the daughter denotations after application of the assignment computed from the new description.

The general definition of the semantic denotation is as follows:

- For all productions of the form $\gamma \to f_\gamma()$: Take a fresh instance $\langle\sigma_\gamma, \delta_\gamma\rangle$ of $\sigma(\gamma)$.

  $[\![f_\gamma()]\!]_{sem} := \langle\overline{\sigma_\gamma}, \delta'_\gamma, top(\delta_\gamma)\rangle$ with

  $$\delta'_\gamma \;=\; \delta_\gamma \bigwedge\{\mathrm{T}(p(top(\delta_\gamma))) = \mathrm{B}(p(top(\delta_\gamma)))\,|\,p \text{ position in } \gamma\}$$

- For all productions of the form $\gamma \to f_{\gamma:p_1,\ldots p_n}(\gamma_1, \ldots, \gamma_n)$: Without loss of generality let $p_1, \ldots, p_k$ $(0 \leq k \leq n)$ be the substitution node positions among the $p_1, \ldots p_n$.

  Take a fresh instance $\langle\sigma_\gamma, \delta_\gamma\rangle$ of $\sigma(\gamma)$.

  $[\![f_{\gamma:p_1,\ldots p_n}(X_1, \ldots, X_n)]\!]_{sem} := \langle\overline{\sigma_\gamma \cup \sigma_{X_1} \cup \cdots \cup \sigma_{X_n}}, \delta', top(\delta_\gamma)\rangle$ with

  $$\begin{array}{rcl}\delta' & = & \delta_\gamma \wedge \delta_{X_1} \wedge \ldots \delta_{X_n} \\ & & \bigwedge_{i=1}^{n} \mathrm{T}(p_i(top(\delta_\gamma))) = \mathrm{T}(\epsilon(top_{X_i})) \\ & & \bigwedge_{i=k+1}^{n} \mathrm{B}(p_i(top(\delta_\gamma))) = \mathrm{B}(f_{X_i}(top_{X_i})) \\ & & \bigwedge\{\mathrm{T}(p(top(\delta_\gamma))) = \mathrm{B}(p(top(\delta_\gamma)))\,|\,p \notin \{p_1, \ldots, p_n\}, \\ & & \qquad\qquad\qquad\qquad\qquad\qquad p \text{ position in } \gamma\}\end{array}$$

Let us go back to the example (32) *John sometimes sometimes loves Mary.* The term describing its derivation was $f_{\alpha_l:1,2,22}(f_{\alpha_j}(), f_{\beta:\epsilon}(f_\beta()), f_{\alpha_m}())$. The computation of the semantic denotation of this term is shown in Fig. 28.

We have shown that for each LTAG G, a GCFG can be defined that generates a term algebra describing the structural analyses of the strings generated by G in the sense of having syntactic denotations that are the derived trees yielding these strings. For this term algebra, there are

(i) a function b giving the semantic denotations of atomic expressions $f()$ in the term algebra ($b(f()) := [\![f()]\!]_{sem}$),

(ii) and rules r_f specifying for each function (syntactic rule) f in the term algebra how to compute $[\![f(\gamma_1, \ldots, \gamma_n)]\!]_{sem}$ from $[\![\gamma_1]\!]_{sem}, \ldots [\![\gamma_n]\!]_{sem}$.

The relationship between the term algebra generated by the GCFG and the semantic denotation given by (i) and (ii) directly corresponds to a property of meaningful terms in a term algebra which Hodges establishes as one of four equivalent ways to characterize a compositional semantics (Hodges, 2001, p. 12, Theorem 4 (b)). Hodges defines a grammar as a set of expressions that can be obtained from atomic expressions by combining them according to a set of syntactic rules. The admissible syntactic combinations are captured by means of a grammatical term algebra, where a term t is grammatical if its value is defined and t is assigned

$$[\![f_\beta()]\!]_{sem} = \langle \sigma_\beta^1, {\delta_\beta^1}', \boxed{11} \rangle \text{ with}$$

$$\begin{aligned}
\sigma_\beta^1 &= \boxed{l_3 : \mathsf{sometimes}'(\boxed{9}),\ \boxed{9} \geq \boxed{10}} \\
{\delta_\beta^1}' &= \mathrm{P}(\mathrm{B}(\epsilon(\boxed{11}))) = l_3 \wedge \mathrm{P}(\mathrm{T}(2(\boxed{11}))) = \boxed{10} \\
&\quad \wedge \mathrm{T}(\epsilon(\boxed{11})) = \mathrm{B}(\epsilon(\boxed{11})) \wedge \mathrm{T}(2(\boxed{11})) = \mathrm{B}(2(\boxed{11}))
\end{aligned}$$

$$[\![f_{\beta:\epsilon}(f_\beta())]\!]_{sem} = \langle \sigma_\beta^2, {\delta_\beta^2}', \boxed{8} \rangle \text{ with}$$

$$\begin{aligned}
\sigma_\beta^2 &= \boxed{l_2 : \mathsf{sometimes}'(\boxed{6}),\ l_3 : \mathsf{sometimes}'(\boxed{9}),\ \boxed{6} \geq \boxed{7},\ \boxed{9} \geq l_2} \\
{\delta_\beta^2}' &= \mathrm{P}(\mathrm{B}(\epsilon(\boxed{8}))) = l_2 \wedge \mathrm{P}(\mathrm{T}(2(\boxed{8}))) = \boxed{7} \\
&\quad \wedge {\delta_\beta^1}' \\
&\quad \wedge \mathrm{T}(\epsilon(\boxed{8})) = \mathrm{T}(\epsilon(\boxed{11})) \wedge \mathrm{B}(\epsilon(\boxed{8})) = \mathrm{B}(2(\boxed{11})) \\
&\quad \wedge \mathrm{T}(2(\boxed{8})) = \mathrm{B}(2(\boxed{8}))
\end{aligned}$$

$$[\![f_{\alpha_j}()]\!]_{sem} = \langle \sigma_{\alpha_j}, \delta'_{\alpha_j}, \boxed{0} \rangle \text{ with}$$

$$\begin{aligned}
\sigma_{\alpha_j} &= \boxed{\mathsf{john}'(x)} \\
\delta'_{\alpha_j} &= \mathrm{I}(\mathrm{B}(\epsilon(\boxed{0}))) = x \\
&\quad \wedge \mathrm{T}(\epsilon(\boxed{0})) = \mathrm{B}(\epsilon(\boxed{0}))
\end{aligned}$$

$$[\![f_{\alpha_m}()]\!]_{sem} = \langle \sigma_{\alpha_m}, \delta'_{\alpha_m}, \boxed{1} \rangle \text{ with}$$

$$\begin{aligned}
\sigma_{\alpha_m} &= \boxed{\mathsf{mary}'(y)} \\
\delta'_{\alpha_m} &= \mathrm{I}(\mathrm{B}(\epsilon(\boxed{1}))) = y \\
&\quad \wedge \mathrm{T}(\epsilon(\boxed{1})) = \mathrm{B}(\epsilon(\boxed{1}))
\end{aligned}$$

$$[\![f_{\alpha_l:1,2,22}(f_{\alpha_j}(), f_{\beta:\epsilon}(f_\beta()), f_{\alpha_m}())]\!]_{sem} = \langle \sigma_{\alpha_l}, {\delta_{\alpha_l}}', \boxed{4} \rangle \text{ with}$$

$$\begin{aligned}
\sigma_{\alpha_l} &= \boxed{\begin{array}{l} \mathsf{john}'(x),\ \mathsf{mary}'(y),\ l_1 : \mathsf{love}'(x, y), \\ l_2 : \mathsf{sometimes}'(\boxed{6}),\ l_3 : \mathsf{sometimes}'(\boxed{9}), \\ \boxed{6} \geq l_1,\ \boxed{9} \geq l_2 \end{array}} \\
\delta'_{\alpha_l} &= \mathrm{I}(\mathrm{T}(1(\boxed{4}))) = \boxed{2} \wedge \mathrm{I}(\mathrm{T}(22(\boxed{4}))) = \boxed{3} \\
&\quad \wedge \mathrm{P}(\mathrm{T}(2(\boxed{4}))) = \boxed{5} \wedge \mathrm{P}(\mathrm{B}(2(\boxed{4}))) = l_1 \\
&\quad \wedge \delta'_{\alpha_j} \wedge {\delta_\beta^2}' \wedge \delta'_{\alpha_m} \\
&\quad \wedge \mathrm{T}(\epsilon(\boxed{0})) = \mathrm{T}(1(\boxed{4})) \\
&\quad \wedge \mathrm{T}(\epsilon(\boxed{1})) = \mathrm{T}(22(\boxed{4})) \\
&\quad \wedge \mathrm{T}(2(\boxed{4})) = \mathrm{T}(\epsilon(\boxed{8})) \wedge \mathrm{B}(2(\boxed{4})) = \mathrm{B}(2(\boxed{8})) \\
&\quad \wedge \mathrm{T}(\epsilon(\boxed{4})) = \mathrm{B}(\epsilon(\boxed{4})) \wedge \mathrm{T}(21(\boxed{4})) = \mathrm{B}(21(\boxed{4}))
\end{aligned}$$

Figure 28
Computation of the semantic denotation for (32) *John sometimes sometimes loves Mary*

a structural analysis. In our case, the GCFG generates all grammatical terms of the LTAG G. (i) and (ii) above determine the semantic denotations for each term. As a result, each term is *μ-meaningful* in the sense of Hodges' Theorem 4, and LTAG semantics fulfills the requirements of a compositional semantics.[25]

6.3 Summary: LTAG and Compositionality

As we have shown, since LTAG belongs to the class of linear context-free rewriting systems, it is possible to define a term algebra describing the syntactic composition (the substitutions and adjunctions) such that the semantics of a term $f(t_1, \ldots, t_n)$ depends only on f and the semantics of the subterms $t_1, \ldots, t_n$. In this sense, LTAG semantics is compositional.

For LRS, it is less obvious whether compositionality can be shown. We still need to identify the relevant structures that determine syntax and semantics. A starting point might be to look for some kind of functor-argument structure, similar to LTAG derivation trees. We leave this issue for further research.

7 Conclusion

We presented and compared two approaches to computational semantics, LRS and LTAG semantics. They are formulated in considerably different grammar frameworks but agree on the use of feature logics as a central mechanism in the specification of dependencies between the meaning of syntactic constituents and their components. This idea sets them apart from most of the current semantic theories of natural languages, which use the lambda calculus for specifying semantic composition.

Beyond their use of feature logic in semantic composition, we can identify a number of additional common characteristics of LTAG semantics and LRS: They both 1. use a Ty2 language for semantics; 2. allow underspecification (scope constraints, $\geq$, in LTAG semantics; component-of constraints, $\lhd$, in LRS); 3. use logical descriptions for semantic computation, including the identification of the arguments of logical functors; 4. use the feature logics for specifying the upper and lower scope boundaries of quantificational operators; 5. are designed for computational applications. Due to these similarities, the analyses of several empirical phenomena and certain generalizations about the nature of semantic composition in natural languages can be formulated in almost identical ways in the two theories. Among these we focussed on the treatment of quantifier scope, and the mechanisms for identifying semantic arguments using attribute values rather than functional application with the lambda calculus.

25 (Hodges, 2001) proposes two alternative characterizations of a compositional semantics. The one we use here is the stronger, more restricted version, which we consider the more interesting notion of compositionality for linguistics.

7.1 Differences between LRS and LTAG

LRS structures are specified by means of a typed feature logic that supports the specification of all aspects of semantic composition. In fact, beyond semantic composition the feature logic can even take over the task of specifying the syntax of the semantic representation language, Ty2. This 'all-in-one' strategy is particularly attractive in combination with a grammar framework such as HPSG, because it makes it possible to investigate the syntax-semantics interface with a uniform model theory that applies to the syntactic structures of natural languages as well as to the semantic representations that are associated with them. From an abstract point of view, the intuitive function of LRS constraints on the meaning of utterances is 1. to specify the meaning contributions of words to the utterances in which they occur, and 2. to govern the way in which a particular mode of syntactic combination restricts the possibilities of putting the meaning contributions of lexical elements together.

In contrast to LRS in HPSG, LTAG is a modularly organized system with mathematically clearly separated subsystems. The syntactic framework is a tree-generating grammar. The elementary trees of the TAG system are linked to underspecified semantic representations that are augmented with feature logical expressions. The underspecification techniques that are applied to the semantic representations come from Hole Semantics (Bos, 1995). A feature logic extension of the underspecified representations is responsible for the treatment of predicate-argument relationships and the scope of quantificational operators. Semantic computation adds feature value equations to the lexical specifications; these feature value equations are triggered by syntactic operations in the derivation of trees. The semantic representation which results from the syntactic derivation is an underspecified representation that awaits further disambiguation. The disambiguation procedure then leads to the interpretation(s) of a sentence in terms of sets of fully specified logical formulas. The disambiguation step can be viewed as another modular extension of the overall architecture and is performed according to the techniques of Hole Semantics.

Both LRS and LTAG semantics use feature logics to express predicate-argument relations and also to treat scope boundaries. However, from a technical perspective they do this in completely different ways. LRS as a whole is formulated in an expressive feature logic. Every element in an HPSG grammar with LRS is a logical description.[26] Linguists call these logical statements the 'grammar principles'. The linguistic expressions that are the subject of linguistic theorizing are perceived as configurations of entities licensed by the totality of logical statements in the grammar. In particular, the Ty2 terms that indicate the real world-meaning of linguistic expressions are also among the structures licensed by the grammar. We can say that they are in the denotation of the set of feature logical state-

26 Apart from the signature, which the linguist has to declare before writing the principles of grammar. See Section 2.1 for a short explanation.

ments that constitute the grammar. The feature logic of LTAG semantics, on the other hand, is simply a restricted first order logic that serves solely to compute underspecified semantic representations. In this architecture the feature logic has nothing to do with the semantic representations linguists are interested in when they want to know the meaning of an utterance. Therefore the models of the feature structure descriptions never play a role in the LTAG architecture.

This difference is related to a much more general difference between Head-driven Phrase Structure Grammar and Tree Adjoining Grammar. HPSG takes a model theoretic view on natural languages. It sees the task of linguists in the logical specification of the well-formed expressions of a natural language with a uniform typed feature logic for all modules of grammar. To make this a feasible enterprise, the feature logic must be very flexible and expressive, because the kinds of principles linguists might want to express and the kinds of structures they might want to characterize cannot be anticipated. The starting point of LTAG is quite different. LTAG belongs to the class of mildly context-sensitive grammar formalisms, which is a class of formal systems with attractive computational properties for parsing. The entire architecture of the semantic framework in LTAG is guided by the desire to uphold its mildly context-sensitive nature. As a consequence, the feature logic extension of the core formalism is kept as weak as possible.

A key aspect of mildly context-sensitive grammars is that they are defined in a way as to guarantee the existence of an underlying context-free structure that uniquely determines both syntactic and semantic composition. The existence of such a context-free structure that links syntax and semantics justifies the claim that LTAG semantics is compositional. In HPSG a corresponding context-free structure might exist for some grammars or even for a particular class of HPSG grammars with LRS, but its existence is not guaranteed by the linguistic framework or the TFL formalism itself. It is the responsibility of the grammar writer to make sure that structures in the denotation of his grammar meet these or similar conditions.

The difference in the use of underspecification in LTAG semantics and in LRS that we discussed in this paper goes in the same direction. LRS employs partial descriptions of fully specified models. It follows immediately that two Ty2 term descriptions in grammatical constraints can denote the same formula in the model of an utterance in the denotation of the grammar. LTAG generates underspecified representations consisting of (pairwise distinct) sub-formulas linked by scope constraints. If a type-identical formula is mentioned twice in grammatical descriptions, the two occurrences of the formula are necessarily distinct tokens. As distinct tokens they will stay distinct throughout all semantic computations during the derivation of a sentence. As first-class citizens of the grammar architecture, the underspecified representations of LTAG semantics also require the explicit definition of a disambiguation procedure.

The heavily parsing-oriented aspect of its overall architecture makes LTAG ultimately less flexible than LRS. Semantic concord cannot be the consequence of (partially) identifying semantic representations of sub-constituents in larger syntactic units. What we get in return are, once more, desirable computational properties: LTAG's semantic representations and the structures that the scope constraints impose on them guarantee that the constraints on underspecified representations resulting from semantic computation are just a slight extension of *normal dominance constraints*, which are known to be polynomially parsable. One of the goals of research in LTAG semantics is to show that its extension of normal dominance constraints still stays within the realm of polynomially parsable systems.

7.2 General Properties of Feature Logic-based Semantic Computation
Despite the architectural differences, the two frameworks for computational semantics share several important characteristics. We believe that these common features are general properties of frameworks with feature logic-based semantic computation. These frameworks can be distinguished in two respects from the influential frameworks in the immediate tradition of generative syntax such as (Heim and Kratzer, 1998):

First, they avoid functional application as the main method of semantic composition, which also means that they do not obligatorily pair up syntactic rules and semantic translation rules. One immediate consequence of not using functional application and similar operations as the mode of semantic composition is that the feature logic-based frameworks do not have to appeal to type shifting the semantics of lexical (or even phrasal) elements either, which is necessary in other theories in order to allow for all necessary functional applications in the course of semantic composition.[27] Similarly, type raising to the worst case is an artefact of the lambda calculus-based systems which is needed to be able to treat all elements of a given syntactic category in the process of semantic composition the same way, even though the basic semantic types of some lexical classes within a given syntactic category could in principle be much simpler. A famous example is the type raising of proper names to quantifiers to obtain a uniform type for all nominal phrases. The feature logic-based systems will always analyze every lexical element with the simplest available typing that is compatible with the empirically observed semantic behavior of the element.

Second, we saw that feature logic constraints permit a straightforward and flexible specification of scope boundaries. In particular, the use of feature logics in combination with underspecification avoids the introduction of otherwise unmo-

27 The families of relations called *argument raising* and *value raising* in the Flexible Montague Grammar of (Hendriks, 1993) are one possible implementation of the technique of type shifting. In a lexicalized version Flexible Montague Grammar is also compatible with HPSG (Sailer, 2003), which makes it possible to compare LRS and a semantics using type shifting operations within one grammar framework; see (Richter, 2004a) for details.

tivated syntactic movement operations such as a tree-configurational mechanism of quantifier raising ('QR'). Consequently, our syntax is very surface-oriented; syntactic structure is assumed only for those units which can be argued for on syntactic grounds. Postulating a level of logical form (often called LF in the literature) to provide an additional layer of syntactic structure for computing the semantics which potentially introduces many empty categories is superfluous. Computational implementations may thus focus on syntactic representations that are known to be tractable more efficiently instead of having to deal with an inconvenient structural overhead with opaque properties, which, moreover, might change dramatically as the semantic theory develops.

It is interesting to note that the use of a standard semantic representation language such as Ty2 in our two frameworks is closely related to the use of feature logics in the combinatorics. Expressions of Ty2 become available as concrete structures due to the existence of independent mechanisms for percolating feature values on the derived syntax tree. In LTAG, the extended domain of locality of the elementary trees provides additional support for a direct specification of semantic representations in a standard higher-order logic.

The large and increasingly important research area of syntactic and semantic licensing requirements is an empirical domain in which a mathematically precise theory of features and feature values provides a firm basis for expressing elegant generalizations. Such contextual factors keep gaining ground in computational linguistics, where they appear in the form of collocation conditions, and they are also of interest in computational pragmatics. A typical syntactic example of a contextual licensing condition is the LTAG analysis of negative concord of Section 5.3; a related LTAG analysis of NPI (negative polarity item) licensing was proposed by (Lichte and Kallmeyer, 2006). Similarly, (Richter and Soehn, 2006) proposes a theory of NPI licensing in HPSG that combines an LRS semantics with elements of a theory of idiomatic expressions. This theory of idioms was originally presented by (Soehn, 2006), who built on previous HPSG work on idioms that had produced a general architecture of a grammar module for the description of various kinds of collocations. Feature logic-based theories of context conditions in semantic representations of the type that we see in the semantic composition mechanisms of LRS and LTAG semantics may thus be viewed as a natural variant and new branch of feature logic-based theories of contextual licensing. In the course of these developments, semantic composition may finally become much more similar to other linguistic mechanisms than was assumed when it was set apart from other modules of grammar by exceptional composition mechanisms.

LTAG semantics as well as LRS have emphasized computational considerations of grammar design from the start. HPSG has always figured prominently in grammar implementation efforts; LRS has been implemented as the CLLRS module of the TRALE grammar development system (Penn and Richter, 2004; Penn and Richter, 2005). However, unlike in our discussion of LTAG semantics, in which we have paid attention to many computational aspects, we largely ignored computational issues in LRS. The reason was that appreciating the relationship between CLLRS and LRS presupposes a much more detailed study of the model theory of LRS than is appropriate in the present context. The starting point of an efficient LRS implementation is the investigation of the intended models of an LRS grammar, and a thorough understanding of the interaction of the LRS constraints with syntactic constraints. On the basis of the models of the logical theory of LRS, CLLRS provides a separate constraint language specifically designed to reason over the intended class of models. Giving up the generality of a feature logic such as RSRL, CLLRS offers new constraint primitives such as component-of constraints and contribution constraints to support precisely those kinds of statements that are prominent in LRS principles. Since CLLRS can be defined as an extension of a standard feature logic, with which it may share meta-variables, the tight integration of syntax and semantics remains possible. The computational efficiency of the resulting system depends on the constraint handling system of CLLRS and its resolution procedures for underspecified descriptions of expressions of the higher-order logic. In current research, optimizing the computational behavior of CLLRS in response to practical experiences with implemented CLLRS grammars is an important issue.[28]

There exist several LTAG parsers and a large coverage grammar for English (XTAG Research Group, 2001). However, this grammar does not include a semantics yet. More recently the Metagrammar (MG) tool developed in Nancy (Crabbé and Duchier, 2004) was augmented by functions for the compact specification of a semantic module in a TAG. (Gardent and Parmentier, 2005) presented a parser for processing syntax and semantics which builds on the grammar format supported by the MG tool.

7.3 Open Questions

An obvious open question is whether HPSG with LRS is a compositional semantics. In Section 6 we sketched a non-trivial notion of compositionality for LTAG semantics which crucially relied on an underlying context-free structure linking the derived trees of the TAG component to underspecified semantic representations. For LRS, we still need to identify the relevant structures that determine a compositional relationship between the syntactic structures and the semantics. However, the fact that such structures exist in a closely related framework such as LTAG semantics indicates that finding them might not be as difficult as a first look at the LRS architecture might suggest.

Another interesting topic for further research is the problem of a more exact specification of the relationship between the feature logic attributes for semantic representations in LTAG and LRS. In the present paper, we focused on how the use of semantic feature values in the two systems leads to systems with very similar

28 For some more remarks on the relationship between LRS and CLLRS, see Section 2.3 above.

overall functions. Pursuing the technical details of the two systems further, it might even be possible to identify translation procedures from one framework to the other. The possibility of translating semantic analyses between two grammars implemented in different frameworks could be a very interesting application for computational grammar development.

As we emphasized throughout this paper, the limited generative capacity of the LTAG formalism is desirable because it guarantees a satisfactory computational behavior of LTAG grammars in the general case. It is not very surprising that this convenience comes at a price. The heavy restrictions on the expressivity of the framework occasionally cause problems: Some natural language phenomena cannot be described within traditional TAG. Most TAG extensions that have been proposed to remedy these problems involve the factoring of elementary trees into multicomponent sets (Weir, 1988; Rambow, 1994; Kallmeyer, 2005). This means that the lexical entries are no longer just single trees; they become sets of trees. If one of these lexical tree sets is used in a derivation step, then all of its elements must be added in this derivation step by substitution or adjunction. If the TAG framework is to reach a better empirical coverage in syntax and in semantics, extending the present syntax-semantics interface to these new TAG variants is an important issue for future research. For example, recent extensions of LTAG to multicomponent sets lead to greater success in the description of word order variability, and this extension in syntactic coverage leads to new questions at the syntax-semantics interface. One of them is the problem of capturing relations between word order and meaning in languages such as German that require a multicomponent extension of LTAG. First ideas on these topics are presented in (Kallmeyer and Romero, 2006). The connection of LTAG semantics to LRS might also be useful here, since the treatment of free word order languages has received much attention in HPSG.

We hope that our comparison of LRS and LTAG semantics will contribute to an increasing and fruitful interaction between the research communities from which the two theories originate. The comparison highlighted some important successful features that the two theories have in common. Due to the significant architectural differences between the two systems, comparing them also improved our understanding of those properties which distinguish both of them as feature logic-based approaches to semantic composition from the current alternative theories of the syntax-semantics interface. At the same time, the differences between LRS and LTAG semantics, in particular the differences in the motivation behind their major design decisions, are substantial enough to make one of the systems occasionally more successful in some tasks than the other. It is again the common core of the two systems that can be useful in transfering successful solutions in one system to the other for their mutual benefit.

Acknowledgments

For many long and fruitful discussions of many aspects of LTAG semantics and LRS, we would like to thank Timm Lichte, Wolfgang Maier, Maribel Romero, Manfred Sailer and Jan-Philipp Söhn. Furthermore, we are grateful to the participants of the workshop on *Typed Feature Structure Grammars* in Aalborg, Denmark, to the audience of our tutorial *Constraint-based Computational Semantics: LTAG and LRS* at the '13th International Conference on Head-Driven Phrase Structure Grammar 2006' in Varna, Bulgaria, and, in particular, to Anders Søgaard and Petter Haugereid and two reviewers for very helpful comments. A much shorter presentation of some aspects of the research reported in this paper appeared in (Kallmeyer and Richter, 2006). Without Janina Radó's help this paper would be much harder to read.

References

Althaus, Ernst, Denys Duchier, Alexander Koller, Kurt Mehlhorn, Joachim Niehren, and Sven Thiel. 2003. An efficient graph algorithm for dominance constraints. *Journal of Algorithms*, 48(1):194–219.

Bos, Johan. 1995. Predicate logic unplugged. In Paul Dekker and Martin Stokhof, editors, *Proceedings of the 10th Amsterdam Colloquium*, pages 133–142.

Copestake, Ann, Dan Flickinger, Carl Pollard, and Ivan A. Sag. 2005. Minimal Recursion Semantics: An introduction. *Research on Language and Computation*, 3:281–332.

Crabbé, Benoit and Denys Duchier. 2004. Metagrammar Redux. In *International Workshop on Constraint Solving and Language Processing*, pages 32–47, Copenhagen.

Frank, Robert. 2002. *Phrase Structure Composition and Syntactic Dependencies.* Cambridge, Mass: MIT Press.

Fuchss, Ruth, Alexander Koller, Joachim Niehren, and Stefan Thater. 2004. Minimal Recursion Semantics as Dominance Constraints: Translation, Evaluation, and Analysis. In *Proceedings of the 42nd Annual Meeting of the Association for Computational Linguistics (ACL'04)*, pages 247–254, Barcelona, Spain.

Gallin, Daniel. 1975. *Intensional and Higher-Order Modal Logic.* North-Holland, Amsterdam.

Gardent, Claire and Yannick Parmentier. 2005. Large scale semantic construction for Tree Adjoining Grammars. In *Logical Aspects of Computational Linguistics, LACL'2005*, pages 131–146, Bordeaux.

Heim, Irene and Angelika Kratzer. 1998. *Semantics in Generative Grammar.* Blackwell.

Hendriks, Herman. 1993. *Studied Flexibility.* ILLC Dissertation Series 1995-5. Institute for Logic, Language and Computation, Amsterdam.

Hodges, Wilfrid. 2001. Formal Features of Compositionality. *Journal of Logic, Language, and Information*, 10:7–28.

Johnson, Mark. 1988. *Attribute-value logic and the theory of grammar.* CSLI Lecture Notes Series. Chicago: University of Chicago Press.

Johnson, Mark. 1990. Expressing disjunctive and negative feature constraints with classical first-order logic. In *Proceedings of the 28th Annual Meeting of the Association for Computational Linguistics*, pages 173–179.

Joshi, Aravind K. 1985. Tree adjoining grammars: How much contextsensitivity is required to provide reasonable structural descriptions? In D. Dowty, L. Karttunen, and A. Zwicky, editors, *Narural Language Parsing.* Cambridge University Press, pages 206–250.

Joshi, Aravind K. and Yves Schabes. 1997. Tree-Adjoning Grammars. In G. Rozenberg and A. Salomaa, editors, *Handbook of Formal Languages.* Springer, Berlin, pages 69–123.

Kallmeyer, Laura. 2005. Tree-local multicomponent tree adjoining grammars with shared nodes. *Computational Linguistics*, 31(2):187–225.

Kallmeyer, Laura and Aravind K. Joshi. 2003. Factoring Predicate Argument and Scope Semantics: Underspecified Semantics with LTAG. *Research on Language and Computation*, 1(1–2):3–58.

Kallmeyer, Laura and Frank Richter. 2006. Constraint-based computational semantics: A comparison between LTAG and LRS. In *Proceedings of the 8th International Workshop on Tree Adjoining Grammar and Related Formalisms (TAG+8)*, pages 109–114, Sydney, Australia, July. The Association for Computational Linguistics.

Kallmeyer, Laura and Maribel Romero. 2006. Quantifier Scope in German: An MCTAG Analysis. In *Proceedings of the 8th International Workshop on Tree Adjoining Grammar and Related Formalisms (TAG+8)*, pages 73–80, Sydney, Australia, July. The Association for Computational Linguistics.

Kallmeyer, Laura and Maribel Romero. 2007. Scope and Situation Binding in LTAG using Semantic Unification. To appear in *Research on Language and Computation*.

Kamp, Hans and Uwe Reyle. 1993. *From Discourse to Logic*. Studies in Linguistics and Philosophy. Dordrecht, Boston, London: Kluwer.

Kasper, Robert. 1997. Semantics of recursive modification. Unpublished Manuscript. The Ohio State University.

Koller, Alexander, Joachim Niehren, and Stefan Thater. 2003. Bridging the gap between underspecification formalisms: Hole semantics as dominance constraints. In *Meeting of the European Chapter of the Association for Computational Linguistics*, pages 195–202, April.

Koller, Alexander, Joachim Niehren, and Ralf Treinen. 2001. Dominance Constraints: Algorithms and Complexity. In M. Moortgat, editor, *Proceedings of the Third International Conference on Logical Aspects of Computational Linguistics (LACL'98), Grenoble, France*, volume 2014 of *Lecture Notes in Computer Science*, pages 106–125, Berlin, December. Springer.

Kupść, Anna. 2000. *An HPSG Grammar of Polish Clitics*. Ph.d. thesis, Institute of Computer Science, Polish Academy of Sciences and Université Paris 7, Warszawa, Poland.

Lichte, Timm and Laura Kallmeyer. 2006. Licensing German Negative Polarity Items in LTAG. In *Proceedings of the 8th International Workshop on Tree Adjoining Grammar and Related Formalisms*, pages 81–90, Sydney, Australia, July. The Association for Computational Linguistics.

Moore, Robert C. 1989. Unification-based semantic interpretation. In *Proceedings of the 27th Annual Meeting of the Association for Computational Linguistics*, pages 33–41.

Nederhof, Mark-Jan. 1997. Solving the correct-prefix property for TAGs. In T. Becker and H.-U. Krieger, editors, *Proceedings of the Fifth Meeting on Mathematics of Language*, pages 124–130, Schloss Dagstuhl, Saarbrücken, August.

Nerbonne, John. 1992. Constraint-based semantics. In Paul Dekker and Martin Stokhof, editors, *Proceedings of the Eighth Amsterdam Colloquium*, pages 425–444. Institute for Logic, Language and Information.

Penn, Gerald and Frank Richter. 2004. Lexical Resource Semantics: From theory to implementation. In Stefan Müller, editor, *Proceedings of the 11th International Conference on Head-Driven Phrase Structure Grammar*, pages 423–443. CSLI Publications.

Penn, Gerald and Frank Richter. 2005. The other syntax: Approaching natural language semantics through logical form composition. In Henning Christiansen, Petter Rossen Skadhauge, and Jørgen Villadsen, editors, *Constraint Solving and Language Processing. First International Workshop, CSLP 2004, Roskilde, Denmark, September 1-3, 2004, Revised Selected and Invited Papers*, volume 3438 of *Lecture Notes in Computer Science*, pages 48–73. Springer.

Pollard, Carl and Ivan A. Sag. 1994. *Head-Driven Phrase Structure Grammar*. Studies in Contemporary Linguistics. Chicago, London: The University of Chicago Press.

Rambow, Owen. 1994. *Formal and Computational Aspects of Natural Language Syntax*. Ph.D. thesis, University of Pennsylvania.

Richter, Frank. 2004a. Foundations of Lexical Resource Semantics. Habilitation Thesis. Eberhard Karls Universität Tübingen.

Richter, Frank. 2004b. *A Mathematical Formalism for Linguistic Theories with an Application in Head-Driven Phrase Structure Grammar*. Phil. dissertation (2000), Eberhard Karls Universität Tübingen.

Richter, Frank and Manfred Sailer. 2001. On the left periphery of German finite sentences. In W. Detmar Meurers and Tibor Kiss, editors, *Constraint-Based Approaches to Germanic Syntax*. CSLI Publications, Stanford, pages 257–300.

Richter, Frank and Manfred Sailer. 2004. Basic concepts of Lexical Resource Semantics. In Arnold Beckmann and Norbert Preining, editors, *ESSLLI 2003 Course Material I*, volume 5 of *Collegium Logicum*. Kurt Gödel Society Wien, pages 87–143.

Richter, Frank and Jan-Philipp Soehn. 2006. 'Braucht niemanden zu scheren': A survey of NPI licensing in German. In Stefan Müller, editor, *Proceedings of the 13th International Conference on Head-Driven Phrase Structure Grammar*, pages 421–440. CSLI Publications.

Sailer, Manfred. 2003. Combinatorial semantics and idiomatic expressions in Head-Driven Phrase Structure Grammar. Phil. Dissertation (2000). Arbeitspapiere des SFB 340. 161, Eberhard Karls Universität Tübingen.

Sailer, Manfred. 2004. Propositional relative clauses in German. In Stefan Müller, editor, *Proceedings of the 11th International Conference on Head-Driven Phrase Structure Grammar*, pages 223–243. CSLI Publications.

Sailer, Manfred. 2006. "Don't Believe" in Underspecified Semantics. Neg Raising in Lexical Resource Semantics. In Olivier Bonami and Patricia Cabredo Hofherr, editors, *Empirical Issues in Formal Syntax and Semantics*, volume 6. Presses de l'Université de Paris-Sorbonne, pages 375–403.

Savitch, Walter J., Emmon Bach, William Marxh, and Gila Safran-Naveh, editors. 1987. *The Formal Complexity of Natural Language*. Studies in Linguistics and Philosophy, edited by-Walter J. Savitch and Emmon Bach and William Marxh and Gila Safran-Naveh. Dordrecht, Holland: Reidel.

Schabes, Yves and Aravind K. Joshi. 1988. An Earley-type parsing algorithm for Tree Adjoining Grammars. In *Proceedings of the 26th Annual Meeting of the Association for Computational Linguistics*, pages 258–269.

Shieber, Stuart M. 1985. Evidence against the context-freeness of natural language. *Linguistics and Philosophy*, 8:333–343. Reprinted in (Savitch et al., 1987).

Soehn, Jan-Philipp. 2006. *Über Bärendienste und erstaunte Bauklötze - Idiome ohne freie Lesart in der HPSG*. Peter Lang (Frankfurt/M). Phil. dissertation (2005). Friedrich-Schiller-Universität Jena.

Vijay-Shanker, K. 1987. *A Study of Tree Adjoining Grammars*. Ph.D. thesis, University of Pennsylvania.

Vijay-Shanker, K. and Aravind K. Joshi. 1985. Some computational properties of Tree Adjoining Grammars. In *Proceedings of the 23rd Annual Meeting of the Association for Computational Linguistics*, pages 82–93.

Vijay-Shanker, K. and Aravind K. Joshi. 1988. Feature structures based tree adjoining grammar. In *Proceedings of COLING*, pages 714–719, Budapest.

Vijay-Shanker, K. and David J. Weir. 1993. Parsing some constrained grammar formalisms. *Computational Linguistics*, 19(4):591–636.

Weir, David J. 1988. *Characterizing mildly context-sensitive grammar formalisms*. Ph.D. thesis, University of Pennsylvania.

XTAG Research Group. 2001. A Lexicalized Tree Adjoining Grammar for English. Technical report, Institute for Research in Cognitive Science, Philadelphia. Available from `ftp://ftp.cis.upenn.edu/pub/xtag/release-2.24.2001/tech-report.pdf`.

Integrating typed feature structures into Combinatory Categorial Grammar

Mark McConville*
University of Edinburgh

Inheritance-driven CCG encapsulates a uniform approach to the elimination of redundancy in CCG lexicons, where grammars incorporate inheritance hierarchies of lexical types, defined over a simple, feature-based category description language. The resulting formalism is partially 'model-theoretic', in that the category notation is interpreted against an underlying set of tree-like typed feature structures. This extension of CCG subsumes a number of other proposed category notations devised to allow for the construction of more efficient lexicons.

1 The CCG formalism

In its most basic conception, a Combinatory Categorial Grammar (henceforth CCG) over alphabet Σ of terminal symbols is an ordered triple $\langle A, S, L\rangle$, where A is an alphabet of saturated category symbols, S is a distinguished element of A, and L is a lexicon, i.e. a mapping from Σ to categories over A. The set of categories over alphabet A is the closure of A under the binary infix connectives / and \ and the associated 'modalities' of (Baldridge, 2002). For example, assuming the saturated category symbols 'S' and 'NP', here is a simple CCG lexicon (with modalities omitted for convenience):

(1) John ⊢ NP
Mary ⊢ NP
loves ⊢ (S\NP)/NP

The combinatory projection of a CCG lexicon is its closure under a finite set of resource-sensitive combinatory operations such as forward application (2), backward application (3), forward type raising (4), and forward composition (5):

(2) $X/Y \quad Y \Rightarrow X$

(3) $Y \quad X\backslash Y \Rightarrow X$

(4) $X \Rightarrow Y/(Y\backslash X)$

(5) $X/Y \quad Y/Z \Rightarrow X/Z$

* Institute for Communicating and Collaborative Systems, School of Informatics, University of Edinburgh, 2 Buccleuch Place, Edinburgh, EH8 9LW, Scotland. Email: Mark.McConville@ed.ac.uk

CCG $\langle A, S, L\rangle$ over alphabet Σ generates string $s \in \Sigma^*$ just in case $\langle s, S\rangle$ is in the combinatory projection of lexicon L. The derivation in Figure 1 shows that CCG (1) generates the sentence *John loves Mary*, assuming that 'S' is the distinguished symbol, and where >**T**, >**B** and > denote instances of forward raising, forward composition and forward application respectively.

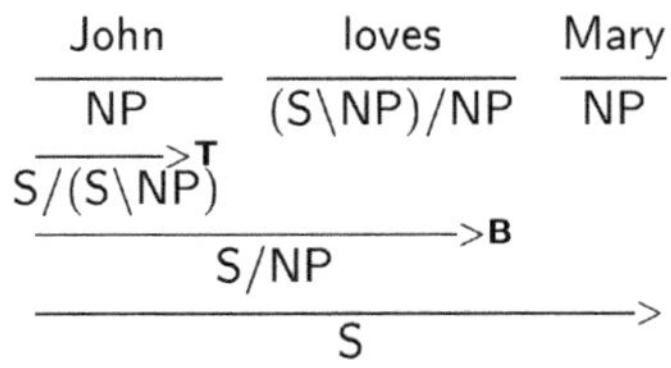

Figure 1
A CCG derivation

A complete introduction to the CCG formalism is found in (Steedman, 2000).

2 Lexical redundancy in CCG

CCG is a particularly interesting and effective theory of human linguistic competence, and forms the basis for efficient practical tools for natural language processing. However, in a number of cases, work has been hindered by the lack of an agreed approach to eliminating redundancy in CCG lexicons. This deficit constitutes a particular problem for radically lexicalised formalisms like CCG, where the customary way of treating bounded dependency constructions such as case, agreement and binding is by means of multiple lexical category assignments. For example, the fragment of English schematised in Table 1, though small, exemplifies non-trivial aspects of case and number agreement.

John		John
he	loves	me
the girl		you
girls		him
I		us
you	love	them
we		the girl
they		girls
girls		girls

Table 1
A fragment of English

Table 2 presents the simplest CCG lexicon for this language. This lexicon contains a number of multiple category assignments: (a) the proper noun *John* and the

$$\begin{aligned}
&\mathsf{John} \vdash \mathsf{NP^{sg}_{sbj}},\ \mathsf{NP_{obj}}\\
&\mathsf{girl} \vdash \mathsf{N_{sg}}\\
&\mathsf{s} \vdash \mathsf{N_{pl}\backslash N_{sg}},\ \mathsf{NP^{pl}_{sbj}\backslash N_{sg}},\ \mathsf{NP_{obj}\backslash N_{sg}}\\
&\mathsf{the} \vdash \mathsf{NP^{sg}_{sbj}/N_{sg}},\ \mathsf{NP_{obj}/N_{sg}},\\
&\qquad \mathsf{NP^{pl}_{sbj}/N_{pl}},\ \mathsf{NP_{obj}/N_{pl}}\\
&\mathsf{I, we, they} \vdash \mathsf{NP^{pl}_{sbj}}\\
&\mathsf{me, us, them, him} \vdash \mathsf{NP_{obj}}\\
&\mathsf{you} \vdash \mathsf{NP^{pl}_{sbj}},\ \mathsf{NP_{obj}}\\
&\mathsf{he} \vdash \mathsf{NP^{sg}_{sbj}}\\
&\mathsf{love} \vdash \mathsf{(S\backslash NP^{pl}_{sbj})/NP_{obj}}\\
&\mathsf{s} \vdash \mathsf{((S\backslash NP^{sg}_{sbj})/NP_{obj})\backslash((S\backslash NP^{pl}_{sbj})/NP_{obj})}
\end{aligned}$$

Table 2
A CCG lexicon

second person pronoun *you* are each assigned to *two* categories, one for each case distinction; (b) the plural suffix *-s* is assigned to *three* categories, depending on both the case and 'bar level' of the resulting nominal; and (c) the definite article *the* is assigned to *four* categories, one for each combination of case and number agreement distinctions. In each of these three cases, there appears to be no pre-theoretically obvious ambiguity involved. Thus, this lexicon violates the following efficiency-motivated ideal on human language lexicons, in the Chomskyan sense of locus of non-systematic information:

ideal of functionality a lexicon is ideally a *function* from morphemes to category labels, modulo genuine ambiguity

Another efficiency-motivated ideal which the CCG lexicon in Table 2 violates is the following:

ideal of atomicity a lexicon is a mapping from morphemes ideally to *atomic* category labels

In the lexicon in Table 2, the transitive verb *love* is assigned to the decidedly non-atomic category label $\mathsf{(S\backslash NP^{pl}_{sbj})/NP_{obj}}$. Lexicons which violate the criteria of functionality and atomicity are not just inefficient in terms of storage space and development time. They also fail to capture linguistically significant generalisations about the behaviour of the relevant words or morphemes.

The functionality and atomicity of a CCG lexicon can be easily quantified. The functionality ratio of the lexicon in Table 2, with 22 lexical entries for 14 distinct morphemes, is $\frac{22}{14} = 1.6$. The atomicity ratio is calculated by dividing the number of saturated category symbol-tokens by the number of lexical entries, i.e. $\frac{36}{22} = 1.6$.

Numerous, more or less *ad hoc* generalisations of the basic CCG category notation have been proposed with a view to eliminating these kinds of lexical redundancy. One area of interest has involved the structure of the saturated category symbols themselves. (Bozsahin, 2002) presents a version of CCG where saturated category symbols are modified by unary modalities annotated with morphosyntactic features. The features are themselves ordered according to a language-particular join semi-lattice. This technique, along with the insistence that lexicons of agglutinating languages are necessarily *morphemic*, allows generalisations involving the morphological structure of nouns and verbs in Turkish to be captured in an elegant, non-redundant format. (Erkan, 2003) generalises this approach, modelling saturated category labels as typed feature structures, constrained by underspecified feature structure descriptions in the usual manner.

(Hoffman, 1995) resolves other violations of the ideal of functionality in CCG lexicons for languages with 'local scrambling' constructions by means of 'multiset' notation for unsaturated categories, where scope and direction of arguments can be underspecified. For example, a multiset category label like $\mathsf{S}\{\backslash\mathsf{NP_{sbj}}, \backslash\mathsf{NP_{obj}}\}$ is to be understood as subsuming both $(\mathsf{S}\backslash\mathsf{NP_{sbj}})\backslash\mathsf{NP_{obj}}$ and $(\mathsf{S}\backslash\mathsf{NP_{obj}})\backslash\mathsf{NP_{sbj}}$.

Computational implementations of the CCG formalism, including successive versions of the Grok/OpenCCG system[1], have generally dealt with violations of the ideal of atomicity by allowing for the definition of macro-style abbreviations for unsaturated categories, e.g. using the macro 'TV' as an abbreviation for $(\mathsf{S}\backslash\mathsf{NP_{sbj}})/\mathsf{NP_{obj}}$. One final point of note involves the project reported in (Beavers, 2004), who implements CCG within the LKB system, i.e. as an application of the Typed Feature Structure Grammar formalism of (Copestake, 2002), with the full apparatus of unrestricted typed feature structures, default inheritance hierarchies, and lexical rules.

3 Inheritance-driven CCG

One of the aims of the project reported here has been to take a bottom-up approach to the problem of redundancy in CCG lexicons, adding just enough formal machinery to allow the relevant generalisations to be formulated, whilst retaining a restrictive theory of human linguistic competence which satisfies the 'strong competence' requirement, i.e. the competence grammar and the processing grammar are identical.

3.1 Type hierarchies

One of the main features of the resulting grammar formalism, which I have called 'inheritance-driven' CCG or I-CCG for short, is that the alphabet of saturated category symbols are organised into a 'type hierarchy', in the sense of (Carpenter, 1992). From this perspective, a type hierarchy is a weak order $\langle A, \sqsubseteq_A \rangle$, where A

1 `http://openccg.sourceforge.net`

is an alphabet of types, $\sqsubseteq_A$ is the 'subsumption' ordering on A (with a least element), and every subset of A with an upper bound has a least upper bound. An example type hierarchy is in Figure 2, where for example types '$\mathsf{Nom}_{\mathsf{sg}}$' and '$\mathsf{NP}$' are compatible since they have a non-empty set of upper bounds, the least upper bound (or 'unifier') being '$\mathsf{NP}_{\mathsf{sg}}$'.

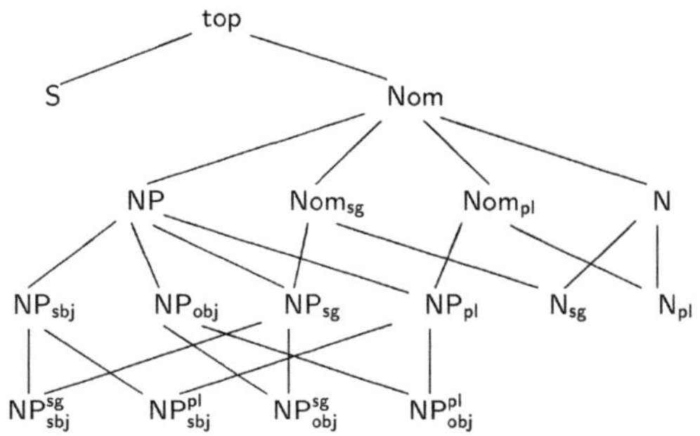

Figure 2
Type hierarchy of saturated categories

By itself, this innovation is enough to eliminate a certain amount of the redundancy inherent in the CCG formalism. For example, the CCG lexicon in Table 3, in conjunction with the type hierarchy in Figure 2, generates the fragment of English in Table 1.

$\mathsf{John} \vdash \mathsf{NP}_{\mathsf{sg}}$
$\mathsf{girl} \vdash \mathsf{N}_{\mathsf{sg}}$
$\mathsf{s} \vdash \mathsf{Nom}_{\mathsf{pl}} \backslash \mathsf{N}_{\mathsf{sg}}$
$\mathsf{the} \vdash \mathsf{NP}_{\mathsf{sg}}/\mathsf{N}_{\mathsf{sg}},\ \mathsf{NP}_{\mathsf{pl}}/\mathsf{N}_{\mathsf{pl}}$
$\mathsf{I, we, they} \vdash \mathsf{NP}^{\mathsf{pl}}_{\mathsf{sbj}}$
$\mathsf{me, us, them} \vdash \mathsf{NP}^{\mathsf{pl}}_{\mathsf{obj}}$
$\mathsf{you} \vdash \mathsf{NP}_{\mathsf{pl}}$
$\mathsf{he} \vdash \mathsf{NP}^{\mathsf{sg}}_{\mathsf{sbj}}$
$\mathsf{him} \vdash \mathsf{NP}^{\mathsf{sg}}_{\mathsf{obj}}$
$\mathsf{love} \vdash (\mathsf{S} \backslash \mathsf{NP}^{\mathsf{pl}}_{\mathsf{sbj}})/\mathsf{NP}_{\mathsf{obj}}$
$\mathsf{s} \vdash ((\mathsf{S} \backslash \mathsf{NP}^{\mathsf{sg}}_{\mathsf{sbj}})/\mathsf{NP}_{\mathsf{obj}}) \backslash ((\mathsf{S} \backslash \mathsf{NP}^{\mathsf{pl}}_{\mathsf{sbj}})/\mathsf{NP}_{\mathsf{obj}})$

Table 3
A type-hierarchical CCG lexicon

Using the lexicon in Table 3, the sentence *girls love John* is derived as in Figure 3: Note that the CCG lexicon in Table 3 comes closer to satisfying the ideal of functionality than does that in Table 2. While the latter has a functionality ratio

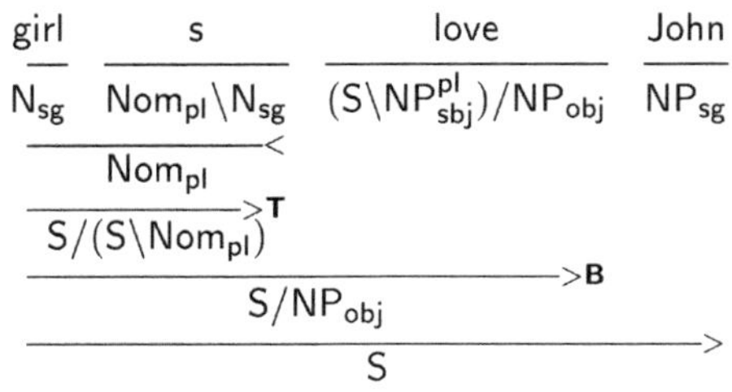

Figure 3
A type-hierarchical CCG derivation

of 1.6, the former's is $\frac{16}{14} = 1.1$.

This improved functionality ratio results from the underspecification of saturated category symbols inherent in the subsumption relation. For example, whereas the proper noun *John* is assigned to two distinct categories in the lexicon in Table 2, in the revised lexicon it is assigned to a single *non-maximal* type '$\mathsf{NP_{sg}}$' which subsumes the two maximal types '$\mathsf{NP^{sg}_{sbj}}$' and '$\mathsf{NP^{sg}_{obj}}$'. In other words, the phenomenon of case syncretism in English proper nouns is captured by having a general singular noun phrase type, which subsumes a plurality of case distinctions.

The CCG formalism which incorporates a type hierarchy of saturated category symbols is equivalent to the 'morphosyntactic CCG' formalism of (Bozsahin, 2002), where features are ordered in a join semi-lattice. Any generalisation which can be expressed in a morphosyntactic CCG can also be expressed in a type-hierarchical CCG, since any lattice of morphosyntactic features can be converted into a type hierarchy. In addition, the revised CCG formalism is equivalent to the formalism described in (Erkan, 2003), where saturated categories are modelled as typed feature structures. Any lexicon from either of these formalisms can be translated into a type-hierarchical CCG lexicon whose functionality ratio is either equivalent or lower.

3.2 Simple category descriptions

A second key feature of the I-CCG formalism involves the incorporation of a flexible description language allowing a more fine-grained specification of sets of categories. This feature-based language is inspired by previous attempts to implement categorial grammars within the unification-based paradigm, e.g. (Uszkoreit, 1986) and (Zeevat, Klein, and Calder, 1987).

The set of simple category descriptions over alphabet A of saturated category symbols is defined as the smallest set Φ such that:

1. $A \subseteq \Phi$

2. for all $\delta \in \{\mathsf{f}, \mathsf{b}\}$, $(\mathsf{SLASH}\ \delta) \in \Phi$

3. for all $\phi \in \Phi$, $(\mathsf{ARG}\ \phi) \in \Phi$

4. for all $\phi \in \Phi$, $(\mathsf{RES}\ \phi) \in \Phi$

Note that category descriptions may be infinitely embedded, in which case they are considered to be right-associative, e.g. RES ARG RES SLASH f.

A simple category description like (SLASH f) or (SLASH b) denotes the set of all expressions which seek their argument to the right/left. A description of the form (ARG ϕ) denotes the set of expressions which take an argument of category ϕ, and one like (RES ϕ) denotes the set of expressions which combine with an argument to yield an expression of category ϕ.

Complex category descriptions are simply sets of simple category descriptions, where the assumed semantics is simply that of conjunction.

3.3 Lexical inheritance hierarchies

A third feature of the I-CCG formalism is that it incorporates a second alphabet of non-terminal symbols, in this case a set of 'lexical types'. The lexical types are organised into an 'inheritance hierarchy', constrained by the simple category descriptions defined in the previous section.

Lexical inheritance hierarchies (Flickinger, 1987) are type hierarchies where each type is associated with a set of expressions drawn from some category description language Φ. Formally, they are ordered triples $\langle B, \sqsubseteq_B, b\rangle$, where $\langle B, \sqsubseteq_B\rangle$ is a type hierarchy, and b is a function from B to $\wp(\Phi)$.

An example lexical inheritance hierarchy over the set of category descriptions over the alphabet of saturated category symbols in Table 2 is presented in Figure 4. The intuition underlying these (monotonic) inheritance hierarchies is that instances of a type must satisfy all the constraints associated with that type, as well as all the constraints it inherits from its supertypes.
This example hierarchy is a *single* inheritance hierarchy, since every lexical type has no more than one immediate supertype. However, *multiple* inheritance hierarchies are also allowed, where a given type can inherit constraints from two supertypes, neither of which subsumes the other. In addition, given some lexical inheritance hierarchy $\langle B, \sqsubseteq_B, b\rangle$, the constraint set of type $t \in B$ is defined as the set of all constraints which are inherited by t, i.e.

(6) $$\bigcup_{t' \sqsubseteq_B t} b(t')$$

3.4 Inheritance-driven CCGs

An I-CCG over alphabet Σ is an ordered 7-tuple $\langle A, \sqsubseteq_A, B, \sqsubseteq_B, b, S, L\rangle$, where $\langle A, \sqsubseteq_A\rangle$ is a type hierarchy of saturated category symbols, $\langle B, \sqsubseteq_B, b\rangle$ is an inheritance hierarchy of lexical types over the set of category descriptions over $A \cup B$, S is a distinguished symbol in A, and lexicon L is a function from Σ to $A \cup B$. Given an appropriate $\sqsubseteq_{A,B}$-compatibility relation on the categories over $A \cup B$,

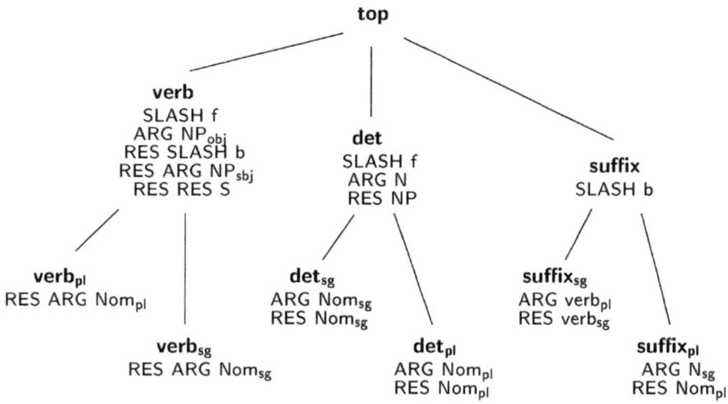

Figure 4
A lexical inheritance hierarchy

the combinatory projection of I-CCG $\langle A, \sqsubseteq_A, B, \sqsubseteq_B, b, S, L\rangle$ can again be defined as the closure of L under the CCG combinatory operations.

The I-CCG lexicon in Table 4, along with the type hierarchy of saturated category symbols in Figure 2 and the inheritance hierarchy of lexical types in Figure 4, generates the fragment of English in Table 1.

$$\begin{array}{l}
\mathsf{John} \vdash \mathsf{NP_{sg}} \\
\mathsf{girl} \vdash \mathsf{N_{sg}} \\
\mathsf{s} \vdash \mathsf{suffix} \\
\mathsf{the} \vdash \mathsf{det} \\
\mathsf{I, we, they} \vdash \mathsf{NP^{pl}_{sbj}} \\
\mathsf{me, us, them} \vdash \mathsf{NP^{pl}_{obj}} \\
\mathsf{you} \vdash \mathsf{NP_{pl}} \\
\mathsf{he} \vdash \mathsf{NP^{sg}_{sbj}} \\
\mathsf{him} \vdash \mathsf{NP^{sg}_{obj}} \\
\mathsf{love} \vdash \mathsf{verb_{pl}}
\end{array}$$

Table 4
An I-CCG lexicon

Using this lexicon, the sentence *girls love John* is derived as in Figure 5, where derivational steps involve 'cache-ing out' sets of constraints from lexical types.

This derivation relies on a version of the CCG combinatory rules defined in terms of the I-CCG category description language. For example, forward application is expressed as follows — for all compex category descriptions Φ and Ψ such that $(\mathsf{SLASH\ b}) \notin \Phi$, and $\{\phi \mid (\mathsf{ARG}\ \phi) \in \Phi\} \cup \Psi$ is compatible, the following

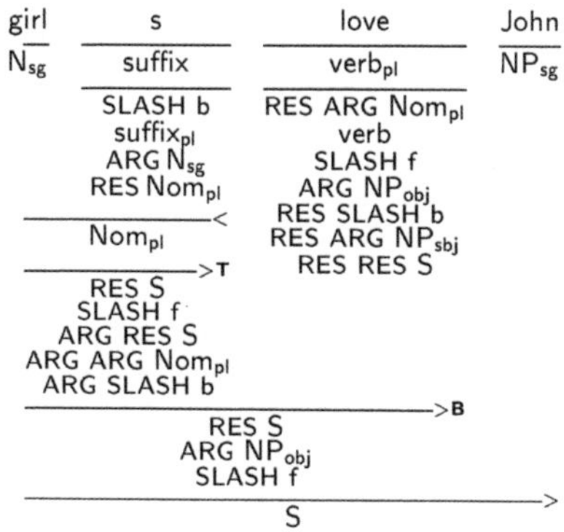

Figure 5
An I-CCG derivation

is a valid inference:

$$\frac{\Phi \qquad \Psi}{\{\phi \mid (\mathsf{RES}\ \phi) \in \Phi\}}>$$

The functionality ratio of the I-CCG lexicon in Table 4 is $\frac{14}{14} = 1$ and the atomicity ratio is $\frac{14}{14} = 1$. In other words, the lexicon is maximally non-redundant, since all the linguistically significant generalisations are encodable within the lexical inheritance hierarchy.

The optimal atomicity ratio of the I-CCG lexicon is a direct result of the introduction of lexical types. In the CCG lexicon in Table 2, the transitive verb *love* was assigned to a non-atomically labelled category $(\mathsf{S}\backslash\mathsf{NP}^{\mathsf{pl}}_{\mathsf{sbj}})/\mathsf{NP}_{\mathsf{obj}}$. In the I-CCG's inheritance hierarchy in Figure 4, there is a lexical type '$\mathsf{verb}_{\mathsf{pl}}$' which inherits six constraints whose conjunction picks out exactly the same category. It is with this atomic label that the verb is paired in the I-CCG lexicon in Table 4.

The lexical inheritance hierarchy also has a role to play in constructing lexicons with optimal functionality ratios. The type-hierarchical CCG lexicon in Table 3 assigned the definite article to two distinct categories, one for each grammatical number distinction. The I-CCG lexicon utilises the disjunction inherent in inheritance hierarchies to give each of these a common supertype 'det', which is associated with the properties all determiners share.

Finally, the I-CCG formalism can be argued to subsume the multiset category notation of (Hoffman, 1995), in the sense that every multiset CCG lexicon can be converted into an I-CCG lexicon with an equivalent or better functionality ratio. Recall that Hoffman uses generalised category notation like $\mathsf{S}\{\backslash\mathsf{NP}_{\mathsf{sbj}}, \backslash\mathsf{NP}_{\mathsf{obj}}\}$ to subsume two standard CCG category labels $(\mathsf{S}\backslash\mathsf{NP}_{\mathsf{sbj}})\backslash\mathsf{NP}_{\mathsf{obj}}$ and $(\mathsf{S}\backslash\mathsf{NP}_{\mathsf{obj}})\backslash\mathsf{NP}_{\mathsf{sbj}}$. Again it should be clear that this is just another way of representing disjunction in a categorial lexicon, and can be straightforwardly converted into a lexical inheritance hierarchy over I-CCG category descriptions.

4 Semantics of the category notation

In the categorial grammar tradition initiated by (Lambek, 1958), the standard way of providing a semantics for category notation defines the denotation of a category description as a set of strings of terminal symbols. Thus, assuming an alphabet Σ and a denotation function $[[\ldots]]$ from the saturated category symbols to $\wp(\Sigma)$, the denotata of unsaturated category descriptions can be defined as follows, assuming that the underlying logic is simply that of string concatenation:

$$(7) \quad \begin{aligned} [[\phi/\psi]] &= \{s \mid \forall s' \in [[\psi]], ss' \in [[\phi]]\} \\ [[\phi\backslash\psi]] &= \{s \mid \forall s' \in [[\psi]], s's \in [[\phi]]\} \end{aligned}$$

This suggests an obvious way of interpreting the I-CCG category notation defined above. Let's start by assuming that, given some I-CCG $\langle A, \sqsubseteq_A, B, \sqsubseteq_B, b, S, L\rangle$ over alphabet Σ, there is a denotation function $[[\ldots]]$ from the *maximal* types in the hierarchy of saturated categories $\langle A, \sqsubseteq_A\rangle$ to $\wp(\Sigma)$. For all non-maximal saturated category symbols ϕ in A, the denotation of ϕ is then the set of all strings in any of ϕ's subcategories, i.e. $[[\phi]] = \bigcup_{\phi \sqsubseteq_A \psi}[[\psi]]$. The denotata of the simple category descriptions can be defined by universal quantification over the set of simple category descriptions Φ:

- $[[\mathsf{SLASH\ f}]] = \bigcup_{\phi,\psi\in\Phi}[[\phi/\psi]]$
- $[[\mathsf{SLASH\ b}]] = \bigcup_{\phi,\psi\in\Phi}[[\phi\backslash\psi]]$
- $[[\mathsf{ARG}\ \phi]] = \bigcup_{\psi\in\Phi}[[\psi/\phi]] \cup [[\psi\backslash\phi]]$
- $[[\mathsf{RES}\ \phi]] = \bigcup_{\psi\in\Phi}[[\phi/\psi]] \cup [[\phi\backslash\psi]]$

This just leaves the simple descriptions which consist of a type in the lexical inheritance hierarchy $\langle B, \sqsubseteq_B, b\rangle$. If we define the constraint set of some lexical type $\phi \in B$ as the set Φ of all category descriptions either associated with or inherited by ϕ, then the denotation of ϕ is defined as $\bigcap_{\psi\in\Phi}[[\psi]]$.

Unfortunately, this approach to interpreting I-CCG category descriptions is insufficient, since the logic underlying CCG is not simply the logic of string concatenation, i.e. CCG allows a limited degree of permutation by dint of the *crossed* composition and substitution operations. In fact, there appears to be no categorial type logic, in the sense of (Moortgat, 1997), for which the CCG combinatory operations provide a sound and complete derivation system, even in the resource-sensitive system of (Baldridge, 2002). An alternative approach involves interpreting I-CCG category descriptions against totally well-typed, sort-resolved feature structures, as in the HPSG formalism of (Pollard and Sag, 1994).

4.1 Category frames

Figure 6 illustrates an example of a kind of feature structure I call 'category frames':

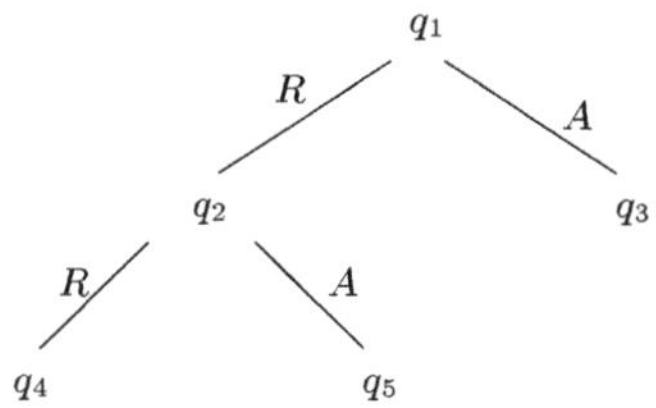

Figure 6
A category frame

Formally, a category frame is an ordered triple $\langle Q, Res, Arg\rangle$, where: (a) Q is a finite, non-empty set of points; (b) Res is the 'result' relation on Q i.e. if $\langle q_i, q_j\rangle \in Res$ then point q_j is a 'result' of point q_i; (c) Arg is the 'argument' relation on Q i.e. if $\langle q_i, q_j\rangle \in Arg$ then point q_j is an 'argument' of point q_i; (d) Res is a functional mapping from Q to Q i.e. every point has at most one result, although not every point has a result; (e) Arg is a functional mapping from Q to Q i.e. every point has at most one argument, although not every point has an argument; (f) the domains of Res and Arg are identical i.e. every point with a result has an argument and vice versa; and (g) where $\prec$ is the transitive closure of $Res \cup Arg$, $\langle Q, \prec\rangle$ is a strict (partial) order with a first/least element i.e. no point is its own result or argument, and no point is the result or argument of a point contained within its own result or argument.

Note that category frames can be, but are not obliged to be, trees. In other words, reentrancy is allowed. All category frames are rooted, all and only non-end points have exactly one result and exactly one argument, and category frames are acyclic.

4.2 Category models

Figure 7 illustrates an example of a 'category model' over the type hierarchy of saturated category symbols in Figure 2. Basically, a category model is a category frame where every end point is annotated with a 'maximal' saturated category symbol (i.e. one which has no subtypes), and every non-end point is annotated with a directionality marker, i.e. f or b.

Formally, a category model over type hierarchy $\langle A, \sqsubseteq_A\rangle$ of saturated category symbols is an ordered 5-tuple $\langle Q, Res, Arg, V_S, V_A\rangle$, where: (a) $\langle Q, Res, Arg\rangle$ is a category frame; (b) V_S is a function from the non-end points of $\langle Q, Res, Arg\rangle$ to $\{/, \backslash\}$ i.e. every non-end point is labelled with exactly one directionality symbol; and (c) V_A is a function from the end points of $\langle Q, Res, Arg\rangle$ to A i.e. every

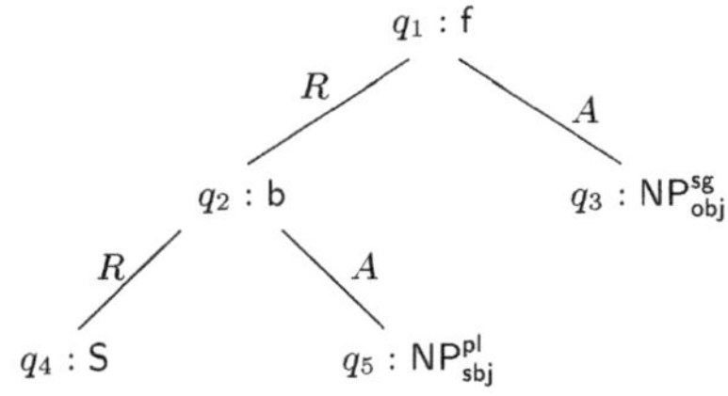

Figure 7
A category model over the type hierarchy in Figure 2

end point in the structure is labelled by exactly one maximal saturated category symbol.

4.3 Global satisfaction

Categorial models, as defined in section 4.2, and the simple category descriptions defined in section 3.2 are linked by the familiar notion of logical satisfaction.

Category model $\mathcal{M} = \langle Q, Res, Arg, V_S, V_A \rangle$ over type hierarchy $\langle A, \sqsubseteq_A \rangle$ of saturated category symbols satisfies simple category description ϕ over $A \cup B$, with respect to lexical inheritance hierarchy $\mathcal{H} = \langle B, \sqsubseteq_B, b \rangle$, written $\mathcal{M} \models_{\mathcal{H}} \phi$, if and only if $\mathcal{M}$ locally satisfies ϕ, with respect to $\mathcal{H}$, from its root point, i.e. $\mathcal{M}, q \models_{\mathcal{H}} \phi$. In other words, global satisfaction is local satisfaction from the root point in a model.

4.4 Local satisfaction

Category model $\mathcal{M} = \langle Q, Res, Arg, V_S, V_A \rangle$ over type hierarchy $\langle A, \sqsubseteq_A \rangle$ of saturated category symbols locally satisfies category description ϕ over $A \cup B$, with respect to lexical inheritance hierarchy $\mathcal{H} = \langle B, \sqsubseteq_B, b \rangle$, from point $q \in Q$, written $\mathcal{M}, q \models_{\mathcal{H}} \phi$, if and only if:

1. where $\phi \in A$: for some $\psi \in A$ such that $\phi \sqsubseteq_A \psi$, $V_A(q) = \psi$, i.e. point q is labelled with some saturated category symbol subsumed by ϕ
2. where $\phi \in B$: for all constraints ψ in the constraint set of ϕ in $\mathcal{H}$, $\mathcal{M}, q \models_{\mathcal{H}} \psi$, i.e. every simple category description inherited by lexical type ϕ is satisfied from point q
3. where $\phi = (\mathsf{SLASH}\ \delta\,)$: $V_S(q) = \delta$, i.e. point q carries the correct directionality symbol
4. where $\phi = (\mathsf{ARG}\ \psi\,)$: $\mathcal{M}, Arg(q) \models_{\mathcal{H}} \psi$, i.e. category description ψ is satisfied from the argument point of q
5. where $\phi = (\mathsf{RES}\ \psi\,)$: $\mathcal{M}, Res(q) \models_{\mathcal{H}} \psi$, i.e. category description ψ is satisfied from the result point of q

To run through a simple example of global satisfaction in I-CCG, note that the category model in Figure 7 satisfies the simple category description '$\mathsf{verb_{pl}}$', with respect to the type hierarchy of saturated category symbols in Figure 2 and the lexical inheritance hierarchy in Figure 4. Where the model is denoted $\mathcal{M}$ and the lexical inheritance hierarchy $\mathcal{H}$, the definition of global satisfaction tells us that $\mathcal{M} \models_{\mathcal{H}} \mathsf{verb_{pl}}$ just in case $\mathcal{M}, q_1 \models_{\mathcal{H}} \mathsf{verb_{pl}}$, since q_1 is the root point of $\mathcal{M}$. The local satisfaction definition then tells us that $\mathcal{M}, q_1 \models_{\mathcal{H}} \mathsf{verb_{pl}}$ if and only if for every simple category description ϕ in the constraint set of $\mathsf{verb_{pl}}$ in $\mathcal{H}$, $\mathcal{M}, q_1 \models_{\mathcal{H}} \phi$, i.e.

(8) $\mathcal{M}, q_1 \models_{\mathcal{H}}$ $\mathsf{RES\ ARG\ Nom_{pl}}$, $\mathsf{SLASH\ f}$, $\mathsf{ARG\ Nom_{obj}}$,
$\mathsf{RES\ SLASH\ b}$, $\mathsf{RES\ ARG\ Nom_{sbj}}$, $\mathsf{RES\ RES\ S}$

With regard to the first of these, $\mathcal{M}, q_1 \models_{\mathcal{H}} \mathsf{RES\ ARG\ Nom_{pl}}$, the following process of deduction shows us that it is true:

(9) $\mathcal{M}, q_1 \models_{\mathcal{H}} \mathsf{RES\ ARG\ Nom_{pl}}$
iff. $\mathcal{M}, q_2 \models_{\mathcal{H}} \mathsf{ARG\ Nom_{pl}}$ [since $Res(q_1) = q_2$]
iff. $\mathcal{M}, q_5 \models_{\mathcal{H}} \mathsf{Nom_{pl}}$ [since $Arg(q_2) = q_5$]

Finally, it is clear that $\mathcal{M}, q_5 \models_{\mathcal{H}} \mathsf{Nom_{pl}}$ since point q_5 is labelled with a saturated category symbol $\mathsf{NP^{pl}_{sbj}}$ which is subsumed by $\mathsf{Nom_{pl}}$ in the type hierarchy in Figure 2.

Proving that the other simple category descriptions listed in (8) are satisfied from the root point in Figure 7 is left as an exercise for the interested reader.

4.5 Combinatory projection of an I-CCG

Given I-CCG $\langle A, \sqsubseteq_A, B, \sqsubseteq_B, b, S, L\rangle$ over alphabet Σ, the combinatory projection of lexicon L is defined recursively. The 'base' is defined as the smallest set L' where for all $\langle s, \phi\rangle \in L$ and all category models $\mathcal{M}$ over $\langle A, \sqsubseteq_A\rangle$ such that $\mathcal{M} \models_{\langle B, \sqsubseteq_B, b\rangle} \phi$, $\langle s, \mathcal{M}\rangle \in L'$. In other words, the base of the combinatory projection of an I-CCG lexicon is a mapping from each lexical form to all the category models which globally satisfy its lexical type.

The combinatory projection of an I-CCG lexicon is then the closure of the base under the small, finite set of CCG combinatory operations discussed in section 1.

5 Conclusion

This paper has focused on an extension of the CCG formalism of (Steedman, 2000), incorporating various aspects of typed feature structure grammars such as lexical inheritance hierarchies and the distinction between structures and structural descriptions, the two notions being linked by logical satisfaction. The resulting formalism, termed 'inheritance-driven' CCG or I-CCG for short, involves two main innovations: (a) the alphabet of saturated category symbols is organised into a type hierarchy; and (b) there is a secondary alphabet of 'lexical types', itself organised into an inheritance hierarchy over a simple, feature-based constraint language. In particular, I presented a detailed semantics for the category description language in terms of a simple notion of tree-like, abstract category models.

The I-CCG formalism was shown to have significant advantages over the baseline CCG formalism, in that it allows us to formulate *non-redundant* natural language lexicons. In addition, I-CCG is shown to subsume a number of other, more or less *ad hoc* extensions to the CCG formalism, which have been developed in order to reduce lexical redundancy, in particular the 'morphosyntactic' CCG of (Bozsahin, 2002) and the 'multiset' CCG of (Hoffman, 1995).

References

Baldridge, Jason. 2002. *Lexically Specified Derivational Control in Combinatory Categorial Grammar.* Ph.D. thesis, University of Edinburgh.

Beavers, John. 2004. Type-inheritance Combinatory Categorial Grammar. In *Proceedings of the 20th International Conference on Computational Linguistics, University of Geneva.*

Bozsahin, Cem. 2002. The combinatory morphemic lexicon. *Computational Linguistics*, 28(2):145–186.

Carpenter, Bob. 1992. *The Logic of Typed Feature Structures.* Cambridge Tracts in Theoretical Computer Science. Cambridge University Press.

Copestake, Ann. 2002. *Implementing Typed Feature Structure Grammars.* CSLI Publications, Stanford CA.

Erkan, Gunes. 2003. A Type System for Combinatory Categorial Grammar. Master's thesis, Middle East Technical University, Ankara.

Flickinger, Daniel Paul. 1987. *Lexical Rules in the Hierarchical Lexicon.* Ph.D. thesis, Stanford University.

Hoffman, Beryl. 1995. *The Computational Analysis of the Syntax and Interpretation of "Free" Word Order in Turkish.* Ph.D. thesis, University of Pennsylvania.

Lambek, Joachim. 1958. The Mathematics of Sentence Structure. *American Mathematical Monthly*, 65:154–170.

Moortgat, Michael. 1997. Categorial type logics. In Johan van Benthem and Alice ter Meulen, editors, *Handbook of Logic and Language.* North Holland, Amsterdam, NL, pages 93–177.

Pollard, Carl Jesse and Ivan A. Sag. 1994. *Head-Driven Phrase Structure Grammar.* The University of Chicago Press.

Steedman, Mark. 2000. *The Syntactic Process.* MIT Press, Cambridge MA.

Uszkoreit, Hans. 1986. Categorial Unification Grammars. In *Proceedings of the 11th International Conference on Computational Linguistics, Bonn*, pages 187–194.

Zeevat, Henk, Ewan Klein, and Jo Calder. 1987. Unification Categorial Grammar. In Nicholas Haddock, Ewan Klein, and Glyn Morrill, editors, *Categorial Grammar, Unification Grammar and Parsing*, Working Papers in Cognitive Science. Centre for Cognitive Science, University of Edinburgh.

Sidder og ... Constructional aspect in Danish

Anne Bjerre*
University of Southern Denmark

Tavs Bjerre†
Aarhus University

1 Introduction

Danish has no (systematic) morphological means of expressing aspect. Instead aspectual differences may be expressed with the help of various verbal constructions. Such aspectual constructions have not received much attention in the Danish linguistic literature, but cf. (Diderichsen, 1946, p. 156), (Hansen, 1967, vol. 3, pp. 30–31), (Jensen, 1985, p. 113), (Brandt, 1992) and (Jørgensen, 2001).

This paper[1] is concerned with the construction shown in (1). We will refer to it as the *sidder og* construction.

(1) Peter sidder og læser en bog.
Peter sits and reads a book

The combination of the two conjuncts makes the construction imperfective, and the *read* event is understood to be in progress and continuous.

The construction is interesting because we cannot predict from the semantics of the two conjuncts the semantics of the coordinated phrase. We will use the term 'constructional aspect' to refer to the aspectual meaning expressed by a construction which is not derivable from the aspectual meaning expressed by the subparts of that construction.

This makes the construction a good candidate for a constructional analysis along the lines of (Ginzburg and Sag, 2000). The construction is further an example of

* University of Southern Denmark, Engstien 1, DK-6000 Kolding, Denmark. Email: bjerre@sitkom.sdu.dk
† Aarhus University, Jens Chr. Skous Vej 7, DK-8000 Aarhus C, Denmark. Email: tavs.bjerre@hum.au.dk
1 We would like to thank two reviewers for their helpful comments.

the subtle interaction between syntactic structure and semantic information. The non-derivational nature of HPSG where the various levels of linguistic description are represented in parallel provides a natural framework for working with such constructions.

2 The *sidder og* construction

The *sidder og* construction consists of two verbal conjuncts, we will refer to them as V1 and V2, respectively, and the conjunction *og*, 'and'. V1 is an intransitive motion or position verb, primarily *går*, 'walk', *løber*, 'run', *står*, 'stand', *sidder*, 'sit' and *ligger*, 'lie', but others may occur.

The construction is mainly characterized by the aspectual information that it introduces, i.e. whether the event expressed by V2 is regarded as completed or not, (Brandt, 1992) and (Hansen, 1967).

We suggest that the construction is used, not to change aspect, but to remove any ambiguity that may be present in a certain sentence, exactly due to Danish not making a formal distinction.

When combined with a clause introducing a point in time the effect comes out quite clearly.

(2) a. Peter sang da Ole kom hjem.
Peter sang when Ole came home

b. Peter sad og sang da Ole kom hjem.
Peter sat and sang when Ole came home

(2a) is ambiguous. Either Peter had already started singing before Ole came home or he started at the time when Ole came home. Not so with (2b) where the singing necessarily started prior to Ole's coming home.

Note that there are also ways to exclude the imperfective aspectual meaning, as shown in (3).

(3) Peter satte sig og sang da Ole kom hjem.
Peter sat down and sang when Ole came home

In (3) the use of *satte sig* forces a reading where the two events occur in sequence and where the second event cannot be imperfective.

3 Aspect and aktionsart of the *sidder og* construction

We have mentioned above that the construction is associated with imperfective aspect. However, to give a more adequate account of the properties of the construction we need to take into account the notion of aktionsart. We understand aktionsart to be aspectual properties contributed by a lexical verb.

We adopt the traditional division of verbs into states, accomplishments, achievements and activities (Vendler, 1957). In addition, we adopt Comrie's semelfactives (Comrie, 1976). In this paper we will not be concerned with states as verbs denoting states do not occur in the *sidder og* construction without coercion.

The verb types may be organized according to the parameters of telicity and duration as in (4).

(4)

	Durative	Punctual
Telic	accomplishment	achievement
Atelic	activity	semelfactive

(5) gives examples of these four different verb types.

(5) a. Peter sidder og synger.
Peter sits and sings

b. Håndklædet ligger og tørrer (i solen).
Towel-the lies and dries (in sun-the)

c. Peter sidder og blinker.
Peter sits and winks

d. Peter sidder og vinder.
Peter sits and wins

As can be seen from (5) all four non-stative verb types enter the *sidder og* construction but with varying effects.

When activity verbs, (5a), and accomplishment verbs, (5b), enter the construction, the durative property of these verbs combine with the imperfective aspect of the construction and the result is that the V2 events get a progressive or continuous reading.

When semelfactive verbs enter the construction, (5c), the combination of the verb's punctual property and the imperfective aspect of the construction results in an iterative reading of the V2 event.

The same is normally the case for achievement verbs, (5d). In (6) the construction does not get an iterative reading even though *døde* is an achievement verb. This however, may be ascribed to the lexical meaning of this particular verb.

(6) a. Jeg følte, at jeg sad og døde lige så stille indefra[2]
I felt that I sat and died ever so slowly from within

4 The constructional approach

In this paper we have chosen a constructional approach to aspect. This is based on the observation that we cannot predict from the semantics of the two verbs involved in our construction what aspectual information is associated with the second event.

This becomes clearest when we look at the examples involving the iterative aspect. In (7) the combination of *sidde* og *blinke* results in an iterative reading of the second event.

(7) Peter sidder og blinker.
Peter sits and winks

The iterative aspect cannot be predicted from either of the verbs. *Sidder* is not iterative, neither in this construction, nor in other contexts. *Blinker* is also not inherently iterative. It may occur in contexts that are either iterative, as in our *sidder og* construction, or just punctual, as shown in (8).

(8) Peter blinker til mig, når jeg skal begynde at synge.
Peter winks at me when I shall start to sing

This means that we cannot assume that *blinker* is lexically specified with an iterative aspectual relation.

5 Related constructions

In this section we will briefly present some constructions that are in one way or another related to the *sidder og* construction.

2 www.annonce-bladet.dk/artikel.asp?mode=full&id=444

5.1 Imperfective constructions

5.1.1 V *og* V

(9) a. Peter læste og læste, men dumpede alligevel.
Peter read and read but failed-the-exam anyway

b. Peter slog og slog.
Peter hit and hit

In (9a) we have an activity verb. The construction expresses that the situation denoted by the verb is extended beyond its normal duration. In (9b) we have a semelfactive verb, and the construction gets an iterative interpretation. State verbs do not occur in this construction. Direct objects do not readily occur with activity verbs, probably because the definite direct object makes the predicate an accomplishment which is characterized by having an endpoint blocking prolongation of the process. If (10) is acceptable at all it can only have an iterative interpretation.

(10) ?Peter læste og læste bogen, men dumpede alligevel.
Peter read and read book-the but failed-the-exam anyway

On the other hand, prepositional objects, which do not make the predicate an accomplishment, are fine in this construction:

(11) a. Peter læste og læste i bogen.
Peter read and read in book-the

b. De drak og drak af flasken.
They drank and drank of bottle-the

5.1.2 *går-(rundt)-og*

(12) Han går (rundt) og er deprimeret.
He walks around and is depressed

This construction is closely related to the *sidder og* construction. Like that it has a continuous or an iterative reading. In contrast to the *sidder og* construction, only the verb *gå*, 'walk', occurs but its lexical meaning has been bleached. In (13) Pia has not necessarily been walking very much during those days.

(13) Pia har gået de sidste dage og tænkt på at få et nyt job.
Pia has walked the last days and thought of to get a new job

If we exchange the verb *gå*, 'walk', with *sidde*, 'sit', the sentence is only acceptable in a situation where Pia has actually been sitting (almost) all of the three days. It would in that case be an instance of the *sidder og* construction.

(14) ?Pia har siddet de sidste dage og tænkt på at få et nyt job.
Pia has sat the last days and thought of to get a new job

5.1.3 *står-og-mangler*

(15) Jeg står og mangler 100 kr. til huslejen.
I stand and miss 100 kr. for rent-the

This construction is similar to the *går-rundt-og* construction. In contrast to the *sidder-og* construction only the verb *står*, 'stand', occurs but with a bleached lexical meaning. V2 in the construction is a state verb or a modal, and the construction expresses that the denoted situation is in some way relevant to - or even critical wrt. - the imminent future. Whereas the situation denoted by the *går-rundt-og* construction has a long duration the situation denoted by this construction has a short duration.

(16) a. Jeg står og skal til New York i morgen.
I stand og shall to New York tomorrow

b. Jeg stod og skulle købe en bil.
I stood and should buy a car

(17) ... de ca. 2-300, som er smidt ud af bistandssystemet, og
... those appr. 2-300, who are kicked out of wellfare system-the, and
nu står og må finde alternative boformer ...[3]
now stand and must find alternative ways of living ...

5.2 Perfective constructions

These constructions are constructions that may be used to force a sequential reading on the involved events.

5.2.1 *går-ud-og*

(18) Hun gik ud og så til maden.
She went out and saw to food-the

3 www.vejle.dk/text2206.asp?conferencesID=68&db_confererenceID=3218&toppost=321

This construction has some similarity to the *sidder-og* construction, in fact, (Brandt, 1992) treats the two constructions as one. There are, however, clear differences. This construction only allows motion verbs, including *tage*, 'take', and *komme*, 'come', but not positional verbs. In contrast to the *sidder-og* construction this construction has a sequential meaning, the situation denoted by V1 precedes the situation denoted by V2, in (19) Michael first runs, then presumably stops running and kisses her.

(19) Michael løb hen og kyssede hende.
Michael ran over and kissed her

V2 may be any kind of verb except state verbs.

5.2.2 *går-hen-og*

(20) Hesten gik hen og døde.
Horse-the went over and died

In this construction neither V1 nor its particle can be exchanged and neither retains its lexical meaning. V2 is an achievement (in some cases perhaps an accomplishment verb) and the construction expresses that the change happens to the surprise of the utterer of the sentence and in some cases perhaps that it happens without or with only little intent on the part of the referent of the subject.

(21) a. Han er gået hen og blevet mormon.
He is gone over and become Mormon

b. Han er gået hen og har fået en kæreste.
He is gone over and has got a girlfriend

5.2.3 *tager-og* (Vannebo, 2003) In this construction the first verb *tage*, 'take', has lost its lexical meaning entirely. In its non-constructional uses *tage* is obligatorily transitive, but in this construction it is obligatorily intransitive. V2 will often be an activity, achievement or accomplishment verb, but also state verbs can occur if the state can be perceived as under the control of the referent of the subject as shown in (22).

(22) a. Tag og slip tasken!
Take and let-go-of bag-the
'(You should) let go of the bag'

b. Du skulle tage og komme forbi Valby.
You should take and come past Valby

c. Tag du nu og vær lidt gladere!
Take you now and be a bit happier

The *tager-og* construction can also be used in assertions, as shown in (23).

(23) ... først tog de og lukkede skadestuen ...[4]
first took they and closed casualty ward-the

Again, the *tager og* construction disambiguates aspectually ambiguous sentences giving them a sequential (perfective) reading, as shown in (24).

(24) a. Peter lavede mad da Lise kom hjem.
Peter cooked when Lise came home.

b. Peter tog og lavede mad da Lise kom hjem.
Peter took and cooked when Lise came home.

(24a) is ambigouos wrt. whether Peter started his cooking prior to Lise's coming home or not, whereas in (24b) the cooking cannot be in progress when she comes home.

In many cases the *tager og* construction is used where there is no need for aspectual disambiguation but it is not clear to us what additional meaning if any it expresses.

6 Pseudocoordination and *sidder og*

The syntactic properties of constructions like the *sidder og* construction have been dealt with in the Nordic literature under the header *pseudocoordination.* The discussion is concerned with whether the construction is really a coordination or whether it may better be treated as some kind of subordinated construction, cf. e.g. (Wiklund, 2005), (Vannebo, 2003), (Lødrup, 2002) and (Johannessen, 1998).

In this section we would like to point out that the Danish constructions dealt with here share many of the syntactic properties mentioned in the literature on pseudocoordination. That we are not dealing with simple coordination is supported by the behaviour of the constructions with respect to a series of syntactic phenomena.

4 www.fyens.de/modeles/debat/topic.php?topicid=102525

6.1 Extraction

One example is its behaviour with respect to the Coordinate Structure Constraint, (Ross, 1967). According to this constraint, a conjunct cannot contain a gap except in 'Across-the-Board' cases where each conjunct has a gap that refers to one and the same filler. (25a) is clearly a violation of this constraint, and the constraint is obeyed in the coordinated VP without *sidder*, (25b).

(25) a. Dette er pigen$_i$ Peter sad og kyssede e_i.
This is girl-the Peter sat and kissed

b. *Dette er pigen$_i$ Peter dansede og kyssede e_i.
This is girl-the Peter danced and kissed

6.2 Word order

The *sidder og* construction and most of the other constructions mentioned above display a number of peculiarities wrt. word order.

6.2.1 Negation In simple coordinated structures the negation typically either follows both conjuncts, (26) (in the case of V coordination) or is inserted in both conjuncts, (27) (in the case of VP/S coordination).

(26) a. Han bor og arbejder ikke i Århus.
He lives and works not in Århus

b. *Han bor ikke og arbejder i Århus.
He lives not and works in Århus

(27) Han læser ikke digte og køber aldrig bøger.
He reads not poems and buys never books

In the *sidder-og* construction the negation follows the first verb as shown in (28).

(28) a. Han sad ikke og spiste.
He sat not and ate

b. *Han sad og spiste ikke.
He sat and ate not

c. *Han sad ikke og spiste ikke.
He sat not and ate not

6.2.2 Time and place adjuncts In simple coordinated structures time and place adjuncts that take scope over both conjuncts must precede or follow these, cf. (29).

(29) a. Peter spiser og sover ude i haven.
Peter eats and sleeps out in garden-the

b. Ude i haven spiser og sover Peter.
Out in garden-the eats and sleeps Peter

c. *Peter spiser ude i haven og sover.
Peter eats out in garden-the and sleeps

In the *sidder-og* construction such adjuncts may also be placed in between the two conjuncts without any difference in meaning, cf. (30).

(30) a. Peter sidder og sover ude i haven.
Peter sits and sleeps out in garden-the

b. Ude i haven sidder Peter og sover.
Out in garden-the sits Peter and sleeps

c. Peter sidder ude i haven og sover.
Peter sits out in garden-the and sleeps

6.2.3 Conjuncts not interchangeable In simple coordinated structures the conjuncts may often be reversed, cf. (31).

(31) a. Børnene dansede og sang.
Children-the danced and sang

b. Børnene sang og dansede.
Children-the sang and danced

This is impossible in the *sidder og* construction.

(32) a. Peter sidder og sover.
Peter sits and sleeps

b. *Peter sover og sidder.
Peter sleeps and sits

6.2.4 Subject position In simple coordinated structures the subject follows both conjuncts if another constituent fills the first slot in the sentence, cf. (33).

(33) a. Kl. 5 spiste og drak Peter.
5 o'clock ate and drank Peter

b. *Kl. 5 spiste Peter og drak.
5 o'clock ate Peter and drank

In the *sidder og* construction and most of the other constructions mentioned here the subject occurs between the conjuncts, cf. (34).

(34) a. Kl. 5 sad Peter og spiste.
5 o'clock sat Peter and ate

b. *Kl. 5 sad og spiste Peter.
5 o'clock sat and ate Peter

In simple coordinated structures with indefinite subjects and *there* insertion the indefinite subject must follow both verbs, cf. (35).

(35) Der bor og arbejder mange mennesker i Århus.
There live and work many people in Århus

In the *sidder og* construction the indefinite subject occurs between the two verbs. This is all the more interesting since indefinite subjects generally occur in the object position following not just the finite verb but also medial adverbs and nonfinite verbs.

(36) Der sad en mand og spiste.
There sat a man and ate

6.3 Conjunction limited

Whereas in simple coordinated structures the conjunction *og* may be exchanged with the conjunctions *eller*, 'or', or *men*, 'but', in the *sidder-og* construction only *og* is used:

(37) a. Peter sidder og sover.
Peter sits and sleeps

b. *Peter sidder eller/men sover.
Peter sleeps or/but sleeps

6.4 Concluding remarks

As we have shown in this section pseudocoordinations behave differently from simple coordinations in a number of respects. This article, however, is not concerned with the question whether the constructions are really coordinations or subordinations, and in the next section we treat the *sidder og* construction as a type of coordination, well aware that from a syntactic point of view the analysis poses problems.

It will, however, be seen that our analysis makes it possible to state the generalizations that the *sidder og* construction does indeed behave as a coordination in certain respects, e.g. it contains a coordinating conjunction and the two conjuncts must have the same morphological form. But at the same time the analysis does not force us to claim that the two types of coordination share all constraints.

7 Formalisation

There are two dimensions in the formalization. On the one hand we have the different types of coordinated constructions, and on the other we have the aspectual information.

The coordinated constructions enter a larger hierarchy of construction types as shown in (38), (Sag and Wasow, 1999).

(38)

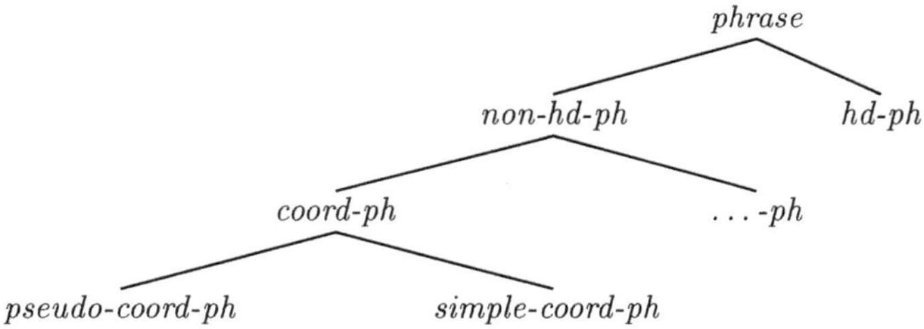

Phrases split into headed and nonheaded phrases, one subtype of nonheaded phrases is coordinated phrases which split into simple (ordinary) coordinated phrases and pseudo-coordinated phrases.

(39) in Figure 1 shows the various types of construction that we have discussed previously. These are all subtypes of *pseudo-coord-ph.*

Most of the constructions we have discussed above are subsumed under the type *V1-og-V2-ph*, constructions containing two different verbs. One of its subtypes, *mot-pos-og-ph*, subsumes all constructions with a motion or position verb as V1. In this paper we concentrate on the *sidder-og-ph* type. Its supertypes, the *pseudo-coord-ph* and the *mot-pos-og-ph*, are constrained as shown in (40) and (41).

The *pseudo-coord-ph* is constrained to contain the coordinating conjunction *og*, 'and'. (40) formalizes the property that the constructions cannot contain other coordinating conjunctions than *og*, i.e. *eller*, 'or'.

(40) $\begin{bmatrix} \textit{pseudo-coord-ph} \\ \text{CONJ-DTR} \mid \text{SYNSEM} \mid \text{LOC} \mid \text{CONT} \mid \text{RELS} \left\langle \textit{\_and\_c\_rel} \right\rangle \end{bmatrix}$

(39)

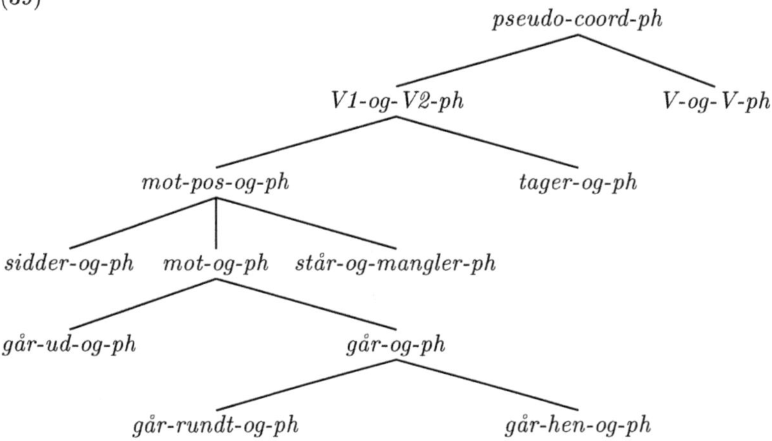

Figure 1

(41) restricts the type of verb that may appear as the left conjunct daugther. Only position and motion verbs occur as left conjunct daugter, i.e. *sidde*, 'sit', *ligge*, 'lie', *gå*, 'go'.

(41) $\begin{bmatrix} \textit{mot-pos-og-ph} \\ \textsc{lconj-dtr} \mid \textsc{synsem} \mid \textsc{loc} \mid \textsc{cont} \mid \textsc{rels} \left\langle \textit{mot\_pos\_rel} \right\rangle \oplus \textit{list} \end{bmatrix}$

Motion and position verbs are specified lexically with a RELS value which is a subtype of *mot_pos_rel*. A part of the hierarchy is shown in (42).

(42)

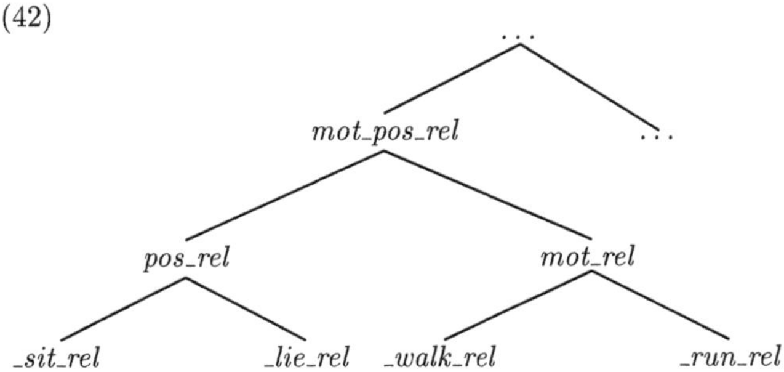

The other dimension is the spectual information. To formalize this we assume a hierarchy of aspectual constructions, as shown in (43).

(43)

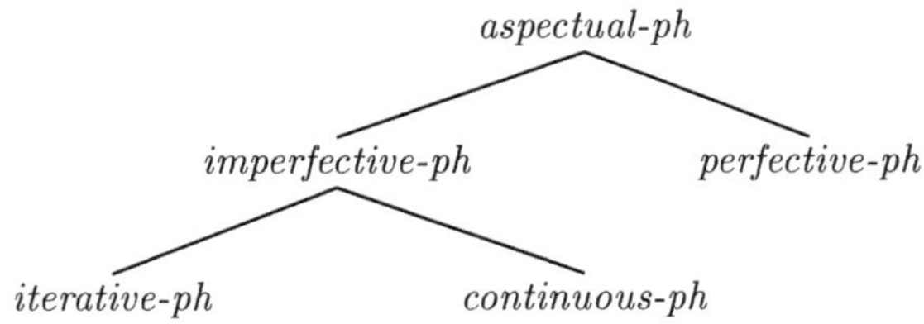

The *imperfective-ph* and *perfective-ph* are constrained as in (44) and (45).

(44) introduces an *imperfective_asp_rel* on the RELS list on the C-CONT (constructional content) path. The C-CONT feature makes it possible for constructions to add semantics, here a relation on the RELS list. This is in contrast to the relations introduced lexically.

(44) $\begin{bmatrix} \textit{imperfective-ph} \\ \text{C-CONT} \mid \text{RELS} \left\langle \textit{imperfective\_asp\_rel} \right\rangle \end{bmatrix}$

Similarly, (45) introduces a *perfective_asp_rel* on the RELS list.

(45) $\begin{bmatrix} \textit{perfective-ph} \\ \text{C-CONT} \mid \text{RELS} \left\langle \textit{perfective\_asp\_rel} \right\rangle \end{bmatrix}$

To account for the constraints on the *iterative-ph* and *continuous-ph*, we need to take into account the aktionsart of the right conjunct daughter in the construction. We therefore introduce a feature representing aktionsart on event indices, cf. (Bonami, 2002) for a similar account of aspect in French.

The attribute AKTIONSART takes the value *aktionsart*. The type *aktionsart* is subtyped as shown in (46).

(46)

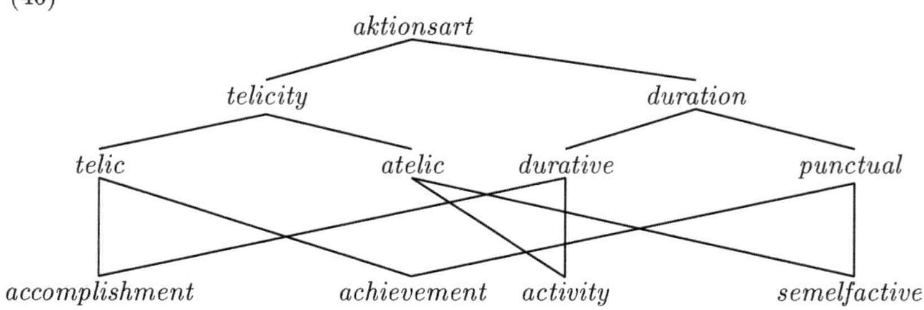

Verbs are specified for an *aktionsart* value in the lexicon, as shown in (47) through (50)[5].

(47)
$$\begin{bmatrix} \text{ORTH} \left\langle \textit{synger} \right\rangle \\ \text{SYNSEM} \mid \text{LOC} \begin{bmatrix} \text{CAT} \begin{bmatrix} \text{HEAD } \textit{verb} \end{bmatrix} \\ \text{CONTENT} \mid \text{HOOK} \mid \text{INDEX} \begin{bmatrix} \text{AKTIONSART } \textit{activity} \end{bmatrix} \end{bmatrix} \end{bmatrix}$$

(48)
$$\begin{bmatrix} \text{ORTH} \left\langle \textit{tørrer} \right\rangle \\ \text{SYNSEM} \mid \text{LOC} \begin{bmatrix} \text{CAT} \begin{bmatrix} \text{HEAD } \textit{verb} \end{bmatrix} \\ \text{CONTENT} \mid \text{HOOK} \mid \text{INDEX} \begin{bmatrix} \text{AKTIONSART } \textit{accomplishment} \end{bmatrix} \end{bmatrix} \end{bmatrix}$$

(49)
$$\begin{bmatrix} \text{ORTH} \left\langle \textit{vinder} \right\rangle \\ \text{SYNSEM} \mid \text{LOC} \begin{bmatrix} \text{CAT} \begin{bmatrix} \text{HEAD } \textit{verb} \end{bmatrix} \\ \text{CONTENT} \mid \text{HOOK} \mid \text{INDEX} \begin{bmatrix} \text{AKTIONSART } \textit{achievement} \end{bmatrix} \end{bmatrix} \end{bmatrix}$$

(50)
$$\begin{bmatrix} \text{ORTH} \left\langle \textit{blinker} \right\rangle \\ \text{SYNSEM} \mid \text{LOC} \begin{bmatrix} \text{CAT} \begin{bmatrix} \text{HEAD } \textit{verb} \end{bmatrix} \\ \text{CONTENT} \mid \text{HOOK} \mid \text{INDEX} \begin{bmatrix} \text{AKTIONSART } \textit{semelfactive} \end{bmatrix} \end{bmatrix} \end{bmatrix}$$

We can now show the constraints that apply to the *iterative-ph* and the *continuous-ph*, cf. (51) and (52).

(51) shows that if the argument of the aspectual relation is *punctual* wrt. aktionsart, the apectual relation is resolved to an *iterative_asp_rel.*

(51)
$$\begin{bmatrix} \textit{iterative-ph} \\ \text{C-CONT} \mid \text{RELS} \left\langle \begin{bmatrix} \textit{iterative\_asp\_rel} \\ \text{ARG0} \mid \text{AKTIONSART } \textit{punctual} \end{bmatrix} \right\rangle \end{bmatrix}$$

Similarly, (52) shows that if the argument of the aspectual relation is *durative* wrt. aktionsart, the apectual relation is resolved to a *continuous_asp_rel.*

(52)
$$\begin{bmatrix} \textit{continuous-ph} \\ \text{C-CONT} \mid \text{RELS} \left\langle \begin{bmatrix} \textit{continuous\_asp\_rel} \\ \text{ARG0} \mid \text{AKTIONSART } \textit{durative} \end{bmatrix} \right\rangle \end{bmatrix}$$

The two dimensions, the coordination constructions and the aspectual information are combined in the types and *iterative-sidder-og-ph*, *continuous-sidder-og-ph*, cf. (53). These types inherit all the constraints specified on their supertypes.

5 The transitive versions of these intransitive entries may have a different value specified for AKTIONSART

We anticipate that more subtypes subsumed by types in the two dimensions may be relevant.

(53)

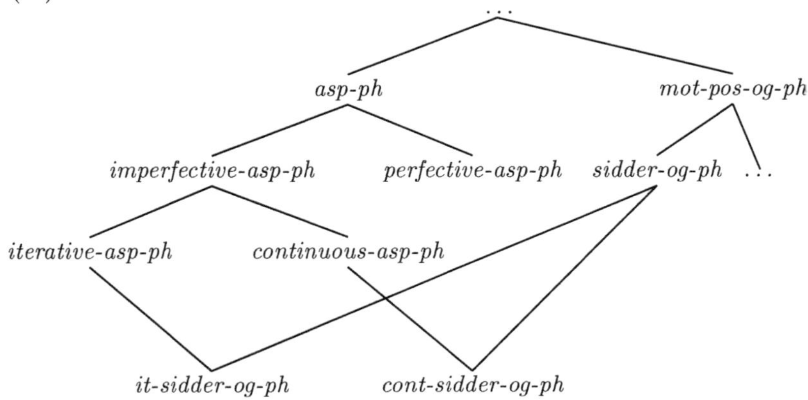

The formalization of the aspectual and coordination construction dimension has been integrated into an MRS style semantic representation, cf. (Copestake et al., 2003).

The RELS and HCONS values of *Peter sidder og blinker*, 'Peter sits and winks', will look like (54), where it can be seen that an *iterative_asp_rel* has been added to the RELS list. The aspectual relation added has been constrained to an iterative relation because the aktionsart of *wink* is *semelfactive*, a subtype of *punctual*. The aspectual relation scopes over the *_wink_rel*. The scope relation is represented by the HCONS feature which encodes restrictions on scope relations.

(54)

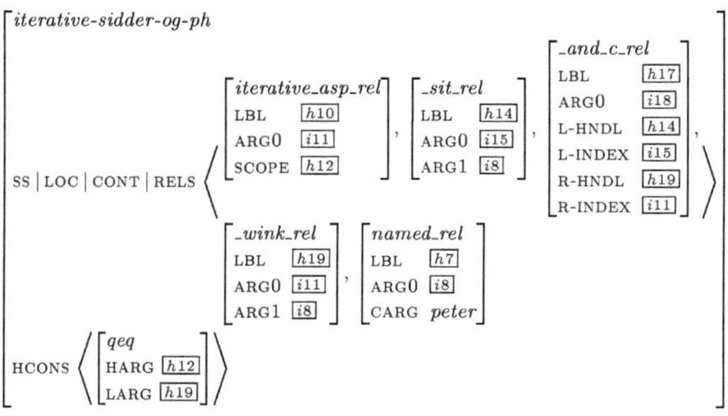

The formalization has been implemented in the LKB system, (Copestake, 2002).

References

Bonami, Olivier. 2002. A syntax-sematics interface for tense and aspect in French. In Frand van Eynde, Lars Hellan, and Dorothee Beermann, editors, *Proceedings of the 8th International HPSG Conference 2001*. CSLI Publications.

Brandt, Søren. 1992. Two problems in Danish verb syntax. *Nordic Journal of Linguistics*, 15:47–64.

Comrie, Bernard. 1976. *Aspect*. Cambridge: Cambridge University Press.

Copestake, Ann. 2002. *Implementing Typed Feature Structure Grammars*. Stanford: CSLI Publications.

Copestake, Ann, Dan Flickinger, Ivan A. Sag, and Carl Pollard. 2003. *Minimal Recursion Semantics. An introduction*. In preparation. Stanford, CA: CSLI.

Diderichsen, Paul. 1946. *Elementær Dansk Grammatik*. København: Gyldendal.

Ginzburg, Jonathan and Ivan Sag. 2000. *Interrogative Investigations: The Form, Meaning and Use of English Interrogatives*. Stanford: CSLI.

Hansen, Aage. 1967. *Moderne Dansk*. Grafisk Forlag.

Jensen, Per Anker. 1985. *Principper for grammatisk analyse*. København: Nyt Nordisk Forlag Arnold Busk.

Johannessen, Janne Bondi. 1998. *Coordination*. Oxford, New York: Oxford University Press.

Jørgensen, Henrik. 2001. Nogle bemærkninger om aspekt i dansk. In Carsten Madsen, Henrik Skov, and Peer E. Sørensen, editors, *Jeget og ordene*. Århus: Klim and Institute for Nordic Languages and Literature, pages 115–136.

Lødrup, Helge. 2002. The syntactic structures of Norwegian pseudocoordinations. *Studia Linguistica*, 56(2):121–43.

Ross, John Robert. 1967. *Constraints on Variables in Syntax*. Ph.D. thesis, MIT.

Sag, Ivan A. and Thomas Wasow. 1999. *Syntactic Theory. A formal Introduction*. Stanford: CSLI.

Vannebo, Kjell Ivar. 2003. *Ta og ro deg ned noen hakk:* on pseudocoordination with the verb *ta* take' in a grammaticalizaation perspective. *Nordic Journal of Linguistics*, 26(2):165–93.

Vendler, Zeno. 1957. Verbs and times. In Zeno Vendler, editor, *Linguistics in Philosophy*. New York: Cornell University Press. 1967., pages 97–121.

Wiklund, Anna-Lena. 2005. *The Syntax of Tenselessness. On Copying Constructions in Swedish*. Umeå: Umeå University.

Aspectual composition in Minimal Recursion Semantics

Maria Flouraki *
University of Essex

Aspectual composition occurs when grammatical aspect and eventuality types combine to trigger particular meanings. This aspectual composition may change the denotation of the eventuality type resulting to aspectual shifts.

One of the languages, where aspectual shifts occur, is Modern Greek, which has a rich aspectual system, involving both morphologically expressed grammatical aspect and eventuality types. Particular emphasis is paid to the interaction between grammatical aspect and eventuality types, since it is due to this interaction that the verbal predicate acquires distinct meanings. The main aim of this paper is to explain potential changes in the meaning of the eventualities caused by this interaction and provide a formal analysis.

To this end, I propose an analysis where the main idea is that grammatical aspect combines with eventuality types and selects eventualities or subeventualities appropriate to its selection restrictions, using information that is already there in the denotation of the eventualities.

1 Introduction

Aspectual composition occurs when grammatical aspect (perfective and imperfective) and eventuality types (accomplishment, achievement, process, state) carried by the verb along with its arguments combine to trigger particular meanings. This aspectual composition may change the denotation of the eventuality type resulting to aspectual shifts (Moens and Steedman, 1988; Jackendoff, 1997; Pustejovsky, 1991; Pulman, 1997; Krifka, 1998; de Swart, 1998; Filip, 2000; Bonami, 2001; Giannakidou, 2002; Egg, 2002; Michaelis, 2003; Michaelis, 2004).

Aspectual shifts are subtypes of type shifts or 'reinterpretations', which are instances of "semantic incompatibility between the immediate subparts of a larger constituent"((Egg, 2002):580). Reinterpretations may occur both in the verbal and nominal domain.

In (1) the verb *freeze* takes as argument a noun denoting a substance (*bottle*), even though its normal argument is a noun denoting a liquid (*water*). The type of the *bottle* has to be reintepretated somehow in order to become an appropriate argument for the verb.

* I would like to thank Louisa Sadler and Doug Arnold for all their help and support. Also, I thank Manfred Sailer for his invaluable comments. This research was suported by ESRC. Email: maria.flouraki@gmail.com

(1) The man froze the bottle.

Reinterpretations are also found in the verbal domain, where aspectual meanings are involved. In (2a) the duration adverbial *for ten minutes* takes as argument the accomplishment eventuality *play the sonata.* This is not a normal input for the adverbial since duration adverbials combine with processes or states. Hence, there is a conflict in the input requirements of the adverbial and an iterative meaning is inferred, which reinterprets the eventuality into a process.

In (2b) the frame adverbial *in a minute* combines with a predicate-argument structure with which it conflicts semantically. Frame advebials combine with accomplishments or achievements, whereas in this case *like him* is a state. An inchoative meaning is inferred that reinterprets the eventuality into an accomplishment.

(2) a. She played the sonata for ten minutes.
b. We liked him in a minute.

In a similar way in (3a) the eventuality *walk a mile* is an accomplishment, which changes into a process in (3b) once the argument gets pluralised (*walk miles*).

(3) a. Mary walked a mile.
b. Mary walked miles.

An instance of this phenomenon is found in Modern Greek (M.G.), where the aspectual shifts observed have a close connection with the interaction between grammatical aspect and eventuality types. In M.G., there is a contrast between perfective and imperfective aspect, morphologically overt in all verbal types. Grammatical aspect combines with eventuality types and affects their meaning.

The accomplishment eventuality *write the letter* in (4) denotes a situation, which starts with the beginning of the *writing* and reaches a culmination with the completion of *the letter.* When this eventuality combines with perfective aspect in (4a), it retains its culmination point and the meaning does not change. When the same eventuality combines with imperfective aspect, it gets a shifted reading in (4b), that is a process or habitual reading. Hence, it is no longer visible when *the letter* reaches its finishing point, its culmination and if it actually does.

(4) a. O Giannis e -graps -e to gramma.
the giannis Aug -write.Perf -3sg.Past the letter
'Giannis wrote the letter' (basic reading)
b. O Giannis e -graf -e to gramma.
the giannis Aug -write.Imperf -3sg.Past the letter
'Giannis was writing the letter' (process reading)
'Giannis used to write the letter' (habitual reading)

The same is the case in (5), which is an instance of an achievement eventuality combined with perfective aspect in (5a) and imperfective aspect in (5b). As was the case with the accomplishment in (4), imperfective aspect modifies the eventuality giving a process or a habitual reading.

(5) a. I Maria kerdis -e sta hartia.
the maria win.Perf -3sg.Past in-the cards
'Maria won in the game of cards' (basic reading)

b. I Maria kerdiz -e sta hartia.
the maria win.Imperf -3sg.Past in-the cards
'Maria was winning in the game of cards' (process reading)
'Maria used to win in the game of cards' (habitual reading)

In (6) the eventuality *love Anna* denotes a situation, which is not clear when it starts and when and whether it finishes. When this eventuality occurs with imperfective aspect in (6a), it gets the default meaning of the eventuality, where no culmination point is denoted and no visible endpoints. In (6b) the same eventuality combines with perfective aspect, which may focus either on the initial stages of the eventuality in which case it acquires an inchoative reading or simply adds both endpoints, in which case there is a bounded reading.

(6) a. O Giannis agapous -e tin Anna.
the giannis love.Imperf -Past.3sg the anna
'Giannis was loving Anna'
'Giannis used to love Anna' (basic reading)

b. O Giannis agapis -e tin Anna.
the giannis love.Perf -Past.3sg the anna
'Giannis loved Anna (and does not love her any more)'
(bounded reading)
'Giannis fell in love with Anna' (inchoative reading)

In the above examples grammatical aspect and eventuality types interact and the meaning of the eventuality is affected by grammatical aspect. When the perfective aspect combines with accomplishments and achievements there is no change in the denotation of the eventuality. As (Smith, 1997) observes perfective aspect and accomplishments - achievements have similar properties. They all have endpoints and reach a culmination. That is why, there is no change in the eventuality denotation once combined with perfective. The same result occurs when imperfective aspect and processes - states combine. No aspectual shifts are observed because they have no endpoints and hence no culmination occurs.

When perfective aspect, though, combines with processes and states, it gives its properties to these eventualities and they acquire both or one endpoint. When, on the other hand, imperfective aspect combines with accomplishments and achievemnts, these eventualities drop their endpoints.

2 Theoretical Background

In order to formalise and explain the interaction between grammatical aspect and eventuality types, it is standard in the literature to assume that there is a functor argument relation: $f(a)$, where f is the functor and a the argument. Where there are aspectual interactions, the relation between functor and argument translates into (7), where there is a functor-argument relation between grammatical aspect and eventuality types.

(7) *aspect(eventuality)*

We may further instantiate the aspectual functor into the perfective functor, which normally takes as argument accomplishments and achievements (8a), as was observed in examples (4a) and (5a) above. The aspectual functor can be also instantiated into an imperfective functor, which normally combines with processes and states in (8b), as shown in example (6a).

(8) a. $perfective(accomplishment \vee achievement)$
b. $imperfective(process \vee state)$

There are cases, though, where the argument is not the appropriate input for the functor. This does not mean that the combination is not acceptable but that reinterpretations occur, which remedy the conflict. Instances of this can be found in (6b), where the perfective aspect combines with a process and in (4b) and (5b), where the imperfective functor occurs with an accomplishment or an achievement respectively.

The main trend in the literature for the explanation of these reinterpretations is the introduction of extralinguistic knowledge. In this case, context plays a major role in the resolution of the conflict and it is manifested with contextually licensed operators.

(Jackendoff, 1997) argues that "the process of composition interpolates a 'coercing function' G to create instead the structure F(G(X)) where X is a suitable argument for G, and G(X) is a suitable argument for F." This means that in type-shifting, the process of semantic composition may add meanings absent in the syntax, in order to ensure that certain functors receive suitable arguments.

A similar explanation comes from (de Swart, 1998) who argues that coercion is "syntactically and morphologically invisible: it is governed by implicit contextual reinterpretation mechanisms triggered by the need to resolve conflicts."((de Swart, 1998):360)

In a similar way aspectual shifts are treated as type coercions by (Moens and Steedman, 1988; Pulman, 1997; Pustejovsky, 1991; Pustejovsky and Bouillon, 1995; de Swart, 1998). The main idea is that the basic aspectual class of an eventuality description may be changed under the influence of tenses, aspectual adverbials and aspectual auxiliares. These are functions, which may coerce eventuality types so as to become appropriate input for them. The reinterpretation, in this case, is achieved with the introduction of operators, which alter the type of the argument so as to become appropriate input for the functor. The licensing of a particular operator depends on context.

Hence, the general relation *f(Op(a))* is used, where the operator *Op* added, is given by pragmatic context. A major drawback of these approaches is that these operators can not be appropriately constrained, so that they occur only where and when needed.[1]

Different solutions have been provided, where the operators are either constrained using a network of contigent aspectual relations (Moens and Steedman, 1988), or a *qualia structure*, where the possible selections are enlisted beforehand (Pustejovsky, 1991) or underspecification in the selection is involved, where the functor does not combine immediately with an argument but there is space in between for other items to intervene, which are left underspecified (Egg, 2002).

The solution pursuit in this paper is different. First of all, I support that grammatical aspect and eventuality types related to it are licensed by morphological material overt in the verbal stem and there is no need for context to interfere. At the same time, following (Michaelis, 2004) and (Pustejovsky, 1991), I develop a highly elaborated inventory of eventuality types, which consists of eventualities and their subeventualities. These interact with grammatical aspect, which adds or selects the whole or subparts of the eventualities according to its selection restrictions. Hence, there is no new material added by context but the one that is already there is appropriately constrained by grammatical aspect.

To this end, this paper is constructed as follows. In section 3.1, I show what is the status of the Modern Greek verbal stem in the HPSG theory and what is the relation between aspectual information and the verbal lexeme. Also, I provide a connection between morphology and semantic representations and introduce some basic concepts of MRS. In section 3.2, I show how MRS can be accomodated to represent grammatical aspect. In 3.3, I move to the representation of subeventual templates as they are constructed in MRS and in 5, I show how the composition between grammatical aspect and eventuality types is achieved in MRS . In section 4, I show how eventuality types and grammatical aspect combine and provide an analysis, where a perfective and an imperfective functor is invloved in 4.1 and 4.2. Finally, I conclude in section 6.

3 The analysis

3.1 Aspectual morphology

In M.G. the verbal lexeme is formed by a variety of stems and inflections added to the stem. The stem realises the grammatical aspect (perfective and imperfective) and the voice (active and medio-passive), whereas the suffixes, added to the stem represent at the same time the tense, person and number and when attached form

1 For a detailed discussion see (Flouraki, 2005).

the fully inflected word. Hence, in M.G. there is cumulative exponence "with every element of form being a partial exponent of several morphosyntactic features" ((Joseph and Smirniotopoulos, 1993): 391). There are the following combinations of features represented in the stem: [perfective, active], [perfective, medio-passive], [imperfective].

The verb *love* in (6), repeated here as (9), has two stems. The stem in (9a) *agapous-*, which realises the combination of features [perfective,active] and the stem in (9b) *agapis-*, which realises the feature [imperfective]. This means that each stem introduces a particular set of features that can not be realised in any other way. The suffix on its part is the same in these two cases and represents the tense that is the past and the person and number, which is the 3rd person singular.

(9) a. O Giannis agapous -e tin Anna.
the giannis love.Imperf -Past.3sg the anna
'Giannis was loving Anna'
'Giannis used to love Anna' (basic reading)

b. O Giannis agapis -e tin Anna.
the giannis love.Perf -Past.3sg the anna
'Giannis loved Anna (and does not love her any more)' (bounded reading)
'Giannis fell in love with Anna' (inchoative reading)

Morphologically, then, the different verbal stems introduce particular sets of features in M.G.. Following (Koenig, 1999), I construct a hierarchy of morphological objects, where the verbal stem is incorporated. This is given in figure 1, where the object *complex-lexeme* is introduced. [2] This has as subtypes the verbal stem (*vb-stem*) and the *word*. The *vb-stem* has as subtypes the perfective stem (*perf-stem*) and the imperfective stem (*imperf-stem*), whereas the *word* has as subtype the *verb-infl*. This realises both the tense and agreement features.

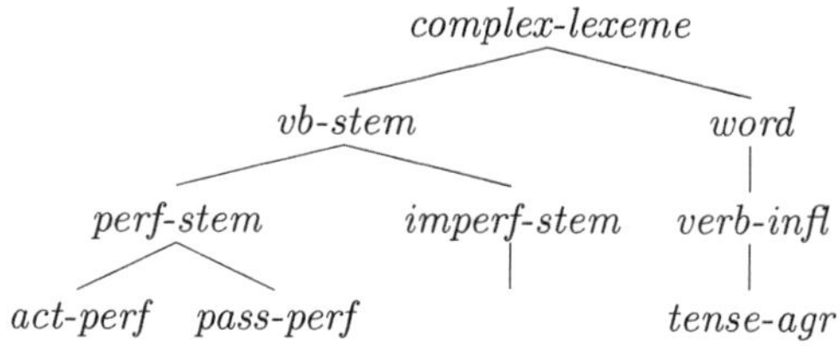

Figure 1
Hierarchy of the verbal lexeme in Modern Greek

Each stem introduces a particular semantic relation as was observed in (9). The perfective stem in (9a) introduces the perfective aspect, whereas the imperfective

2 For more details see Koenig(1999).

stem in (9b) the imperfective aspect. These semantic relations are represented using Minimal Recursion Semantics (MRS)(Copestake et al., 2000). MRS is a metalanguage, which describes semantic structures within the framework of HPSG (Pollard and Sag, 1994).

In order to understand the overall semantics of the verbal lexeme, I will explain first how it is realised in MRS and then incorporate the aspectual information.

According to the MRS architecture, a semantic object is created of type *mrs*, which has appropriate attributes and values. For instance, the verb *love* shows a semantic relation: *love(x,y,e)*, where x and y are the participants of this relation and e the eventuality variable. In MRS, this is represented as a *love-rel*, where the feature L(a)B(e)L is introduced along with appropriate arguments for the relation. The LBL identifies the relation and connects it with potential other relations introduced by a phrase. The arguments show the participant roles in the relation and are represented as ARG1 x and ARG2 y. The eventuality variable is represented with ARG0 z. This is coindexed with the INDEX feature in HOOK, which represents the eventuality type of the whole phrase. The HOOK attribute "is used to group together the features that specify the parts of an MRS which are visible to semantic functors" ((Copestake et al., 2000):24). In semantic composition the HOOK of the mother is always the HOOK of the semantic head daughter.

Each lexical item has a single distinguished main EP, which is captured by the feature KEY. Usually the key EP is equal to the LTOP of a phrase, as is the case in (10).

(10)
$$
\left[\begin{array}{l} \textit{mrs} \\ \text{HOOK} \left[\begin{array}{l}\text{LTOP } \boxed{1}\\ \text{INDEX } \boxed{z}\end{array}\right] \\ \text{RELS} \left\langle \left[\begin{array}{l} \textit{love-rel}\\ \text{LBL } \boxed{1} \\ \text{ARG1 } \boxed{x}\ \textit{ref-ind} \\ \text{ARG2 } \boxed{y}\ \textit{ref-ind}\\ \text{ARG0 } \boxed{z}\end{array}\right], \ldots \right\rangle \end{array}\right]
$$

Explicit lexical material, that is the stem in M.G., introduces aspectual information. This aspectual information will be represented in the form of different relations. Hence, the constraint in (11) is introduced, which states that the *vb-stem* introduces two relations: a grammatical aspect relation *aspect-rel* and an eventuality type relation *eventuality-rel.* The question that will concern us in the next section is what will be the connection between the relations representing the aspectual information and the *verb-rel* as given in (10).

(11) $\textit{vb-stem} \Longrightarrow \left[\text{RELS}\left\langle \begin{bmatrix} \textit{aspect-rel} \\ \text{LBL } \textit{handle} \\ \ldots \end{bmatrix}, \begin{bmatrix} \textit{eventuality-rel} \\ \text{LBL } \textit{handle} \\ \ldots \end{bmatrix} \right\rangle\right]$

3.2 Aspectual Representations

As we saw in the previous section, grammatical aspect and eventuality types are represented within the verbal lexeme itself. Hence, having in mind the MRS architecture, we have to enrich the semantic representation of the *verb-rel*, so as to incorporate the aspectual information. The arguments showing the participant roles stay as such but the argument representing the verbal eventuality has to become more complex in order to show the aspectual interaction. Hence, ARG0 in (10) takes as value a feature structure, where different relations are introduced.

These relations represent both the grammatical aspect functor and the eventuality type argument. They have to be introduced within the verbal lexeme since in M.G. grammatical aspect and eventuality types are instantiated in the verb. (Koenig and Davis, 2003) apply MRS to the lexemic level, where semantic decomposition is achieved by introducing more than one relation in the EP's semantic type. Also (Bonami, 2001) decomposes the verbal lexeme so as to accomodate the tense functor in French. In his analysis, the verbal lexeme introduces not one but three relations. There is a *tense-rel*, a *verb-rel* and an *asp*(ectual)-*op*(erator)-*rel*, representing the contextual operators discussed in section 2. The idea is that the *asp-op-rel* binds with an eventuality through the B(ounded) EV(ventuality) feature and reinterpets it into another eventuality with the eventuality (EVY) feature. Then, the *tense-rel* combines with the reinterpreted eventuality through BEV as shown in (12).

(12) $\left[\text{RELS}\left\langle \begin{bmatrix} \textit{tense-rel} \\ \text{LBL } \boxed{1} \\ \text{SCOPE } \boxed{2} \\ \text{BEV } \boxed{y} \end{bmatrix}, \begin{bmatrix} \textit{asp-op-rel} \\ \text{LBL } \boxed{2} \\ \text{EVY } \boxed{y} \\ \text{BEV } \boxed{x} \\ \text{SCOPE } \boxed{3} \end{bmatrix}, \begin{bmatrix} \textit{verb-rel} \\ \text{LBL } \boxed{3} \\ \text{EVY } \boxed{x} \\ \text{ACTOR } \textit{idn-ind} \\ \text{UNDER } \textit{idn-ind} \end{bmatrix} \right\rangle\right]$

In the case of aspectual composition, I provide an alternative where the relations introduced by the verbal lexeme are just an aspectual relation of type *aspect-rel* and an eventuality relation of type *eventuality-rel*[3].

Each relation is part of a hierarchy of relations given in figure 2, where the *aspect-rel* is a subtype of the *scopal-rel*, which introduces the feature SCOPE. This means that this particular relation has to take scope over another one. The

3 The *tense-rel* is a relation that is introduced by the Greek verbal lexeme but for the purposes of this paper it will not be discussed here

aspect-rel has as subtypes the perfective (*perf-rel*) and the imperfective relation (*imperf-rel*), corresponding to the perfective and imperfective aspect respectively. The *eventuality-rel* is a *non-scopal* relation and has as subtypes the eventualities *transition-rel*, for accomplishments and achievements [4], *process-rel* and *state-rel* for processes and states respectively.

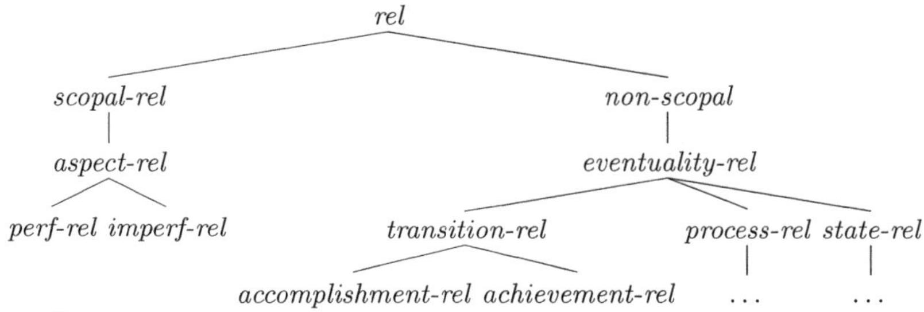

Figure 2
Hierarchy of relations

The *aspect-rel* introduces the features LBL and BINDS guaranteed by the constraint in (13). The LBL has as value the type *handle*, which identifies the relation and shows its scopal connection with the other relations. The *aspect-rel* combines with an eventuality through the BINDS feature and gives back the same or a different eventuality represented by the EVENT-STR(ucture) feature. Both BINDS and EVENT-STR take as value an *event-str*, which represents the subparts of the eventualities, as we will see in the following section.

$$(13) \quad \textit{aspect-rel} \Longrightarrow \begin{bmatrix} \text{LBL } \textit{handle} \\ \text{SCOPE } \textit{handle} \\ \text{EVENT-STR } \textit{event-str} \\ \text{BINDS } \textit{event-str} \end{bmatrix}$$

3.3 Subeventual templates

As was mentioned in section 2, a way to eliminate the contextual operator is to decompose the eventualities into subparts. In this way, grammatical aspect will be able to select the appropriate subpart in each case.

(Pustejovsky, 1991) argues that verbal predicates have subeventual structure, which provides a template for verbal decomposition and lexical semantics. In his theory, there are three basic eventuality types: states, processes and transitions. States are evaluated relative to no other eventualities, while processes denote a sequence of events, which identify the same semantic expression. Transitions are complex types, equivalent to accomplishments and achievements. These consist

4 This categorisation belongs to (Pustejovsky, 1991)

of a process and a state subevent and denote a transition from the process of an eventuality coming about, to the state of being about through the culmination point. Hence, if we take the accomplisment *build the house*, the first subevent is the process, which leads to the completion of the house, whereas the second subevent is the state that represents the completion stage.

The ordering of these subevents is guaranteed by the temporal relation *exhaustive ordered part of* ($\prec$), which holds between an event e_1 and another e_2, iff e_1 temporally precedes e_2. Hence, in accomplishments and achievements, there is an event structure, where the process temporally precedes the state. For instance, in the achievement *reach the top*, the process of reaching the top precedes the state of being at the top.

In order to differentiate accomplishments from achievements, Pustejovsky introduces another kind of relation: the *event headedness*. This "provides a way of foregrounding and backgrounding of event arguments" and indicates their "relative prominence". The head indicates the most prominent subevent, which contributes to the 'focus' of interpretation. In the case of accomplishments, the head is the process while in the case of achievements the head is the state. As far as the processes and states are concerned, they consist only of one eventuality and the focus is on that eventuality.

Following (Pustejovsky, 1991), I support that each *eventuality-rel* introduces an event structure (EVENT-STR), whose value is a feature structure, that consists of different subeventualities indicated by the features EVENT1 and EVENT2.

The *transition-rel* in (14) introduces apart from the attribute LBL, the attribute EVENT-STR, which takes as values a subeventual structure that consists of two eventualities: EVENT1 has a *process* as its value and EVENT2 a *state* type. Their temporal ordering is guaranteed through the RESTR(iction) attribute, which states that there is a precedence temporal relation between EVENT1 and EVENT2.

$$(14) \quad \textit{transition-rel} \Longrightarrow \begin{bmatrix} \text{LBL } \textit{handle} \\ \text{EVENT-STR } \boxed{3} \begin{bmatrix} \text{EVENT1 } \boxed{1}\textit{process} \\ \text{EVENT2 } \boxed{2}\textit{state} \\ \text{RESTR } \left\{ \boxed{1} \prec \boxed{2} \right\} \end{bmatrix} \end{bmatrix}$$

In order to differentiate the *accomplishment-rel* from the *achievement-rel* an extra feature is introduced, the EV(entuality)-FOC(us), which takes as value one of the two subevents of the event structure. In the case of accomplishments, the EV-FOC has as value the EVENT1 as shown in (15), while in the case of achievements the EV-FOC has as value the EVENT2 in (16).

$$(15) \quad \textit{accomplishment-rel} \Longrightarrow \begin{bmatrix} \text{LBL } \textit{handle} \\ \text{EVENT-STR } \boxed{3} \begin{bmatrix} \text{EV-FOC } \boxed{1} \end{bmatrix} \end{bmatrix}$$

$$(16)\quad achievement\text{-}rel \Longrightarrow \begin{bmatrix} \text{LBL } handle \\ \text{EVENT-STR } \boxed{3} \begin{bmatrix} \text{EV-FOC } \boxed{2} \end{bmatrix} \end{bmatrix}$$

The *process-rel* in (17) introduces an EVENT-STR with an eventuality attribute EVENT1, which denotes a *process* and an EVENT2, which is coindexed with the first subevent.[5] This is the case because processes do not consist of different subparts. Subsequently, the RESTR is empty and the EV-FOC is coindexed with EVENT1.

$$(17)\quad process\text{-}rel \Longrightarrow \begin{bmatrix} \text{LBL } handle \\ \text{EVENT-STR } \boxed{3} \begin{bmatrix} \text{EVENT1 } \boxed{1} process \\ \text{EVENT2 } \boxed{1} \\ \text{RESTR } \{\} \\ \text{EV-FOC } \boxed{1} \end{bmatrix} \end{bmatrix}$$

The second step in the representation of aspectual meaning is to combine these subeventual templates with grammatical aspect. An issue that arises is how we can indicate that grammatical aspect combines with certain eventuality types and changes nothing in their denotation while with others there are aspectual shifts as we saw in section 1. This is an issue, I am going to explore in the following section, where selectional constraints on grammatical aspect will be introduced.

4 Aspectual combinations

Following (Michaelis, 2003; Michaelis, 2004), I support that as in Romance languages, perfective and imperfective aspect in M.G. are type-selecting operators, reflecting the eventuality type of their arguments. Hence, the perfective functor in (18a) combines with non-stative eventualities (-ST) and returns bounded ones (+BD), while the imperfective functor in (18b) combines with stative ones (+ST) and returns unbounded ones (-BD).

(18) a. $\lambda e_{+BD}.perf(\lambda e'_{-ST}.write'(mary', the.letter')(e'))(e)$
b. $\lambda e_{-BD}.imperf(\lambda e'_{-ST}.run'(mary')(e'))(e)$

Even though these two classes of operators have a distinct function, they can potentially modulate when it is necessary the aspectual properties of their argument and can denote event types and place constraints upon the lexically expressed types they combine with. According to Michaelis, this kind of combination between functor and argument is guaranteed with the *Aktionsart preservation principle*, which states that that no extra material is needed intervene

5 Many thanks to Manfred Sailer for pointing this out.

in the functor argument relation. She supports that "In an aspectual mapping, whether implicit or explicit, input and output types must share some portion of their respective causal and/or temporal representations." ((Michaelis, 2004):16)

The *Aktionsart Preservation principle* guarantees that no extra material is needed interve in the functor-argument relation and this is the basis of the theory assumed here. Hence, the perfective and the imperfective functor take as argument particular eventualities and when the argument is not the appropriate input for the functor, the functor selects or adds a subpart to the eventuality it combines with. The mechanism works thanks to the introduction of subeventual structure, where subeventualties can be added or chosen in each case.

In order to depict the selectional restrictions of grammatical aspect in HPSG, I assume that there is a perfective and an imperfective functor, which place different constraints according to what the argument is.

4.1 Perfective functor

The perfective functor (F_{perf}) defined in (19) normally selects transition eventualities. Since the output of this functor is the same as the input, it is a type-selecting operator. This is guaranteed by the constraint in (19a), which states that when the argument of the perfective functor is an EVENT-STR, which consists of EVENT1 with value *process* and EVENT2, then the outcome is the same event-structure.

(19) a. $F_{perf}\left(\boxed{1}\begin{bmatrix}\text{EVENT1 } \textit{process} \\ \text{EVENT2 } \textit{state}\end{bmatrix}\right) = \boxed{1}$

b. $F_{perf}\left(\begin{bmatrix}\text{EVENT1 } \boxed{1} \textit{ process} \\ \text{EVENT2 } \boxed{1}\end{bmatrix}\right) = \begin{bmatrix}\text{EVENT1 } \boxed{1} \\ \text{EVENT2 } \textit{state}\end{bmatrix}$

However, the *perf-rel* may combine with a *process-rel* in which case the functor operates on the eventuality and alters the second subevent into a state so as to get a *transition-rel.* This is ensured by the constraint in (19) which states that when there is an eventuality consisting of EVENT1 of value *process* and EVENT2, that has the same value as EVENT1, then the outcome is an event structure, where EVENT2 gets as value a *state.*

Hence, when there is a *transition-rel*, the *perf-rel* selects through the BINDS feature the whole EVENT-STR indicated with the tag $\boxed{3}$ in (20). The output of this combination is the same as the input, as it is licensed by the constraint in (19a).

$$(20)\quad \begin{bmatrix} \text{KEY } \boxed{1} \\ \text{RELS } \left\langle \begin{bmatrix} \textit{perf-rel} \\ \text{LBL } \boxed{1} \\ \text{SCOPE } \boxed{2} \\ \text{EVENT-STR } F_{perf}(\boxed{6}) \\ \text{BINDS } \langle \boxed{3} \rangle \end{bmatrix}, \begin{bmatrix} \textit{transition-rel} \\ \text{LBL } \boxed{2} \\ \text{EVENT-STR } \boxed{3} \begin{bmatrix} \text{EVENT1 } \boxed{4}\textit{process} \\ \text{EVENT2 } \boxed{5}\textit{state} \\ \text{RESTR } \{\boxed{4} \prec \boxed{5}\} \end{bmatrix} \end{bmatrix} \right\rangle \end{bmatrix}$$

When the *perf-rel* combines with a *process-rel*, the constraint in (19b) applies. Hence,the *perf-rel* selects an eventuality of type *process* through the BINDS feature and alters the second subevent into a *state*. This changes the *process* eventuality into a *transition* in (21).

$$(21)\quad \begin{bmatrix} \text{KEY } \boxed{1} \\ \text{RELS } \left\langle \begin{bmatrix} \textit{perf-rel} \\ \text{LBL } \boxed{1} \\ \text{SCOPE } \boxed{2} \\ \text{EVENT-STR } F_{perf}(\boxed{6}) \\ \text{BINDS } \langle \boxed{3} \rangle \end{bmatrix}, \begin{bmatrix} \textit{process-rel} \\ \text{LBL } \boxed{2} \\ \text{EVENT-STR } \boxed{3} \begin{bmatrix} \text{EVENT1 } \boxed{1}\textit{process} \\ \text{EVENT2 } \boxed{1} \\ \text{RESTR } \{\} \end{bmatrix} \end{bmatrix} \right\rangle \end{bmatrix}$$

4.2 Imperfective functor

The imperfective functor is a type-selecting operator as well. It selects process eventualities and returns an output of the same eventuality as the input. When it combines with transition eventualities, it selects only the *process* subeventuality which is appropriate for its selection type.

The constraint in (22a) guarantees that, when the input is a *process*, the output is a *process* as well. When the input is a *transition* then the output is just the *process* subevent (22b).

$$(22)\quad \text{a. } F_{impf}\left(\boxed{2}\begin{bmatrix} \text{EVENT1 } \boxed{1}\textit{process} \\ \text{EVENT2 } \boxed{1} \end{bmatrix}\right)=\boxed{2}$$

$$\text{b. } F_{impf}\left(\begin{bmatrix} \text{EVENT1 } \boxed{1}\textit{process} \\ \text{EVENT2 } \textit{state} \end{bmatrix}\right)=\begin{bmatrix} \text{EVENT1 } \boxed{1} \\ \text{EVENT2 } \boxed{1} \end{bmatrix}$$

When the imperfective functor indicated by the *imperf-rel* combines with eventualities of type *process-rel*, it selects through the BINDS feature the whole EVENT-STR of the *eventuality-rel*. The EVENT-STR of the *imperf-rel* is the same as the EVENT-STR of the *process-rel*.

(23)
$$\left[\begin{array}{l} \text{KEY } \boxed{1} \\ \text{RELS } \left\langle \left[\begin{array}{l} \textit{imperf-rel} \\ \text{LBL } \boxed{1} \\ \text{SCOPE } \boxed{2} \\ \text{EVENT-STR } F_{impf}\big(\boxed{6}\big) \\ \text{BINDS } \boxed{3} \end{array}\right], \left[\begin{array}{l} \textit{process-rel} \\ \text{LBL } \boxed{2} \\ \text{EVENT-STR } \boxed{3} \left[\begin{array}{l} \text{EVENT1 } \boxed{1}\textit{process} \\ \text{EVENT2 } \boxed{1} \\ \text{RESTR } \{\} \end{array}\right] \end{array}\right] \right\rangle \end{array}\right]$$

When the *transition-rel* combines with the *imperf-rel*, then the *imperf-rel* strips the *transition-rel* of its culmination point and consequent state, which is the EVENT2 (24). This is guaranteed by the constraint in (22b).

(24)
$$\left[\begin{array}{l} \text{KEY } \boxed{1} \\ \text{RELS } \left\langle \left[\begin{array}{l} \textit{imperf-rel} \\ \text{LBL } \boxed{1} \\ \text{SCOPE } \boxed{2} \\ \text{EVENT-STR } F_{impf}\big(\boxed{6}\big) \\ \text{BINDS } \left\langle\boxed{3}\right\rangle \end{array}\right], \left[\begin{array}{l} \textit{transition-rel} \\ \text{LBL } \boxed{2} \\ \text{EVENT-STR } \boxed{3} \left[\begin{array}{l} \text{EVENT1 } \boxed{4}\textit{process} \\ \text{EVENT2 } \boxed{5}\textit{state} \\ \text{RESTR } \left\{\boxed{4} \prec \boxed{5}\right\} \end{array}\right] \end{array}\right] \right\rangle \end{array}\right]$$

5 Composition

The relations introduced by the verbal lexeme i.e. *aspect-rel* and *eventuality-rel* have to combine to denote the semantics of the overall verbal lexeme. The HOOK feature is introduced in order to achieve semantic composition. The value of the attribute HOOK, as we saw in section 3.1, has the attributes LTOP and the INDEX defined on it. The LTOP is equated with the highest scopal relation and the INDEX represents the eventuality of the complete utterance.

In the case of the verbal EP in M.G., there is an interaction between grammatical aspect and eventuality types, which determines the eventuality type of the overall verbal lexeme. This interaction is represented by the *aspect-rel* and the *eventuality-rel*. The *aspect-rel* has a fixed scope over the *eventuality-rel* and bears the feature SCOPE. How is then the LTOP of the overall EP determined? When there is a scopal combination the LTOP of the verbal EP is equated with the KEY of the relation that bears the SCOPE feature and the INDEX is coreferential with the EVENT-STR of the relation that scopes over all the others. Hence, in figure 5, the INDEX is coindexed with the EVENT-STR of the *perf-rel*, that determines the final aspectual information of the verbal phrase, whereas the LTOP is coindexed with the LBL of the *verb-rel*.

$$
\begin{bmatrix}
\text{HOOK} & \begin{bmatrix}\text{LTOP} & \boxed{1}\\ \text{INDEX} & \boxed{4}\end{bmatrix}\\
\text{RELS} & \left\langle \begin{bmatrix} \textit{verb-rel} & \\ \text{ARG0} & \begin{bmatrix} \text{RELS} & \left\langle \begin{array}{l} \begin{bmatrix}\textit{perf-rel} & \\ \text{LBL} & \boxed{1}\\ \text{SCOPE} & \boxed{2}\\ \text{EVENT-STR} & f_{perf}\left(\boxed{4}\right)\\ \text{BINDS} & \left\langle\boxed{3}\right\rangle\end{bmatrix}, \\ \begin{bmatrix}\textit{transition-rel} & \\ \text{LBL} & \boxed{2}\\ \text{EVENT-STR} & \boxed{3}\begin{bmatrix}\text{EVENT1} & \boxed{5}\textit{process}\\ \text{EVENT2} & \boxed{6}\textit{state}\\ \text{RESTR} & \left\{\boxed{5}\prec\boxed{6}\right\}\end{bmatrix}\end{bmatrix} \end{array}\right\rangle\end{bmatrix}\end{bmatrix}\right\rangle
\end{bmatrix}
$$

6 Conclusion

In this paper, I have presented a formal analysis of the combination between grammatical aspect and eventuality types. I have shown that in M.G., there are eventuality types, which combine with the morphologically overt grammatical aspect. This combination triggers particular meanings, which depend on the eventuality type used. There is the view that when the meanings inferred are the non-standard ones, they can be explained with the use of contextual operators.

I argue against such a contextual interpretation on the ground that it is not possible to appropriately constrain contextual operators. Thus, I provide an analysis where the eventualities consist of subeventual templates and grammatical aspect selects each time an appropriate subeventuality as input according to its selectional restrictions. Particular meanings are inferred, which are already there in the denotation of the eventuality and they just need to be picked up by grammatical aspect. Hence, no extra material intervenes in the denotation.

References

Bonami, Olivier. 2001. A syntax - semantics interface for tense and aspect in french. In Frank van Eynde, Lars Hellan, and Dorothy Beerman, editors, *Proceedings of the 8th International HPSG conference*. CSLI publications.

Copestake, Ann, Dan Flickinger, Carl Pollard, and Ivan A. Sag. 2000. Minimal recursion semantics: An introduction. *Journal of Research on Language and Computation*, 3(0):281–332.

de Swart, Henriette. 1998. Aspect shift and coercion. *Natural Language and Linguistic Theory*, 16:347–385.

Egg, Markus. 2002. Semantic construction for reinterpretation phenomena. *Linguistics*, 40:579–609.

Filip, Hana. 2000. The quantization puzzle. In James Pustejovsky and Carol Tenny, editors, *Events as Grammatical Objects*. CSLI Press, Stanford, pages 3–60.

Flouraki, Maria. 2005. *Aspect in Modern Greek: an HPSG analysis*. Ph.D. thesis, University of Essex.

Giannakidou, Anastasia. 2002. A puzzle about until and the present perfect. In Artemis Alexiadou, Monika Rathert, and Arnim von Stechow, editors, *Perfect Explorations*. Mouton de Gruyter.

Jackendoff, Ray. 1997. *The Architecture of the Language Faculty*. Cambridge, MA: MIT Press.

Joseph, Brian and Jane Smirniotopoulos. 1993. The morphosyntax of the modern greek verb as morphology and not syntax. *Linguistic Inquiry*, 24(2):338–398.

Koenig, Jean-Pierre. 1999. *Lexical Relations*. Stanford, CA: CSLI Publications.

Koenig, Jean-Pierre and Anthony Davis. 2003. Semantically transparent linking in HPSG. In Stefan Müller, editor, *Proceedings of the HPSG-2003 Conference, Michigan State University, East Lansing*, pages 222–235, Stanford. CSLI Publications.

Krifka, Manfred. 1998. The origins of telicity. In Susan Rothstein, editor, *Events and Grammar*. Kluwer Academic Publishers, Great Britain, pages 197–235.

Michaelis, Laura. 2003. Headless constructions and coercion by construction. In E.J. Francis and L.A. Michaelis, editors, *Mismatch: Form-Function Incongruity and the Architecture of Grammar*. CSLI Publications, Stanford, pages 259–310.

Michaelis, Laura A. 2004. Type shifting in construction grammar: An integrated approach to aspectual coercion. *Cognitive Linguistics*, 15:1–67.

Moens, Marc and Mark Steedman. 1988. Temporal ontology and temporal reference. *Computational Linguistics*, 14:15–28.

Pollard, Carl J. and Ivan A. Sag. 1994. *Head-Driven Phrase Structure Grammar*. Chicago: University of Chicago Press.

Pulman, Stephen G. 1997. Aspectual shift as type coercion. *Transactions of the Philological Society*, 95(2):279–317.

Pustejovsky, James. 1991. The syntax of event structure. *Cognition*, 41:47–81.

Pustejovsky, James and Pierrette Bouillon. 1995. Aspectual coercion and logical polysemy. *Journal of Semantics*, 12:133–162.

Smith, Carlota. 1997. *The Parameter of Aspect*. Dodrecht, The Netherlands: Kluwer Academic Publishers.

A constructional approach to syntax and the treatment of passive in Norwegian

Petter Haugereid*
Norwegian University of Science and Technology

A syntax-based approach to argument structure for HPSG is presented, where it is assumed that argument structure frames are syntactic constructs and that passive is a syntactic element. This makes it possible to avoid stipulating detailed information about argument structure in open class lexical entries.

1 Introduction

Different phenomena in the discussion around argument structure such as unaccusativity and unergativity, valence alternations and voice are in frameworks such as LFG and HPSG accounted for by means of subcat stipulations in lexical entries. In this paper, an alternative approach is presented, where five syntactic argument roles called arg1-role, arg2-role, arg3-role, arg4-role and arg5-role are assumed in order to account for the creation of argument frames. The arg1-role corresponds to the external argument role in GB/Minimalism. The arg2-role corresponds to the deep direct object role, the arg3-role corresponds to the deep indirect object role, the arg4-role corresponds to so-called delimiters, that is, resultatives and end-of-paths. The arg5-role corresponds to other PP complements that serve as preconditions for the event. The five argument roles are realized by syntactic entities such as phrase structure rules, inflections and function words. The approach has much of the formal inventory of an HPSG grammar (see e.g. (Pollard and Sag, 1994)). All the constituents in the grammar (lexical and syntactic) are represented as typed feature structures. But the idea that argument structure is a syntactic construct is taken from Minimalism (See (Borer, 2005a), (Borer, 2005b), (Åfarli, 2003) and (Åfarli, 2006)). With such a syntactic approach to argument structure, a verb is by default compatible with all possible argument frames. This is different from other HPSG approaches where verbs are listed with particular argument frames in the lexicon. The ideas are implemented in an HPSG gram-

* Norwegian University of Science and Technology, Dragvoll, N-7491 Trondheim, Norway. Email: petterha@hf.ntnu.no.

mar (Norsyg) for Norwegian, which covers all argument frames for verbs listed in lexical resources for Norwegian such as Troll and NorKompLeks.[1]

The paper opens with a presentation of the five argument roles in Section 2. Then the basic syntactic machinery is presented in Section 3, and finally, an analysis of passive for Norwegian is given in Section 4.[2]

2 Argument roles

As mentioned in the introduction, five argument roles are assumed in this approach: The arg1-role (external argument), the arg2-role (deep direct object), The arg3-role (deep indirect object), the arg4-role (delimiter) and the arg5-role (argument that precedes the event).

2.1 Arg1-role

The arg1-role corresponds to the external argument in GB/Minimalism, and can be seen as the initiator of the event. The arg1-role can be realised as an NP subject like in (1a). It can also be realised as the passive auxiliary as shown in (1b) or with the infinitival marker as shown in (1c). In (1c) the infinitival marker is realised as the arg1-role of *sleep*.

(1) a. **John** sleeps.
    b. John **is** admired.
    c. John tries **to** sleep.

2.2 Arg2-role

The arg2-role corresponds to the deep direct object. It can be realised as the direct object like in (2a). In (2a) the argument is an NP, but it can also be a subordinate clause (see 2b) or an infinitival clause (see (2c)). The arg2-role can be realised as the subject if the clause is unaccusative (see (2d)), or if the clause has passive voice (see (2e)). Like the arg1-role, the arg2-role can also be realised as an infinitival marker (see (2f)).

(2) a. John admires **Mary**.
    b. John claims **that he didn't sleep**.
    c. John tries **to smile**.
    d. **The man** came.
    e. **John** is admired.
    f. John tries **to** come.

1 See `http://www.hf.ntnu.no/hf/isk/Ansatte/petter.haugereid/norsyg.html` for a short description of the grammar and download instructions.

2 A mechanism for arriving at the correct word order is implemented in Norsyg, but it will not be discussed in this paper.

2.3 Arg3-role

The arg3-role corresponds to the deep indirect object. It can be realised as the indirect object, like in (3a). It can be realised as the subject if the clause has passive voice (see (3b)). It can also be realised as the infinitival marker if the infinitival clause has passive voice (see (3c)).

(3) a. John gave **Mary** flowers.
b. **Mary** was given flowers.
c. Mary hoped **to** be given flowers.

2.4 Arg4-role

The arg4-role corresponds to so-called delimiters, that is, arguments that typically say where the arg2-role ends up. The arg4-role can be realised as a resultative like in (4a) and (4b) or a end-of-path like in (4c).[3]

(4) a. The lecture bored the students **to death**.
b. John drank the glass **empty**.
c. John threw the stone **into the water**.

2.5 Arg5-role

The arg5-role corresponds to PP arguments that serve as a precondition to the event. It can be a source as in (5a) or an instrument as in (5b). The distinction between arguments that precede the event (what here is referred to as the arg5-role) and arguments that follow the event (the arg4-role) can also be found in (Croft, 1991, 183-240).

(5) a. Water dripped **from the roof**.
b. John painted the wall **with a big brush**.

2.6 Constellations of argument roles

Argument frames are assumed to be constellations of argument roles. The argument frame of an unergative intransitive verb like *sleep* consists of only one argument *arg1*, and it is called an *arg1-frame* (see 1a). The argument frame of a transitive verb like *admire* consists of an arg1-role and an arg2-role, and is called an *arg12-frame* (see 2a). An unaccusative verb like *come* has only an arg2-role, and so its argument frame is an *arg2-frame* (see 2d). A ditransitive frame is

3 There can be only one delimiter. Consider, for instance:

(i) a. John kicked the ball flat.
b. John kicked the ball flat out of the room.

In (ia), *flat* is ambiguous. It can be interpreted both as a resultative or as an adjunct. In (ib), *flat* can only have one reading, namely as an adjunct. That is because an end-of-path *out of the room* is added. See also (Winkler, 1997, 375) for similar observations.

called an *arg123-frame* (see 3a), and a transitive frame with a delimiter is called an *arg124-frame* (see e.g. 4a). It is also possible to have no argument roles, as illustrated with *rain* in (6), where the subject is an expletive. This argument frame is called an *arg0-frame*.

(6) It rains.

2.7 The valence mechanism

Instead of the valence features that are used in HPSG (see Figure 1), valence features for each of the argument roles are assumed, as illustrated in Figure 2.[4] In HPSG, subcategorization information is specified on the valence lists. The subject of a verb is on the SUBJ list and the complements are on the COMPS list. Lexical entries of verbs have detailed information about the syntactic arguments and how these arguments are linked to the verb semantically. Verb alternations are accounted for by means of multiple lexical entries or lexical rules. The arguments are canceled off as they are realized. That means that at sentence level, the valence lists are empty.

Instead of having valence features that reflect the surface function of the arguments (SUBJ and COMPS), valence features that reflect the "deep" function of the arguments are assumed in this approach, where ARG1 is the initiator, ARG2 is the undergoer, ARG3 is the beneficiary and ARG4 is the delimiter. The values of the different ARG-features in this approach are *synsem*'s, that is, structures with syntactic and semantic information (Pollard and Sag, 1994, 15-21). A feature LINK is added that tells whether an argument is realized or not.

valence	
SUBJ	*list*
SPR	*list*
COMPS	*list*
SPEC	*list*

Figure 1
valence in HPSG

valence	
VAL-TYPE	*link*
ARG1 | LINK	*link*
ARG2 | LINK	*link*
ARG3 | LINK	*link*
ARG4 | LINK	*link*

Figure 2
New valence features

Verbs are specified with regard to what argument frame they have via the feature VAL-TYPE (see Figure 2). The transitive verb *admire* is given the VAL-TYPE value *arg12*, as illustrated in Figure 3. Note that the arg2-role of *admire* is constrained to be a nominal via the ARG2 feature.

Some verbs like *eat* are compatible with more than one argument frame. *eat* can be both transitive as in (7a) (*arg12-frame*) and unergative intransitive as

4 The arg5-role is not displayed here, and will not be discussed further in this paper.

$$\begin{bmatrix} \textsc{stem} \left\langle \textit{admire} \right\rangle \\ \textsc{synsem} \mid \textsc{loc} \begin{bmatrix} \textsc{cat} \mid \textsc{val} \begin{bmatrix} \textsc{val-type}\ \textit{arg12} \\ \textsc{arg2} \mid \textsc{local} \mid \textsc{cat} \mid \textsc{head}\ \textit{nominal} \end{bmatrix} \\ \textsc{cont} \mid \textsc{rels} \left\langle \begin{bmatrix} \textsc{pred}\ \textit{\_admire\_v\_rel} \end{bmatrix} \right\rangle \end{bmatrix} \end{bmatrix}$$

Figure 3
Lexical entry of *admire*

in (7b) (*arg1-frame*). These verbs are given VAL-TYPE values that reflect what argument frames they can appear in. In the case of *eat* the VAL-TYPE value is *arg1-12*. I will come back to these cases in Section 3.4.

(7) a. John eats fish.
    b. John eats.

3 Syntax

Four classes of rules make up the basis of the syntactic analysis:

- Valence rules:

  — Binary valence rules: Realize arguments in their canonical position.
  — Extraction valence rules: Extract arguments that are realized by the head filler rule.
  — Unary valence rules: Realize the unexpressed subject. Apply to functional elements such as infinitival markers and imperative morphology.

- Force rules. Apply at the top of the tree. Categorize the clause as a proposition, question or command, and check that all the arguments are realized.

- Head filler rule. Applies at the bottom of the tree. Realizes the element on the SLASH list as its first daughter.

- Merge rule. Combines the projection that realizes the subject (the left branch) with a non-finite verbal category.

3.1 Valence rules

There are four realizations of each of the valence rules above (except for the unary rules), one for each of the argument roles. The arg1 binary rule is illustrated in Figure 4.[5]

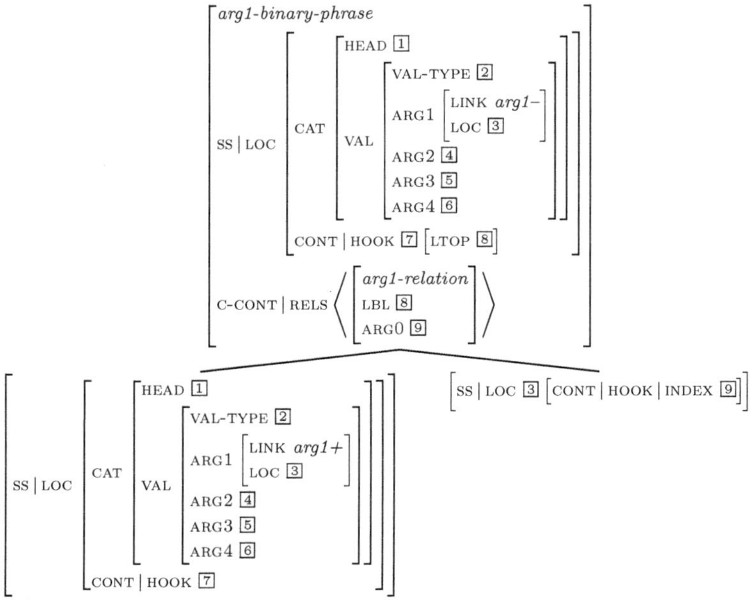

Figure 4
Arg1 binary rule

The rule in Figure 4 shows how the ARG1|LINK value is switched from a positive value in the head daughter *arg1+* to a negative value in the mother *arg1−*. All the other valence features are copied up. The rule also introduces a Parsons-style[6] arg1-relation in C-CONT|RELS that links the non-head daughter to the LTOP of the head projection. C-CONT stands for constructional content, and relations that enter the C-CONT|RELS list are included in the semantic composition. The arg2, arg3 and arg4 binary rules are similar to the arg1 binary rule, except that

5 I refer to instantiations of phrase types as *rules* and to phrase types as *phrases*
6 (Parsons, 1990) gives the following logical form for 'Brutus stabs Caesar':

$$(\forall e)[Stabbing(e)\&Subject(e, Brutus)\&Object(e, Caesar)]$$

where the form

$$(\forall e)[Stabbing(e, Brutus, Caesar)]$$

is given an underlying event analysis. The event variable e binds the three subevents together. Instead of using the event variable to bind the subevents together, I follow (Copestake, 2003) and use the labels of the subevents to tie them together.

corresponding LINK values are switched and corresponding Parsons-style relations are introduced.

The valence extraction rules are similar to the binary rules except that the argument is not realized as the non-head daughter, but inserted into the SLASH list of the head daughter. An abbreviated version of the arg1 extraction rule is given in Figure 5.

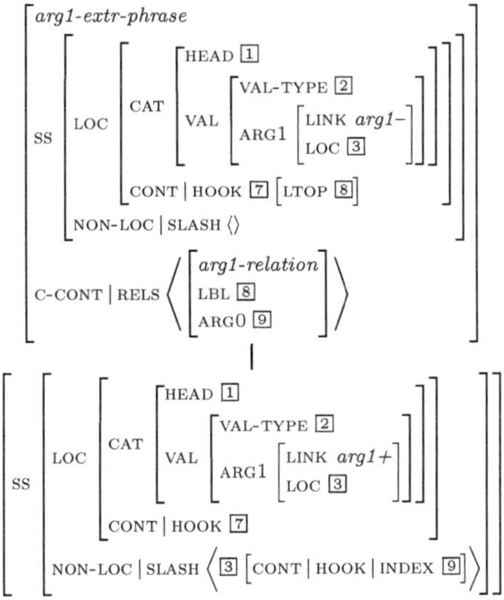

Figure 5
Arg1 extraction rule

By doing linking with Parsons-style semantics as illustrated here, it is possible to underspecify the arity of the semantic predicate. It will be the syntactic rules that in the end determine the number of semantic arguments, since the semantic arguments directly correspond to the syntactic rules. If the verb *eat* occurs in a transitive clause as in (7a), the number of semantic arguments will be two, as illustrated in (8a). If *eat* occurs in an intransitive frame (see (7b)), the number of arguments will be one, as illustrated in (8b).

(8) a.

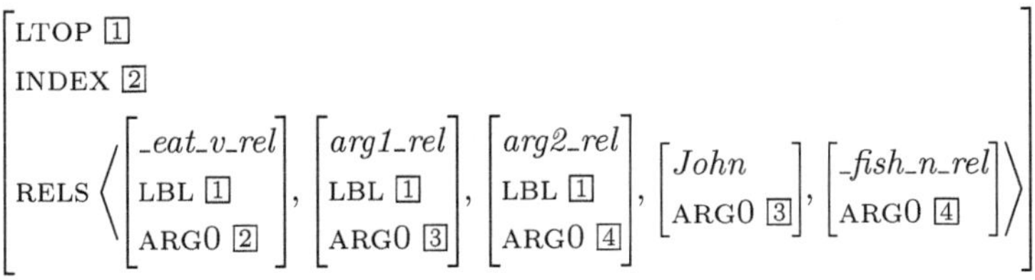

b. $\begin{bmatrix} \text{LTOP } \boxed{1} \\ \text{INDEX } \boxed{2} \\ \text{RELS } \left\langle \begin{bmatrix} \textit{\_eat\_v\_rel} \\ \text{LBL } \boxed{1} \\ \text{ARG0 } \boxed{2} \end{bmatrix}, \begin{bmatrix} \textit{arg1\_rel} \\ \text{LBL } \boxed{1} \\ \text{ARG0 } \boxed{3} \end{bmatrix}, \begin{bmatrix} \textit{John} \\ \text{ARG0 } \boxed{3} \end{bmatrix} \right\rangle \end{bmatrix}$

As is shown in (8), the argument relations are linked to the predicate via the LBL of the relation. The semantic representations are called RMRSs (see (Copestake, 2003)). An approach that does linking in the syntax has an advantage to approaches that do linking in the lexicon, since the latter approaches must specify precisely in the lexical entries how many semantic arguments they have, and so there is no room for underspecification.

3.2 Force rules

Force rules are unary rules that apply at the top of the sentence and mark the sentence as a proposition, question or command. All the valence features of the daughter are constrained to have a negative LINK value, and the SLASH list is constrained to be empty. This is illustrated for the yes-no force rule in Figure 6.

$$\begin{bmatrix} \textit{yes-no-phrase} \\ \text{SS} \mid \text{LOC} \begin{bmatrix} \text{CAT} \mid \text{HEAD } \boxed{1} \\ \text{CONT} \mid \text{HOOK } \boxed{2} \begin{bmatrix} \text{INDEX} \mid \text{MESSAGE } \textit{yes-no-ques\_m\_rel} \end{bmatrix} \end{bmatrix} \end{bmatrix}$$

$$\Big|$$

$$\begin{bmatrix} \text{SS} \begin{bmatrix} \text{LOC} \begin{bmatrix} \text{CAT} \begin{bmatrix} \text{HEAD } \boxed{1} \\ \text{VAL} \begin{bmatrix} \text{ARG1} \mid \text{LINK } \textit{arg1–} \\ \text{ARG2} \mid \text{LINK } \textit{arg2–} \\ \text{ARG3} \mid \text{LINK } \textit{arg3–} \\ \text{ARG4} \mid \text{LINK } \textit{arg4–} \end{bmatrix} \end{bmatrix} \\ \text{CONT} \mid \text{HOOK } \boxed{2} \end{bmatrix} \\ \text{NON-LOC} \mid \text{SLASH } \langle\rangle \end{bmatrix} \end{bmatrix}$$

Figure 6
Yes-no force rule

3.3 Head filler rule

The head filler rule applies at the bottom of the tree. This differs from the general assumption that the head filler rule applies at the top of the tree. It is the fact that the extraction rule always dominates the head filler rule that makes it possible to have the head filler rule at the bottom of the tree.[7] The extraction rule enters the extracted element into the SLASH list of the daughter, as I showed in Figure

7 The fact that the the head filler rule is at the bottom of the tree, and not at the top, is not relevant for my analysis of passive, so I will not go further into the reasons why I have chosen this analysis here.

4. It is then copied from mother to head daughter until it reaches the head filler rule that fills it in. The head filler rule is illustrated in Figure 7.

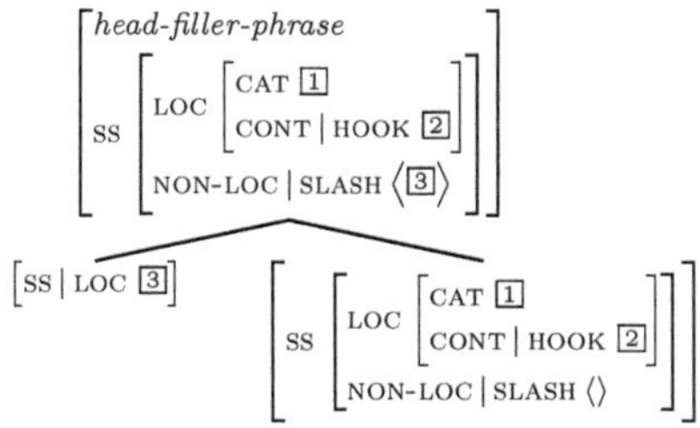

Figure 7
Head filler rule

Since Norwegian is a V2 language, I assume that the constituent before the finite verb in a main clause is extracted and filled in by the head filler rule. This also holds for the subject of the main clause.[8] So the analysis of an intransitive sentence becomes like the one in Figure 8.[9]

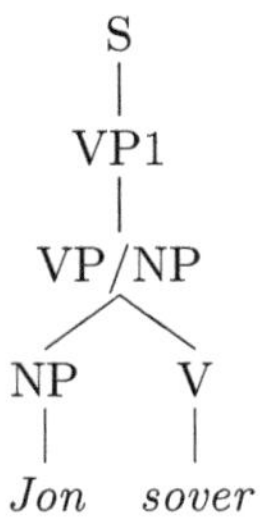

Figure 8
Analysis of *Jon sover* ('Jon sleeps')

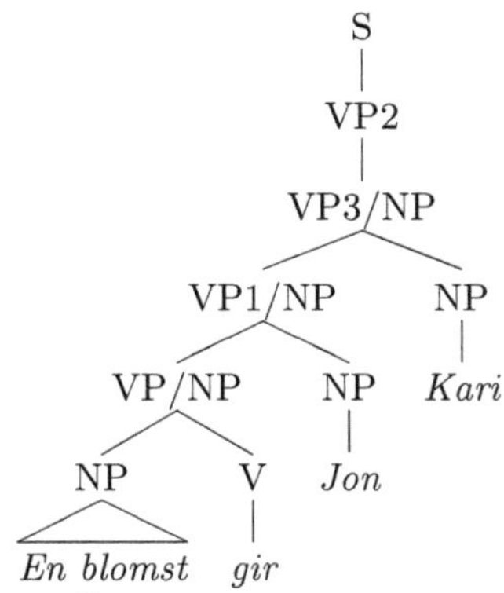

Figure 9
Analysis of *En blomst gir Jon Kari* ('A flower Jon gives Kari')

In Figure 8 the top unary rule (S) is the main clause force rule. The second rule (VP1) is the arg1 extraction rule, which inserts the extracted argument into the SLASH list of its daughter. The third rule (VP/NP) is the head filler rule which fills in the extracted subject.

8 A similar procedure is discussed in (Pollard and Sag, 1994, 381) and is applied for Norwegian in (Ellingsen, 2003).
9 The use of integers in the labels of the tree are there to show that an argument role has been realized by a rule. So the node VP1 indicates that the phrase has head value verb and that it realizes the arg1-role.

Figure 9 shows the analysis of a ditransitive sentence where the direct object is topicalized. The topicalized element is inserted into the SLASH list by the arg2 extraction rule (VP2), and transported down the tree until the head filler rule (VP/NP) fills it in.

3.4 The valence mechanism

In order to achieve that a verb only occurs in the appropriate argument frames, a type hierarchy of linking types is introduced. Figure 10 illustrates how argument frame types are subtypes of certain constellations of LINK values. The top types in the hierarchy (*arg1+*, *arg1–*, *arg2+*, *arg2–*, *arg3+*, *arg3–*, *arg4+* and *arg4–*) are possible LINK values. They say whether an argument is realized or not. If an arg1 rule and an arg2 rule have applied in a clause, the LINK values of the head word of the clause projection will have the LINK values *arg1+*, *arg2+*, *arg3–*, and *arg4–*. These values are unified in the head word and unified with the VAL-TYPE value. As the hierarchy in Figure 10 shows, the greatest lower bound of *arg1+*, *arg2+*, *arg3–*, and *arg4–* is *arg12*, and if this type is not compatible with the VAL-TYPE value of the main verb, the parse fails. As I showed in Figure 3, the transitive verb *admire* has the VAL-TYPE value *arg12*.

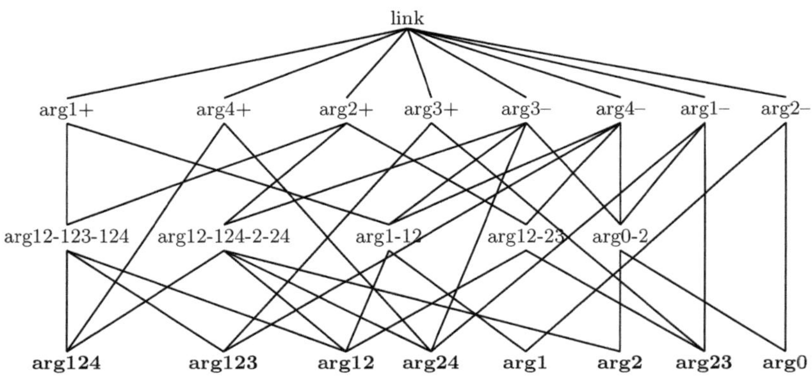

Figure 10
The *link* hierarchy

The bottom types in Figure 10 are possible argument frames. The hierarchy also has a number of intermediate types. These are designed for verbs that can enter more than one argument frame. The type *arg1-12* for example has two subtypes, *arg1* and *arg12*. This means that a verb like *eat*, that is specified with *arg1-12* as value of VAL-TYPE, will be compatible with both the arg1 frame and the arg12 frame.

The tree in Figure 11 illustrates in detail how the LINK values end up in the head word. Here the head word is the verb *beundrer* ('admires'). The tree also shows how the linking relations are introduced, and how they connect the predicate to the arguments.

3.5 Merge rule

In the approach suggested in this paper, the main verb of the clause is not necessarily the head word of the clause. In a subordinate clause the complementizer will be the head word and in a main clause with an auxiliary, the finite auxiliary will be the head word. The function of the main verb in these cases will be to give the head projection its valence requirements. This is done in a rule called *merge rule* which copies the valence requirements of the non-head daughter onto the head projection. The *merge rule* is illustrated in Figure 12.

In the merge rule the value of VAL in the second daughter is unified with the VAL values of the first daughter and the mother. This ensures that the head projection gets the valence requirements of the main verb. The merge rule makes use of a feature MERGE. This feature lets auxiliaries constrain the tense of the verbal constituent that they combine with.

The first daughter serves as the syntactic head of the rule (the rule is head-initial), while the second daughter serves as the semantic head. The HOOK (that is, the LTOP and the INDEX) of the second daughter is unified with the HOOK of the mother. The merge rule takes as its first daughter a constituent that has realized the subject, and as its second daughter a verbal category that conforms with the tense requirements of the first daughter. This is exemplified in Figure 13.

In Figure 13 the auxiliary *har* ('has') is the head word. The subject is realized by the arg1 extraction rule (AUXP1) in combination with the head filler rule (AUXP/NP) before the main verb is combined with the head projection by the merge rule (AUXP). The main verb transfers its valence requirements to the head projection and ensures that a proper argument frame is generated.

4 Passive

In this section I will show how the arg1-role can be expressed as passive voice. I follow the assumption of (Jaeggli, 1986), (Baker, 1988) and (Åfarli, 1992) that there is an element PASS. But instead of assuming that this element is a verb internal argument, I assume that it is a syntactic element that has two realizations in Norwegian, namely as a passive auxiliary *bli* (*bli-passive*) and as an *s*-morpheme that is attached to the finite main verb (*s-passive*). A constructional approach to passive is also suggested in (Åfarli, 2006). First I will present some data.

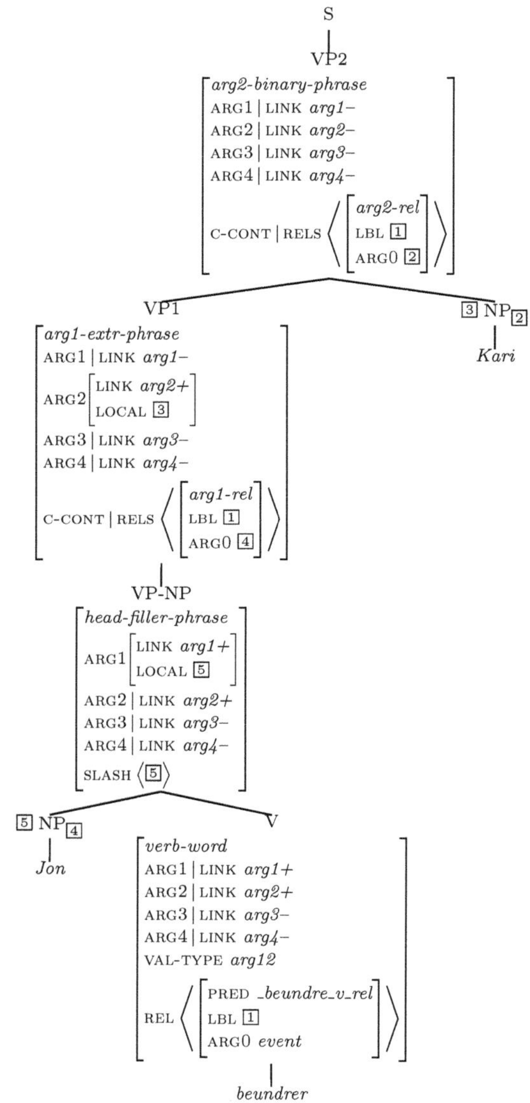

Figure 11
Transitive main clause

4.1 Data

In Norwegian there are two kinds of passive, periphrastic passive (*bli*-passive) and morphological passive (*s*-passive). The periphrastic passive uses the auxiliary *bli*,

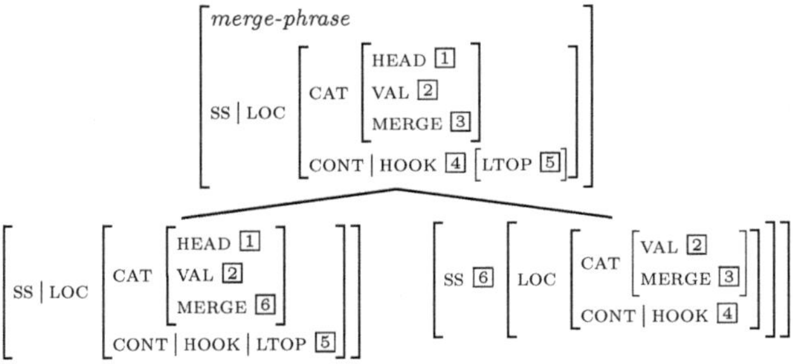

Figure 12
Merge rule

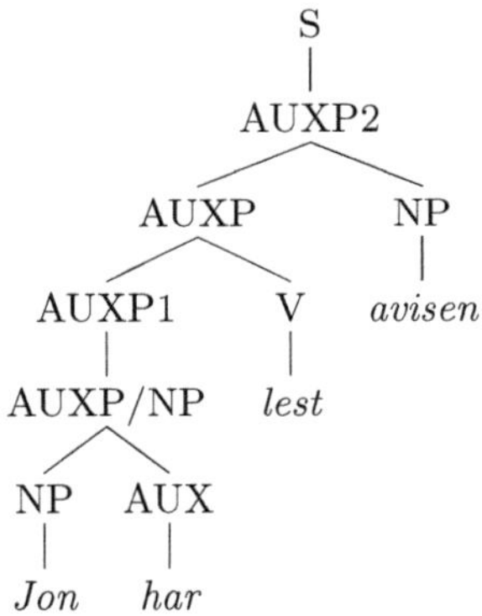

Figure 13
Analysis of *Jon har lest avisen* ('Jon has read the newspaper')

(see (9b)), and the morphological passive attaches the suffix *-s* to the finite main verb (see (9c)). There is a slight semantic distinction between the two forms, which I will not go into (see (Hovdhaugen, 1977, 35-39), (Engdahl, 2001) and (Engdahl, 2006)). The data I present here are well known in the literature (see e.g. (Hovdhaugen, 1977) and (Åfarli, 1992)).

(9) a. En spiller smasher ballen.
a player smashes ball-DEF
'A player smashes the ball.'

b. Ballen blir smashet.
ball-DEF becomes smashed
'The ball is smashed.'

c. Ballen smashes.
ball-DEF smash-PASS
'The ball is smashed.'

In the examples (9b) and (9c), the subject (*Ballen*) would have been the direct object if the sentences were active. In (10), the three passive variants of the active clause *Jon gir Marit en is* (Jon gives Marit an ice cream) are given.[10]

(10) a. Marit blir gitt en is.
Marit becomes given an ice-cream
'Marit is given an ice cream.'

b. En is blir gitt Marit.
an ice-cream becomes given Marit
'Marit is given an ice cream.'

c. Det blir gitt Marit en is.
it becomes given Marit an ice-cream
'Marit is given an ice cream.'

In (10a) what would have been the indirect object in an active clause is the subject. In (10b) what would have been the direct object in active is the subject, and in (10c) the expletive *det* is the subject.

4.2 The passive types

The passive auxiliary is assumed to be different from other words that may be the head word of a clause, in that it does not unify the LINK values in VAL, but rather in a feature called FIRST-VAL. The auxiliary is assumed to introduce an arg1-relation in the same fashion as for example the arg1 binary rule (see Figure 4). The auxiliary does however not have a head daughter to relate its valence features to. (In the arg1 binary rule the ARG1|LINK value is switched from *arg1−* in the mother to *arg1+* in the head daughter.) Instead the passive auxiliary relates its valence features to FIRST-VAL as shown in Figure 14.[11] If the passive auxiliary is the head word of the projection, the LINK values are unified in FIRST-VAL.

The *s-pass-word*, is an inflectional rule that adds an *s*-morpheme to main verbs.

Since the passive auxiliary and the passive inflection absorb the arg1-role of the verb, the subject must be realized by an element that does *not* have the arg1-role.[12]

10 The examples in (10) have *s*-passive counterparts.
11 The reason for having the FIRST-VAL feature in HEAD is that it will then be accessible to the merge rule in case the auxiliary is *not* the head word of the clause. In the implemented grammar it is the FIRST-VAL feature and not the VAL feature that is copied from the non-head daughter to the head daughter in the merge rule. But for expository reasons I have not shown that in the analyses given here.
12 It has been brought to my attention that in Yucatec Maya the verb corresponding to *learn* may have

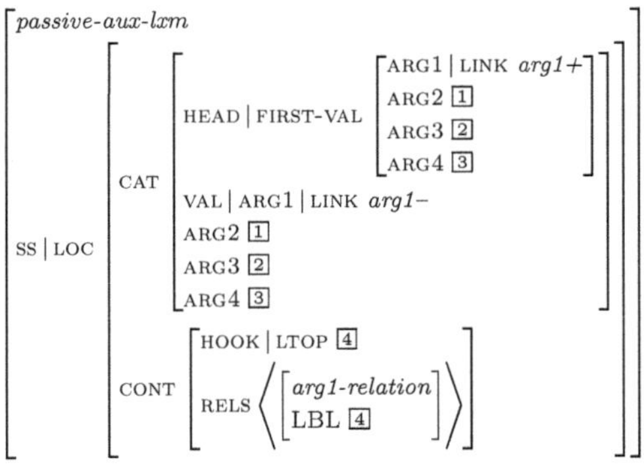

Figure 14
The *passive-aux-lxm* type

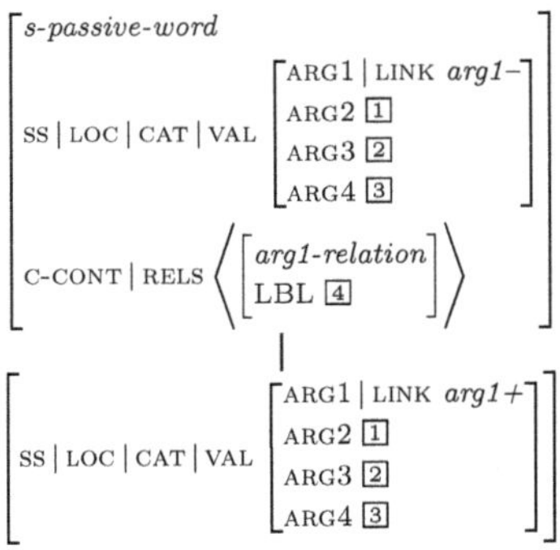

Figure 15
The *s-passive-word* type

4.3 Analysis

The tree in Figure 16 shows in detail how linking is done in a passive transitive clause with the auxiliary *bli*. There are two different signs that do linking in the tree. The passive auxiliary (AUX1) adds an *arg1-relation* and shifts the *arg1–* link type in VAL to *arg1+* in FIRST-VAL. This ensures that the arg1-role is realized.

---

the following chain of suffixes: V – PASS – CAUS – PASS, and that the meaning corresponds to *being taught*, as illustrated in (i) (see (Müller, To appear 2006)). A possible approach to such examples would be to assume that there are two argument frames, one for the learning predicate and one for the causative morpheme, and that the two passive morphemes each realize an arg1-role.

(i) k=u ká`an -s -á`al le teòria-o`
INCOMPL=3.ERG learn.PASS -CAUS -PASS.IMPF Det theory-D1

'The theory is being taught.'

(Somebody causes that the theory is being learned)

The arg2-extr-phrase (AUX2) adds an *arg2-relation* that it links to the extracted *local* and shifts the *arg2–* link type in the mother to *arg2+* in the daughter. This realizes the arg2-role. The tree shows how all the link types *arg1+*, *arg2+*, *arg3–* and *arg4–* end up in the FIRST-VAL of the auxiliary. The tree does not show that the types are unified, since that would make the illustration more difficult to follow. When the types are unified, we get the type *arg12*, exactly like in the active counterpart in Figure 11.

5 Conclusion

I have presented a constructional approach to syntax where different constellations of five syntactic argument roles are assumed to constitute argument structure frames. This, together with a hierarchy of *link* types (see Figure 10) has made it possible to give packed representations of possible argument frames of verbs without the use of lexical rules or multiple lexical entries. The assumption that *passive* is a syntactic element also has made it possible to account for passive without the use of multiple lexical specifications.

References

Åfarli, Tor. 1992. *The Syntax of Norwegian Passive Constructions.* Amsterdam: Benjamins.

Åfarli, Tor. 2003. Har verbet argumentstruktur? *Motskrift*, 2:87–99.

Åfarli, Tor. 2006. Passive and argument structure. *Passivization and Typology, Form and Function*, pages 373–382.

Baker, Mark C. 1988. *Incorporation. A Theory of Grammatical Function Changing.* The University of Chicago Press.

Borer, Hagit. 2005a. *Structuring Sense. An Exo-Skeletal Triology. Volume I. In Name Only.* Oxford University Press.

Borer, Hagit. 2005b. *Structuring Sense. An Exo-Skeletal Triology. Volume II. The Normal Course of Events.* Oxford University Press.

Copestake, Ann. 2003. Report on the design of rmrs (preliminary version). Technical report, Cambridge, April 11,.

Croft, William. 1991. *Syntactic Categories and Grammatical Relations.* Chicago.

Ellingsen, Liv. 2003. Norwegian word order in head-driven phrase structure grammar. phenomena, analysis, and implementation. Master's thesis, Institutt for Lingvistiske Fag, Universitetet i Oslo.

Engdahl, Elisabet. 2001. Scandinavian passives in hpsg. In A. Holmer, J-O. Svantesson, and Å. Viberg, editors, *Proceedings of the 18th Scandinavian Conference of Linguistics*, pages 23–36, Lund. Universitetstryckeriet.

Engdahl, Elisabet. 2006. Semantic and syntactic patterns in swedish passives. *Demoting the Agent. Passive, middle and other voice phenomena*, pages 21–45.

Hovdhaugen, Even. 1977. Om og omkring passiv i norsk. In Thorstein Fretheim, editor, *Sentrale problemer i norsk syntaks.* Universitetsforlaget, pages 15–46.

Jaeggli, Osvaldo. 1986. Passive. *Linguistic Inquiry*, 17:587–622.

Müller, Stefan. To appear 2006. Phrasal or lexical constructions? *Language*, 82(4).

Parsons, Terence. 1990. *Events in the Semantics of English. A Study of Subatomic Semantics.* Current Studies in Linguistics Series, volume 19. Cambridge, MA: MIT Press.

Pollard, Carl J. and Ivan A. Sag. 1994. *Head-Driven Phrase Structure Grammar.* Chicago: University of Chicago Press.

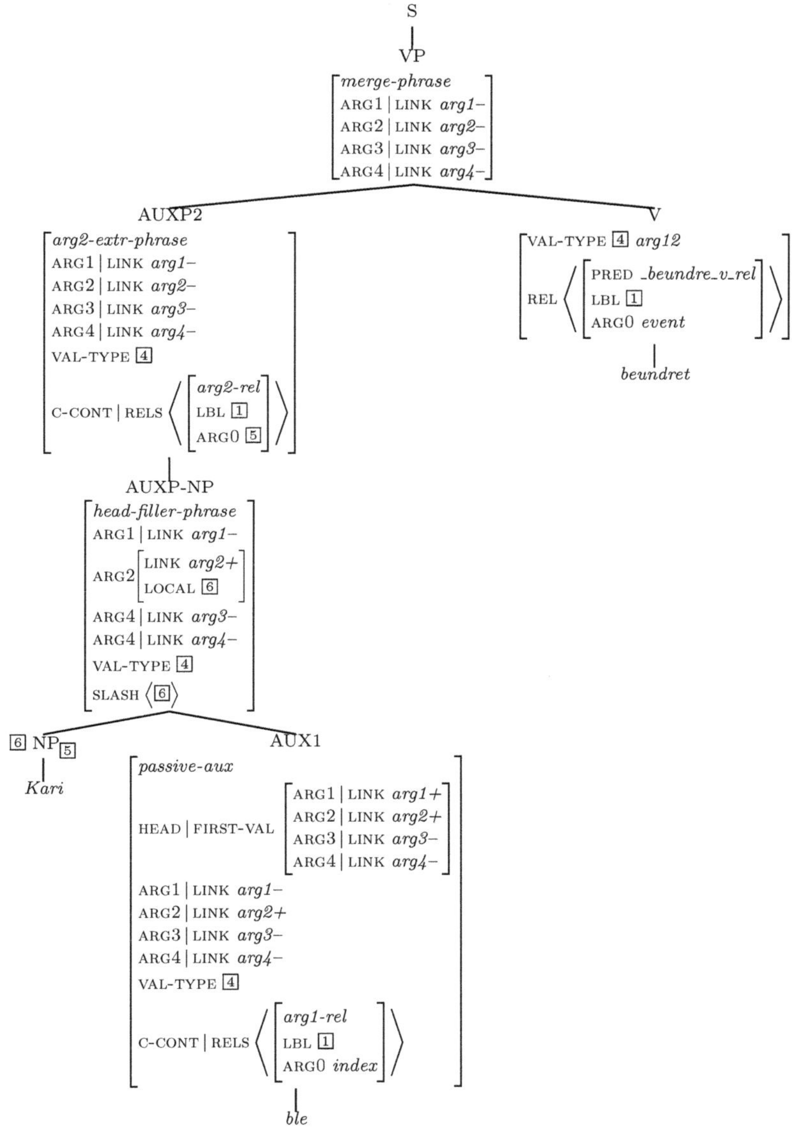

Figure 16
Transitive main clause with periphrastic passive

Winkler, Susanne. 1997. *Focus and Secondary Predication.* Berlin and New York: Mouton de Gruyter.

Ontology-based question answering with feature structures

Patrizia Paggio
Dorte Halstrup Hansen
Lene Offersgaard
University of Copenhagen*

Abstract

This paper describes the Danish grammar resources developed within the European project MOSES (Modular and Scalable Environment for the Semantic Web). In particular we discuss the way in which the Danish feature structure grammar developed previously by means of the LKB platform has been adapted to work in the MOSES application, and how the PET parser used to run the grammar was modified to function in the MOSES architecture. The approach taken in MOSES is unique in its integration of deep processing with domain knowledge representation. We conclude that feature structures are an adequate means of expressing the necessary relations between linguistic and ontological knowledge in the type system, the grammar rules and the lexicon.

1 Natural language processing and question answering in the MOSES project

The objective of MOSES was to develop an ontology-based methodology to create, maintain and search semantically structured Web contents in a federation of sites (Atzeni et al., 2004) (Paggio et al., 2004). The methodology has been implemented in a test bed consisting of an agent-based knowledge management system and an ontology-based search engine for the Web sites of the two European universities of Roma Tre and Copenhagen.

The use of natural language processing is an important aspect of MOSES in that it provides the system with an intuitive and user-friendly interface. Conversely, MOSES constitutes a non-traditional and challenging application for natural language processing for several reasons. First of all, although it can be seen as a question answering (QA) application from the point of view of the interaction with the user, MOSES differs from classical QA systems, see e.g. (Moldovan and

* University of Copenhagen, Centre for Language Technology, Njalsgade 80, DK-2300 Copenhagen S, Denmark. Email: {patrizia|dorte|loff}@cst.dk

Surdenau, 2003), because it is ontology-based and relies on the topic maps formalism (Garshol, 2003) for the representation of Web contents. This means that the linguistic components, instead of looking for answers in texts as is customary in QA, must interface to the topic maps knowledge structure both in question analysis and answer generation.

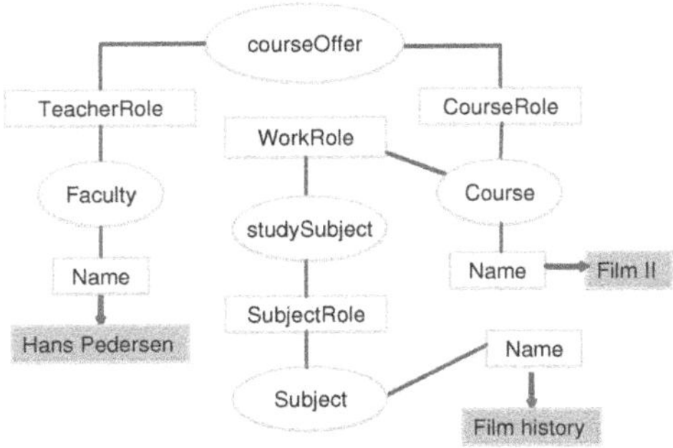

Figure 1
A topic map example

An example of topic map is shown in Figure (1). It consists of three different relations, or associations[1] as they are called in topic maps, that combine occurrences of the three classes *Faculty*, *Course* and *Subject*. In the MOSES system, topic map occurrences covering a good portion of the people, courses and research activities at the two universities are represented in the knowledge base by using the XTM topic map language. A topic map may often be a very complex and rich structure consisting of a large number of associations, and the XML code will be quite difficult for a human to decipher. Therefore, being able to transform the information contained in a topic map into natural language output is quite an important task. Likewise, it is important to query the topic map knowledge base in such a way that only the information that is relevant to the user question – often a fraction of an entire topic map – is retrieved.

Figure (2) illustrates how question answering is carried out at the level of a single MOSES site. The user's questions are analysed and a semantic representation of their content is sent to the content matcher, which after further processing sends the query to the knowledge base. The relevant topic maps are extracted and returned to the answer generator, which renders them in the form of an answer in natural language. The figure also shows that both question analysis and generation are equipped with lexical and ontological resources. In fact, their domain ontology is a copy of the ontology that constitutes the backbone of the knowledge structure, and the ontology drives both analysis and generation processes. We see

1 Topic map associations are n-ary, and have named arguments.

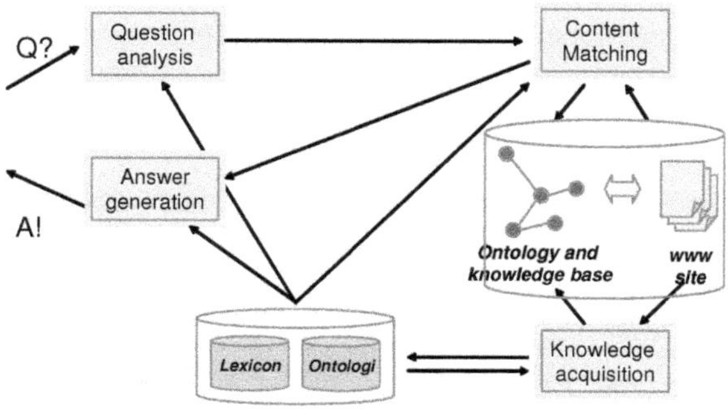

Figure 2
Ontology-based question answering in MOSES

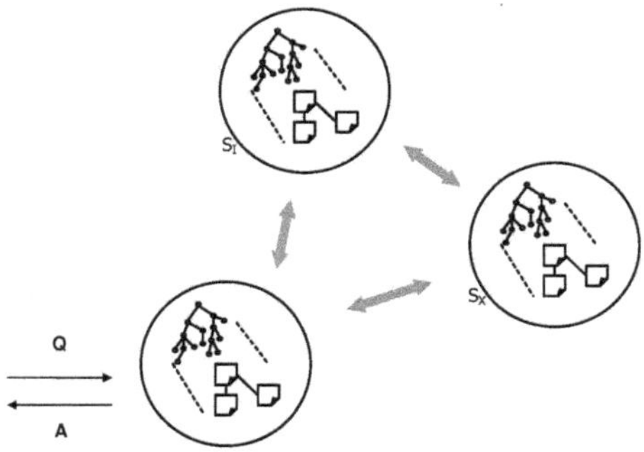

Figure 3
Ontology-based question answering in a federation of sites

the tight integration between domain ontology and deep linguistic processing, together with the interaction with topic maps, as interesting and unique features of natural language processing in MOSES.

Another challenge related to natural language in the project is multilinguality, with the added complexity of a distributed environment in which different ontological views of the domain have to be accommodated.

Figure (3) illustrates the MOSES federated scenario, which is made up of several sites, each equipped with a local version of the domain ontology and with specialised natural language components. The distributed approach has the advantage of making it possible for MOSES to integrate nodes (i.e. different sites, different knowedge bases and different language interfaces) where QA processing is carried out following quite different linguistic styles, and using different software tools, provided the semantic representations produced by the analyser and accepted by the generator can be interfaced with the topic maps formalism. A pre-requisite for this is that natural language components and knowledge structure share the same ontology at the local level. The treatment of different natural languages has been tested in the project by developing components for Danish and Italian.

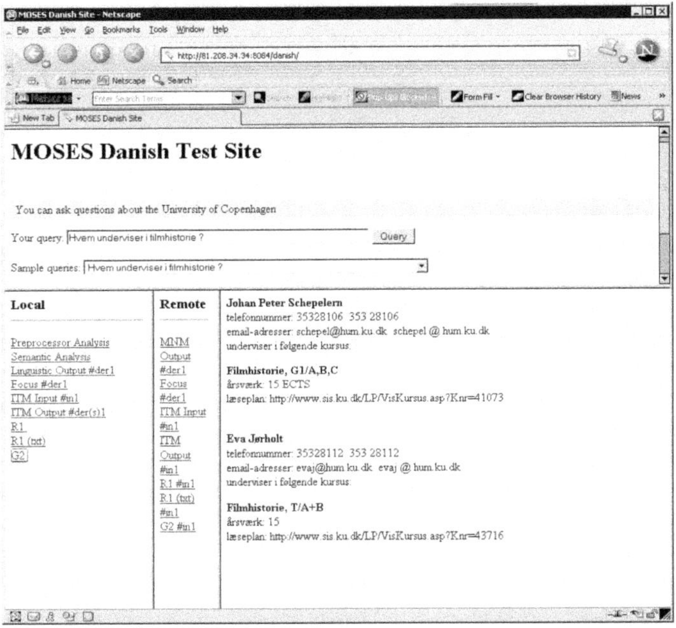

Figure 4
The MOSES prototype

Figure (4) is a screen dump of the Danish MOSES prototype, an experimental interface where the user – here the MOSES developer – can ask questions in Danish and inspect the system's results. In the lower left part of the screen are gathered the intermediate results produced by the Danish linguistic preprocessing tools and parser, as well as the XML query generated by the content matcher. The lower middle section is reserved to results from the remote (Italian) site. Finally, the lower right part contains the answer in Danish

In the rest of the paper, we deal with the requirements to the language interfaces (Section 2); we then go through the methodology applied in question analysis, with particular focus on the treatment of Danish, where feature structures play a central role (Section 3); and finally we discuss issues related to evaluation and system development, including our treatment of unknown words (Section 4).

2 Requirements to question analysis

The requirements posed to question analysis in MOSES include structural as well as linguistic aspects. Whereas the former concern the type of navigation that a question answering framework would be able to replace, the latter have to do with syntactic form as well as content. In this paper we are only concerned with linguistic requirements.

Prospective users were asked to construct questions that dealt with university employees, courses and research activities. Paraphrases of these questions were then added by the system's developers to enlarge the coverage, and the questions were then classified. A classification of question types often quoted in the QA literature is that in (Lauer, Peacock, and Graesser, 1992), which mainly builds on speech act theory. Another influential, more syntactically-oriented approach is (Harabagiu et al., 2001), where to each syntactic category correspond one or several possible answer types, or focuses (a person, a date, a name etc.). Our approach builds on the same idea, with the added dimension that the focus has to correspond to an ontological class. From the point of view of the linguistic analysis, therefore, both syntactic category and ontological content are the central dimensions of sentence classification.

Syntactic categories are e.g. yes/no questions, what-questions, who-questions etc. Subtypes relate to the position inside the question where the focus is expressed, e.g. depending on whether the wh-pronoun is a determiner, or the main verb is a copula. The content consists of the classes and relations from the ontology that the question instantiates, the focus class constraint, and a count feature indicating the number of instances to be retrieved. An example of classification is shown in Table 1.

Sentence 1	Who teaches film history?
Content	Focus: Faculty Count: all courseOffer(Faculty,Course) studySubject(Course,Subject: *film history*)
Form 1	Hvem underviser i filmhistorie?
Syntactic type Subtype	Hvem (Who) non-copula verb
Form 2	Hvem afholder kurser i filmhistorie?
Syntactic type Subtype	Hvem (Who) non-copula verb

Table 1
Question classification example

3 Question analysis

Question analysis is carried out in the MOSES linguistic module associated with each system language. No constraints are posed on how the conceptual representation should be produced, nor on the format of the output of each linguistic module. However, the building blocks of the linguistic output must be the classes, instances and relations of the corresponding ontology. The output is transformed into an XML query understandable to the knowledge base by the content matcher. Two independent modules have been developed for Danish and Italian language analysis. They have a similar architecture (both use preprocessing, i.e. POS-tagging and lemmatising, prior to syntactic and semantic analyses), but specific parsers. In the Italian analyser the syntactic parser produces quasi-logical forms (Basili and Zanzotto, 2002) that are then provided an interpretation by means of the LASIE interpreter (Humphreys et al., 1998). On the other hand the Danish parser, an adapted version of PET (Callmeier, 2000), produces for each input sentence a set of typed feature structures corresponding to all the possible semantic interpretations of the question. In other words, although syntactic and semantic analysis are tightly integrated in the grammar as is customary for contraint-based grammars inspired by the HPSG paradigm, e.g. (Flickinger, 2000), only the semantic information is retained in the output. Both representation types have proven adequate to express the desired conceptual content.

To understand how the relation between lexical and grammatical knowledge on the one hand, and conceptual knowledge on the other, is exploited in the linguistic analysis, let us consider an example:

IT: Chi insegna il corso sulla storia del cinema?
DA: Hvem underviser i filmhistorie?
(Who teaches film history?)

Informally, the content of the Italian and Danish questions, both roughly equivalent to the English translation in parentheses, can be summarised as being about three classes of objects: one or more unknown teachers (belonging to the *Faculty* class), one or more courses and a course subject with name "film history". The three objects are related to each other by relations, so that the teachers teach the courses, and the courses have as their subject "film history". Furthermore, in both questions we are interested in finding all the relevant teachers. Since the Danish and Italian ontologies provide slightly different views of the university domain, and use different names for classes and relations, the semantic representations constructed by the two natural language analysers differ somewhat. The formalisms in which these representations are couched are also, as was mentioned earlier, not the same. However, both will be made up of the same semantic blocks, i.e. variables and a number of class, relation and value constraints over the variables.

3.1 Representing the content of questions

In the analysis of Danish questions we take advantage of the expressive power of typed feature structures to express the desired content.

$$\begin{bmatrix} \textit{cont} \\ \text{FOCUS } \boxed{1} \\ \text{COUNT } \textit{all} \\ \text{LOA } \left\langle \begin{array}{l} \textit{courseOffer}\begin{bmatrix} \text{TEACHER } \boxed{1} \\ \text{COURSE } \boxed{2} \end{bmatrix} \\ \textit{studySubject}\begin{bmatrix} \text{WORK } \boxed{2} \\ \text{SUBJECT} \mid \text{NAME } \textit{film-history} \end{bmatrix} \end{array} \right\rangle \end{bmatrix}$$

Figure 5
Feature structure representation of question content

Figure 5 shows the feature structure representation of the content of the Danish question "Hvem underviser i filmhistorie" produced by the Danish analyser. At the highest level, the FOCUS attribute refers to the semantic class the knowledge structure is to be queried for, while the value of COUNT indicates that we are interested in all the topics belonging to this class, and LOA (list of associations) contains a list of relevant semantic relations, in this case *courseOffer* and *studySubject*, that further constrain the topics in question. Each relation is in turn a feature structure and has a number of attributes corresponding to semantic roles. The value of a semantic role is a domain class. The indices in the feature structure allow us to express token identity between values of different attributes. In this case, the FOCUS is identical to the value of TEACHER, and identity is also enforced between the COURSE and the WORK roles in the two associations.

The system's content matcher maps the content of the feature structure onto an XML query that looks more or less as follows:

```
<query>
  <topic-filter types="Faculty">
    <role-filter types="TeacherRole">
      <association-filter types="courseOffer">
        <role-filter types="CourseRole">
          <topic-filter types="Course">
            <role-filter types="WorkRole">
              <association-filter types="studySubject">
                <role-filter types="SubjectRole">
                  <topic-filter ids="film-history"/>
                </role-filter>
                ...
  </topic-filter>
```

Role, association and topic class names correspond to some of those in the topic map in Figure 1.

The information about the question focus is retained by the content matcher and sent on to the answer generator that decides how to prune the retrieved topic map so that it provides a relevant answer to the user's question. In this particular case, for example, the answer will be constructed so that the focus is on the names of the teachers rather those of the courses.

3.2 Ontological and semantic feature types

The semantic types of which the output of the Danish analysis component is built, are part of the system's feature type system. It consists of about 200 classes and 50 relations, the same as in the ontology underlying the knowledge structure. The type system was originally developed in the LKB system (Copestake, 2002), which is based on a formalism very similar to that used in PET. The topmost type in the ontology is called *topic*, and comprises the two subtypes *entity*, which groups the various ontology classes, and *association*, which subsumes the various relation types. Entities split into *universal* on the one hand, where abstract types such as *time* or *degree* are defined, and *individual* on the other, which subsumes i.a. *person*, *location* and *activity*.

Unlike the knowledge base, this linguistic ontology makes no explicit distinction between classes and members of the classes (called occurrences in topic maps). The properties of occurrences, however, are defined by means of type attributes, e.g. the attribute NAME, which pertains to all entities, or the attribute SALARY, which characterises employees:[2]

(1) *Entity* := *topic* & [NAME *string*]

(2) *Enployee* := *Person* & [SALARY *Salary*]

The *association* type is used to define the domain ontology associations, which are n-ary relations among ontology classes in which each class plays a specific role. The role name corresponds in our implementation to an attribute of the feature type that identifies the association. For example, the *courseOffer* association type looks as follows:

(3) *courseOffer* := *association* &

$$\begin{bmatrix} \text{COURSE } \textit{Course} \\ \text{PROVIDER } \textit{Organisation} \\ \text{TEACHER } \textit{Faculty} \end{bmatrix}$$

2 In the following examples, the LKB user language is used, where := means 'is a subtype of', and attributes are added after the & symbol.

A peculiarity of the linguistic association types that distinguishes them from the related associations in the topic maps is that an attribute cannot be introduced into the type system more than once. This means that if any two associations share one or more semantic roles, either they must subsume each other, or they must both inherit the role from a common supertype. For instance the two associations *courseOffer* and *courseDuration* both share a COURSE attribute: since neither of them subsumes the other, they are defined as sutypes of a common more generic *courseAssoc*, where the attribute in question is introduced.

The ontological types, i.e. entity classes and associations, interact with more general semantic types to yield semantic representations like the one in Figure 5. The most general of these is *cont*, which comprises different subtypes used to express the content of nominal objects on the one hand (*nom-obj*) and verbal objects on the other (*verb-obj*). A subtype of *verb-obj* is *question*, which expands to the feature structure below:

(4) $\begin{bmatrix} \textit{question} \\ \text{FOCUS } \textit{topic} \\ \text{COUNT } \textit{count} \\ \text{LOA } \textit{list-of-associations} \end{bmatrix}$

The value of FOCUS is a *topic*, and will be token-identical to the value of one of the semantic roles in the list of associations. The type *count* receives one of the three possible values *all*, *one* or *count*, depending on the quantification of the topic in focus. The list of associations will consist of zero, one or several relations that constrain the interpretation of the focus.[3]

3.3 Grammar rules

The grammar consists of a subset of the syntactic types in which a dominance and precedence relation between nodes is defined. These types, also called schemata, or rules, are used by the chart parser to build syntactic structures. The parsing process is based on the unification of compatible feature structures. The MOSES grammar consists of relatively few quite general syntactic schemata in the spirit of Head-driven Phrase Structure Grammar (Pollard and Sag, 1994), that are expanded out into a larger number of more specific grammar construction types such as declarative clause or question as described in (Neville and Paggio, 2001). The general syntactic and semantic principles are, in other words, not specific to MOSES. In particular the enforcement of the ontological semantic constraints falls out from the general semantic principle according to which the content of a phrase is identical to the content of the head daughter.

3 The list will be empty if the question only asks for a class, e.g. all teachers.

$$\begin{bmatrix} \textit{wh-interrog-cl} \\ \text{SYNSEM} \mid \text{LOC} \mid \text{CONT } \textit{question} \begin{bmatrix}\text{FOCUS } \boxed{1} \\ \text{COUNT } \boxed{2}\end{bmatrix} \\ \text{NON-HD-DTR} \mid \text{SYNSEM} \mid \text{NON-LOC} \mid \text{QUE } \textit{wh-nom-obj} \begin{bmatrix}\text{RESTR } \boxed{1} \\ \text{WH-COUNT } \boxed{2}\end{bmatrix} \end{bmatrix}$$

Figure 6
Wh-question rule

Grammar rules that introduce domain constraints specific to MOSES are those defining the various question types spelled out in the question classification. There are types for wh-questions and yes/no-questions.

In Figure 6 we show a wh-question rule in simplified form. The rule states that the content of a wh-question is of type *question*. In addition, it states that the values for FOCUS and COUNT unify with values in the feature structure corresponding to the wh-pronoun that makes up the non-head daughter of the construction. In particular, FOCUS will unify with the wh-pronoun's semantic restriction RESTR. The rule type that accounts for yes/no questions, which we do not show here, sets the value of FOCUS to being *polarity*.

3.4 Lexical types

Typed feature structures have proved an adequate formalism not only to define the domain ontology and the necessary semantic constraints in grammar rules, but also to express the necessary relations between lexical and syntactic features on the one hand, and domain content on the other. These relations are defined in the individual lexical entries.

A straightforward example is the entry for *universitet* (university), the content of which is a nominal object restricted to being of type *University*, which is a domain ontology class. Syntactic features are omitted apart from the HEAD value *noun*.

(5)
$$\begin{bmatrix} \textit{lex-phrase} \\ \text{ORTH “universitet”} \\ \text{SYNSEM} \mid \text{LOC} \begin{bmatrix} \text{CAT} \mid \text{HEAD } \textit{noun} \\ \text{CONT} \begin{bmatrix} \textit{nom-obj} \\ \text{RESTR } \textit{University} \end{bmatrix} \end{bmatrix} \end{bmatrix}$$

Another example is the entry for the verb *undervise* (teach) shown in Figure 7.

Here, token identity is enforced between the content of the first verbal argument and the TEACHER role in the *courseOffer* relation, and between the content of the second argument and the SUBJECT role in the *studySubject* relation. The same strategy is used to map semantic arguments onto conceptual content in the case of the deverbal noun *undervisning* (teaching). The fact that the noun has semantic arguments (which are of course not always realised) and

$$\begin{bmatrix} \text{ORTH “undervise”} \\ \text{SYNSEM} \begin{bmatrix} \text{ARG-ST} \left\langle \begin{array}{l} \begin{bmatrix}\text{CONT } \boxed{1}\end{bmatrix} \\ \begin{bmatrix}\text{CONT } \boxed{2}\end{bmatrix} \end{array} \right\rangle \\ \text{CONT} \mid \text{LOA} \left\langle \begin{array}{l} \textit{courseOffer}\begin{bmatrix}\text{TEACHER } \boxed{1} \\ \text{COURSE } \boxed{3}\end{bmatrix} \\ \textit{studySubject}\begin{bmatrix}\text{WORK } \boxed{3} \\ \text{SUBJECT } \boxed{2}\end{bmatrix} \end{array} \right\rangle \end{bmatrix} \end{bmatrix}.$$

Figure 7
Danish lexicon entry

that it has a very similar behaviour to that of the corresponding verb from the point of view of semantics, can be seen in the following examples:

(6) Har Pedersen undervisning dette semester?
(Does Pedersen have any teaching this semester?)
Hvem har undervisning i filmhistorie?
(Who does teaching in film history?)

In conclusion, the approach taken in the MOSES lexicon is an attempt to abstract away from syntactic descriptions and constraints and focus instead on the semantic restrictions that bind words to their semantic arguments.

4 Development and evaluation

The Danish analysis component developed for MOSES builds as already mentioned on previous work. The preprocessing tools, which have not been discussed in this paper, already existed but had to be adapted to the domain. In particular, specific rules were added manually to the Named Entity Recogniser to categorise names of departments and courses; the POS-tagger was modified to accept the new name tags; finally, the lemmatiser was retrained on 450,000 word forms, corresponding to 60,000 different lemmas, which produced 44,000 automatically discovered lemmatisation rules. Similarly, the generic grammar resources previously implemented in the LKB framework had to be extended with ontological types and ontological constraints to be added to grammar rules and lexical entries.

The coverage of the resulting grammar has been tested on a list of 85 questions of varying syntactic complexity spanning a reasonable range of semantic relations. Of these, 65 were analysed correctly, 3 produced an incorrect analysis, and 17 failed to produce an analysis. These results make it clear that although the grammar is able to produce correct semantic representations in a number of non-trivial cases, more robustness should be added to produce at least partial analyses for the cases that fall outside of the implemented coverage. In fact, ensuring rubustness is more important than limiting overgeneration, firstly because the integration of domain knowledge in itself keeps ambiguity low, secondly because the content matcher weeds out competing semantic representations that would produce the same answer.

In addition to grammar development, a good deal of work was also put into engineering aspects that had to do with i. integration of the linguistic analysis with the rest of the system, ii. integration of the various analysis steps with each other, and iii. adaptation of the parser in the PET software.

The two main changes concerning the parser, which are the most relevant of these adaptations in the perspective of this paper, are a modification of the output, and the new treatment of unknown words. As already mentioned, the MOSES version of the PET parser only outputs the semantic part of the entire complex feature structure corresponding to each sentence analysis. This implies that the entire feature structure is analysed to find the semantic CONT feature which has an instantiated FOCUS attribute. This CONT feature is then extracted from the chart of the parser and printed as output from the PET parser.

The other change concerns the treatment of unknown words, and was implemented after the evaluation had been carried out to add robustness to the system.

4.1 Treating unknown words

To implement a treatment of unknown words we took advantage of a mechanism already present in PET, modulo some re-programming to make it compatible with the MOSES semantics. This PET mechanism allows parsing of unkown words based on POS-tags. POS-tags are input to PET using the special yy-format, which also gives the possibility to get links to the input tokens using the content of a specialised WLINK feature. In the extraction of the semantic part of the parsing output a special treatment of the WLINK element has been implemented to extract the corresponding input tokens.

From a linguistic point of view, the primary element of the mechanism for the treatment of unknown words are the so-called generic lexicon entries, which apply to unknown POS-tagged words. In order to ensure that unknown words contribute to the semantic representation, generic entries must provide an interpretation which is as underspecified as possible. In the case of nouns, this amounts to not providing any interpretation, so that the semantic restriction is provided by the semantic relations in which the noun will fill up a semantic role.

For instance, in the input question *Hvilken gæsteprofessor underviser i filmhistorie?* (Which guest professor teaches film history) the noun *gæsteprofessor* is not in the lexicon. Since it is POS-tagged as a noun, it will unify with the generic lexicon entry for nouns, which simply tells the parser to copy the word onto the value of a special feature called WLINK and to assign it other features typical of a noun, like [HEAD *noun*]. In the final representation, the word will fit into

$$\begin{bmatrix} \textit{cont} \\ \text{FOCUS } \boxed{1} \\ \text{COUNT } \textit{all} \\ \text{LOA } \left\langle \begin{array}{l} \textit{courseOffer}\begin{bmatrix}\text{TEACHER } \boxed{1} \begin{bmatrix}\textit{Faculty}\\ \text{WLINK “gæsteprofessor”}\end{bmatrix} \\ \text{COURSE } \boxed{2}\end{bmatrix} \\ \textit{studySubject}\begin{bmatrix}\text{WORK } \boxed{2} \\ \text{SUBJECT} \mid \text{NAME } \textit{film-history}\end{bmatrix}\end{array}\right\rangle \end{bmatrix}$$

Figure 8
Semantic interpretation and unknown words (here the word *gæsteprofessor*)

the TEACHER semantic role, and inherit *Faculty* as a semantic class type, as illustrated in Figure 8.

In other cases, e.g. unknown verbs, constructing an interpretation is much more difficult, in that generally it is the verb that provides the semantic predicate that is the backbone of the analysis. In this case, therefore, generic lexical entries provide default interpretations that are left for the content matcher to interpret. A generic lexical entry for divalent verbs looks as follows:

(7)
$$\begin{bmatrix} \textit{lex-generic-v} \\ \text{SYNSEM} \mid \text{LOC} \begin{bmatrix} \text{CAT v} \\ \text{ARG-ST} \left\langle \begin{array}{l} [\text{LOC} \mid \text{CONT } \boxed{1}] \\ [\text{LOC} \mid \text{CONT } \boxed{2}] \end{array} \right\rangle \\ \text{CONT} \begin{bmatrix} \textit{verb-obj} \\ \text{LOA} \left\langle \begin{bmatrix} \textit{dummy-binary-rel} \\ \text{DUMMYARG1 } \boxed{1} \\ \text{DUMMYARG2 } \boxed{2} \end{bmatrix} \right\rangle \end{bmatrix} \end{bmatrix} \end{bmatrix}$$

Similar lexical entries are defined for monovalent and trivalent verbs. In general, the mechanism is quite efficient, and yields results that cover unknown words of different syntactic categories and with different grammatical functions. Of course, the more underspecified the resulting semantic interpretation is, the less precise the XML query to the knowledge base will be.

5 Conclusion

Our expectations when we started developing the Danish analysis component for the MOSES project, was that it would be a challenging and interesting application for the existing Danish LKB grammar. After almost three years of grammar and system development efforts, we still believe the work was well worth its while.

The grammar has grown and has a much better syntactic coverage, in spite of the fact that its general syntactic structure has not been dramatically changed to meet project-specific requirements. From the point of view of semantics, on the other hand, all the domain knowledge that has been added to the type system as well as the grammar and the dictionary, is of course specific to the application domain, and would have to be replaced if the domain were changed. However, the domain knowledge is mainly concentrated in the CONT part of the lexicon entries and in the part of the type system that defines concepts and associations, and can therefore be omitted without much damage to the grammar's syntactic backbone. In general, we believe our work has demonstrated that feature structure types are an adequate means of expressing ontological knowledge and interfacing to the XML query language.

Another aspect that merits some reflection is the engineering consideration that full parsing and deep processing of the kind described here are still too fragile in real applications. In spite of the pipelined architecture in which full parsing is backed up by more robust preprocessing steps, more robustness is still needed. In MOSES we have taken a little further step in this direction by experimenting with a new treatment of unknown words. Even in this respect, feature structure types have provided an expressive representation language that allows for the necessary interplay between ontological requirements and lexical underspecification.

References

Atzeni, Paolo, Roberto Basili, D. H. Hansen, Paolo Missier, Patrizia Paggio, Maria Teresa Pazienza, and Fabio Massimo Zanzotto. 2004. Ontology-based question answering in a federation of university sites: The MOSES case study. In *NLDB*, pages 413–420.

Basili, Roberto and Fabio Massimo Zanzotto. 2002. Parsing engineering and empirical robustness. *Journal of Natural Language Engineering*, 8(2), June.

Callmeier, Ulrich. 2000. PET – a platform for experimentation with efficient HPSG processing techniques. *Natural Language Engineering. Special Issue on Efficient Processing with HPSG.*

Copestake, Ann. 2002. *Implementing Typed Feature Structure Grammars.* CSLI Publications. Stanford University.

Flickinger, Dan. 2000. On building a more efficient grammar by exploiting types. *Journal of Natural Language Engineering*, 6(1):15–28.

Garshol, Lars Marius. 2003. Living with Topic Maps and RDF. Technical report, Ontopia.

Harabagiu, Sandra, Dan Moldova, Marius Pasca, Rada Mihalcea, Mihai Surdeanu, Rhzvan Bunescu, Roxana Girju, Vasile Rus, and Paul Morrescu. 2001. The role of lexico-semantic feedback in open domain textual question-answering. In *Proceedings of the Association of Computational Linguistics.* July.

Humphreys, K., R. Gaizauskas, S. Azzam, C. Huyck, B. Mitchell, H. Cunningham, and Y. Wilks. 1998. University of Sheffield: Description of the LASIE-II system as used for MUC-07. In *Proceedings of the Seventh Message Understanding Conferences (MUC-7).* Morgan Kaufman.

Lauer, Thomas W., Eileen Peacock, and Arthur C. Graesser, editors. 1992. *Questions and Information Systems.* Hillsdale, NJ: Lawrence Erlbaum.

Moldovan, D. and M. Surdenau. 2003. On the role of IR and IE in question answering systems. In Maria Teresa Pazienza, editor, *Information Extraction in the Web Era.* Springer, pages 129–147.

Neville, Anne and Patrizia Paggio. 2001. Developing a Danish grammar in the GRASP project - a construction-based approach to topology and extraction in Danish. *Electronic Notes in Theoretical Computer Science*, 53.

Paggio, Patrizia, Dorte Haltrup Hansen, Roberto Basili, Maria Teresa Pazienza, and Fabio Massimo Zanzotto. 2004. Ontology-based question analysis in a multilingual environment: the

MOSES case study. In *Proceedings of OntoLex 2004: Ontologies and Lexical Resources in Distributed Environments. Workshop held at LREC 2004*, pages 1–8, May.

Pollard, Carl and Ivan A. Sag. 1994. *Head-Driven Phrase Structure Grammar*. Chicago: The University of Chicago Press.

Peter Lang · Internationaler Verlag der Wissenschaften

Jacek Waliński / Krzysztof Kredens /
Stanisław Goźdź-Roszkowski (eds.)

Corpora and ICT in Language Studies

PALC 2005

Frankfurt am Main, Berlin, Bern, Bruxelles, New York, Oxford, Wien, 2007.
451 pp., num fig., tab. and graph.
Łódź Studies in Language. Edited by Barbara Lewandowska-Tomaszczyk.
Vol. 13
ISBN 978-3-631-56099-0 · pb. € 69.–*

Information and communication technology (ICT) has dramatically altered the world's social and economic landscape and is now gaining momentum in the realm of language studies. *Corpora and ICT in Language Studies* attempts to signal and document this phenomenon by bringing together twenty-nine contributions authored by both seasoned researchers and newcomers to the field. The contributions range from more traditional corpus-based or corpus-driven studies to those incorporating ICT as an integral part of their methodology. The volume includes a selection of conference papers given at PALC 2005, the fifth conference in the biennial cycle of meetings organized by the Department of English Language at Lodz University, as well as a number of invited papers. The papers are grouped in three parts: corpora in empirical language studies, cognitive linguistics and e-learning.

Contents: Information and communication technology · New digital technologies · Knowledge acquisition and corpus tools · Corpora in empirical language studies · Cognitive corpus linguistics · e-learning · Learner corpus

Frankfurt am Main · Berlin · Bern · Bruxelles · New York · Oxford · Wien
Distribution: Verlag Peter Lang AG
Moosstr. 1, CH-2542 Pieterlen
Telefax 00 41 (0) 32 / 376 17 27

*The €-price includes German tax rate
Prices are subject to change without notice

Homepage http://www.peterlang.de